Vol. II

90 Client-directed Energetic Protocols to Accelerate Trauma Recovery & Healing:

Innovations *in* Healing Trauma

Books also by Leland W. Howe, Ph.D.

The Companion Guide for Grab the Tiger by the Tail

Grab the Tiger by the Tail

How to Raise Children in a TV World (co-author)

Taking Charge of Your Life

Personalizing Education: Values Clarification and Beyond (co-author)

Values Clarification: A Handbook for Teachers and Students (co-author)

Facing Down Your Trauma Tiger

Vol. II

90 Client-directed Energetic Protocols to Accelerate Trauma Recovery & Healing:

Innovations in Healing Trauma

Leland W. Howe, PhD
with Rev. Karen Arndorfer & Terrie MacNicol, CET

Copyright © 2024 by Leland W. Howe, Ph.D.

90 Client-directed Energetic Protocols to Accelerate Trauma Recovery & Healing: Innovations in Healing Trauma, Vol. II

All rights reserved. Except as permitted under U.S. Copyright Act of 1976, no part of this publication may be reproduced, distributed, or transmitted in any form or by any means, or stored in a database or retrieval system, without the prior written permission of the publisher.

ISBN 979-8-9875745-2-2

First edition, December 2024

Cover illustration by Jay Stoner, Lexington, KY

Book & cover design by Terrie MacNicol, Leslie, MI

IHT Press

5090 Chinook Lane

Lyons, MI 48851

Printed in the United States of America

Dedication

To Sandy, my wonderful wife, whose support, editorial suggestions which greatly improved this book, editing, and frequent reminders to energetically ground myself during the creation of this work.

To my grandfather, Herbert Howe, who really listened to me as a troubled boy and teenager. The only advice that he ever gave me was to 'grab the tiger by the tail' and fight for the life I want. (In this case, to fight for clients' health and happiness by helping them heal their trauma.)

To Joel Nigg whose inspired wisdom helped shape the ideas in this book.

To Terrie MacNicol who provided inspired creative suggestions, editing, and layout work to prepare this book for publication.

To my colleague, Karen Arndorfer, and her talented husband, Rob Curtner, who have supported me with their love and wisdom throughout the creation of this Energetic Therapy approach.

Table of Contents

Table of Client-directed Energetic Protocols x

Preface xv

Chapter 1: Facing Down Your Trauma Tiger 1

Chapter 2: Case Demonstration on How to Use the Energetic Therapy Protocols 11

Chapter 3: A Case Demonstration on How to Use The Toxic Shame Busting Protocol 71

Chapter 4: Case Examples of Using the Start-Up Protocol to Help Clients Self-diagnose 97

Chapter 5: The Body Knows Best 105

Chapter 6: Jump Starting a Strong Energy Charge to Help Move Clients' Trauma Healing Therapy Forward 133

Chapter 7: Using the Vibration & Slow Movement Stretching

Protocols to Help Clients Restructure Their Energetic Holding Defenses 155

Chapter 8: Creating a Spiritual Bridge to Help Clients Heal Trauma 183

Chapter 9: Helping Clients Let Go of a Trauma Memorial 203

Chapter 10: Using The Toxic Shame Busting Protocol to Help Clients Get Rid of Their Debilitating Toxic Shame 209

Chapter 11: More on Innovations in Healing Trauma & Energetic Therapy 227

References 261

About the Authors 267

For More Information 269

Table of Client-directed Energetic Protocols

1. The Hair-pin Energetic Grounding Protocol.................18, 147
2. The Client is in Charge Agreement Protocol.........................19
3. The Healing Power of the Group Protocol............................20
4. The Validation Protocol 20
5. The Assisted Hair-pin Energetic Grounding Protocol 22
6. The Downhill Ski Energetic Grounding Protocol..23,   147
7. The Small Pressure Roller Protocol 25
8. The Foot Saver Protocol 26
9. The Spontaneous Movement Protocol 28, 105, 118
10. The Personal Support Protocol 30
11. The Pressure Roller Protocol...31, 50
12. The Heroic Story Protocol 33
13. The Identifying the Inner Judge Protocol 35
14. The Just Be With Your Body Protocol....................................36
15. The Defending Against the Inner Judge Protocol.................36
16. The Subtle Energy Protocol 37
17. The Tune-in for Resonance Protocol......................................37

18. The Building a Strong Energetic Charge
    in the Body Protocol..39
19. The Wall-sit Energetic Grounding Protocol..........................40
20. The Dis-identifying with the Inner Judge Protocol..............42
21. The Advocate Protocol..43
22. The Take-it-in Protocol...44
23. The Toxic Waste Dump Protocol...45
24. The Take Your Anger at God to God.................................46, 196
25. The God has Already Forgiven Me Protocol...................47, 197
26. The God has Already Forgiven Them Protocol.............48, 197
27. The Scissors Kicking Protocol...49
28. The Air-hammer Protocol..49
29. The Large Pressure Roller Protocol.......................................50
30. The Shake-Rattle-&-Roll Trauma Healing Protocol.....51, 181
31. The Start-up Protocol...52
32. The Energetic Holding Defenses Restructuring Protocol....55
33. The Arm & Shoulder Pillow Lift Protocol.............................57
34. The Kicking Large Pillows Protocol.......................................58
35. The Foam Hand Gripper Jaw Release Protocol....................58
36. The Bonger Percussion Protocol...59
37. The Wolf-bite Protocol...60
38. The If-I-Could-Let-Myself-See Protocol................................61
39. The Personal Tug-Of-War Protocol..61

40. The Energetic Client-directed Therapy Journal Record Protocol 64

41. The Group Feedback Whip Protocol 65

42. The I-Learned Statements Protocol 65

43. The Session Rating & Feedback Evaluation Protocol 65

44. The Paired Energetic Grounding Protocol 67

45. The Group Hug Protocol 69

46. The Toxic Shame Busting Protocol 72, 89, 209, 216-221

47. The Energetic Peer Co-counseling Protocol 75, 89, 94, 234-235

48. The Covering Shame Protocol 78

49. The Bunker Busting Protocol 79

50. The Extolling Protocol 83, 93

51. The Shower of Golden Light Protocol 88

52. The Intuition Protocol 130

53. The Whack-A-Judge Energy Jump Start Protocol 143

54. The Bouncing Jump Start Protocol 144

55. The Hammer Heals Kicking Jump Start Protocol 144

56. The Team/One-On-One Tug of War Energy Jump Start Protocol 145

57. The Get-A-Leg-Up Energetic Grounding Protocol 148

58. The Bridge Energetic Grounding Protocol 150

59. The Backup Energetic Grounding Protocol 151

60. The Vibration Protocols 155

61. The Slow Movement Stretching Protocols 155
62. The Trampoline Release Protocol 168
63. The Pressure Roller Release Protocol 169
64. The Pressure Stool Release Protocol 171
65. The Pelvic Lift Stretching Release Protocol 172
66. The Open Clam Shell Stretching Release Protocol 172
67. The Closed Clam Shell Stretching Release Protocol 173
68. The Butt Squeeze Release Protocol 173
69. The Leg Lift Stretching Release Protocol 173
70. The Torso-Pelvic Lift Stretching Release Protocol 174
71. The Reverse Belly Bow Stretching Release Protocol 174
72. The Standing Bow Release Protocol 174
73. The Head Lift Release Protocol 175
74. The Arm Lift Release Protocol 175
75. The Jaw Drop Release Protocol 175
76. The Jaw Bite Release Protocol 176
77. The Releasing Fascia in Your Feet & Ankles Protocol 177
78. The Releasing Fascia in Your Knees & Hips Protocol 177
79. The Releasing Fascia in Your Shoulders
    & Arms Protocol 178
80. The Releasing Fascia in Your Neck Protocol 178
81. The Neck Stretching Release Protocol 179
82. The Releasing Fascia in Your Back & Chest Protocol 179

83. The Shake-Rattle-And-Roll Trauma Release
    & Healing Protocol 181

84. The Classical Stretch Protocols 182

85. The Spiritual Bridge Protocols 194-195

86. The Getting On My Knees to Ask God
    for Help Protocol 196

87. The Learning Life's Lesson Protocol 201

88. The Releasing Your Trauma Memorial Protocol 204

89. The Bi-lateral Tapping Protocol 228, 232-233

90. The Sleep Disturbance Remedy Protocol 239, 240-241

Preface

One of the most powerful ways to help trauma victims get in touch with and follow their body's cellular and healing wisdom comes directly out of the new brain research. It involves teaching trauma victims how to follow their body's spontaneous energetic impulses or movements wherever they lead. Brain researchers have discovered that energetic and imaged movement is central to almost every part and function of our brain. Thus, helping trauma victims allow and follow their spontaneous movements naturally leads to almost instant access to their buried, repressed, and forgotten trauma memories, feelings, and emotions and the cognitive information that they need to help them heal their trauma as well as solve personal problems, develop more functional and successful behaviors and responses, rewire their brain with more functional neural pathways, remove chronic tension from their body, and restructure their Energetic Holding Defenses. Learning to be in touch with, allow, and follow their inner body wisdom in the form of spontaneous movements is a vital and powerful way to help trauma victims reach their goal of living a life filled with health, well-being, and happiness.

Another early influence came from reading Peter A. Levine's *Waking the Tiger: Healing Trauma* (1997). It had a profound impact on my practice of energetic psychotherapy as I realized that my clients' own natural healing process of thawing and shaking out the frozen trauma in their bodies could be relied on when the right therapeutic conditions of safety, support, and encouragement were provided. I provide numerous case examples which point to the effectiveness of tapping clients' natural healing process of ridding their bodies of frozen trauma.

Then I read John L. Ratey's, *A User's Guide to the Brain* [2001] which further impacted on my practice of doing energetic psychotherapy. One sentence, in particular, really got my attention. It reads, "But, mounting evidence shows that movement is crucial to every other brain function, including memory, emotion, language, and learning." I had already encouraged my clients to follow their own trauma healing impulses and movements and here was confirmation that I was on the right path. It was the birth of the Spontaneous Movement Protocol which became a Mega Star mainstay in my client-directed Energetic Therapy approach.

Using the Spontaneous Movement Protocol helped my clients peel away the layers of their trauma until they finally reached its core. When this happened, clients often encountered stiff resistance which kept them from making further trauma healing progress. My training in the medical model Energetic Therapy had prepared me to help my clients overcome this resistance using character analysis and applying it to help clients remove their energetic muscular blocks to moving forward. However, I was reluctant to abandon my use of a client-centered, client-directed approach to solve this problem. Fortunately, I was able to develop a protocol to help my clients self-diagnose their own primary and secondary Energetic Holding Defenses which they had adopted in order to protect themselves against re-experiencing the trauma and pain caused by their abusive or neglectful childhood caretakers. I called it the Startup Protocol because the Energetic Holding Defense/s 'program' which clients had adopted resembled the Startup program on a computer. The central part of this Startup Protocol consisted of a descriptive check list of nine

Energetic Holding Trauma Defenses which clients then used to compare themselves against and find the best diagnostic match/s.

I then developed four more mainstay innovations which also became Mega Stars in my Client-centered, Client-directed Energetic Therapy approach. (These were in addition to the already named Mega Star Spontaneous Movement Protocol and the Startup Protocol). One was the Restructuring Protocol which my clients used to self-release the particular muscular tension that kept their Energetic Holding Defense in place. The second innovation was the use of Energetic Grounding Protocols to help keep clients grounded in their physical body rather than doing their Energetic Therapy in an ungrounded way from their ego alone. The third innovation was the use of Energetic Therapy Outcome Review Protocols which clients completed to provide me feedback regarding their satisfaction with their therapy progress. This protocol was also used to help improve their therapy process. The fourth innovation was the use of the Energetic Peer Co-counseling Protocol, which was designed to help clients direct their trauma healing therapy more affordably.

This Innovations in Healing Trauma handbook lays out the work that I and my colleagues are doing to move the Energetic Trauma Healing Therapy approach forward. It presents numerous additional Innovative Trauma Healing Protocols which we have developed along with our clinical evidence for its effectiveness in the form of case examples as well as a limited Energetic Therapy outcomes research study presented in Chapter 9.

> Leland W. Howe, Ph.D,
> Director of The Center for Innovations
> in Healing Trauma
> Lyons, MI 48851
> 8/15/2022

Facing Down Your Trauma Tiger

(Note: If you are a Therapist, this chapter is written as if to speak directly to your client/patient. If you are a current client/patient of a Therapist, or wish to become one, simply read the following and then give it to your Therapist or prospective Therapist and encourage him or her to use the Client-directed Energetic Therapy Protocols you select, or the full Client-directed Energetic Therapy approach, with you.)

Coming face to face with your childhood and adult trauma can be a traumatic experience. Your body has undoubtedly protected you by repressing your past trauma, so you are not feeling the continuous pain and reactive presence of it. However, your buried-hidden trauma may still show up as you relive your trauma in nightmare dreams and daytime flashbacks, or as crippling depression and anxiety, as well as a host of other debilitating conditions. Nor does it allow you to be fully in the present moment or live a joy filled life. It is always lurking in the shadows, casting a cloud of self-doubt and uncertainty over your life.

When you decide to face down your trauma tiger, it can be a daunting and frightening challenge. However, your body wisdom will help you, if you let it. Your body wants to heal your trauma and is designed to do so. If the conditions are made right, the wisdom of your body will help you mobilize and direct your energy and efforts forward toward full trauma recovery. There will be times in healing your trauma (or if you are a Therapist helping your clients heal their trauma) when using the right Energetic Trauma Healing Protocols can make all the difference. My favorite is the Mega Star of the Energetic Trauma Healing Protocol tool kit, the Spontaneous Movement Protocol. This powerful, innovative protocol asks you to set a healing intention and then let a spontaneous movement arise from your body, which if you follow where the movement leads—to feelings, thoughts, buried memories, and further movements—will advance your trauma healing therapy ahead at a rapid pace. And, there are numerous other innovative Energetic Trauma Healing Protocols which I employ when the healing situation calls for their use. This is especially true of the Energetic Grounding Protocols as well as the other dozens of Client-directed Energetic Therapy Protocols in this handbook such as the Advocate Protocol, The Toxic Shame Busting Protocol and, The Validation Protocol just to name a few.

Thus, this *Innovations in Healing Trauma Vol. II* sets forth a wide variety of Energetic Trauma Healing Protocols that can be used in trauma healing settings using any type of trauma healing approach. An abundance of these Energetic Trauma Healing Protocols are presented in Chapters 2 and 3. I also provide case demonstrations throughout this handbook on how to use them in trauma healing settings.

The impetus for this Innovations in Healing Trauma handbook was born with my first Client-directed Energetic Therapy client many years ago when the mistakes I made, especially in her first session, caused me to realize that my training as a psychotherapist left a lot to be desired. These mistakes literally set me on a new and unexpected trauma healing course right from the beginning of my career as a body-oriented psychotherapist. This eventually led me to forge a new Client-centered, Client-directed Energetic Therapy approach using the Spontaneous Movement Protocol as the main go-to healing protocol to help clients direct their trauma healing therapy. Since movement is connected to every part of the human brain, it allowed clients to tap into buried-hidden childhood and adult trauma memories, feelings, and emotions. When they followed the innate impulses of their own body-mind-wisdom to heal, their Energetic Trauma Healing Therapy moved ahead at lighting speed, figuratively speaking.

When my clients got stuck or their therapy slowed and stalled, I created new Energetic Trauma Healing Protocols to help them get unstuck and move forward. These new, innovative Trauma Healing Protocols are the focus of this Client-directed Energetic Therapy handbook. I provide an abundance of case material to illustrate how I use them in my own Energetic Trauma Healing Therapy practice. As well, my colleagues and I conduct training seminars and workshops for other Therapists in how to use these Client-directed Energetic Therapy Protocols.

I have also shared these Energetic Trauma Healing Protocols with other colleagues and Therapists who use a more conventional, medical-model-diagnosis-prescription trauma healing methods; gratifyingly they report these innovative Trauma Healing Protocols help them achieve successful trauma healing outcomes with their clients which was an unexpected but welcomed surprise to me.

What This Innovations in Healing Trauma Handbook Is All About

In a nutshell, these Client-directed Energetic Therapy Protocols presented here follow the therapeutic formula created by the famous psychotherapist, Milton Erickson. He mystified his colleagues and students who furiously tried in vain to figure out the reason for his amazing therapeutic success (de Shazer,1994). So, what was the simple reason for his success? It was exactly what Erickson said it was, except no one listened to or believed what he said. For him, it was all about listening to his clients and letting them lead and direct their trauma healing where they wanted to go. That was his simple formula and, this is what this Innovations in Healing Trauma handbook is all about—listening to clients and letting them lead and direct their trauma healing where they want to go with the help of these Client-directed Energetic Therapy Protocols.

This does not mean that your Therapist, if she or he uses these Client-directed Energetic Therapy Protocols to help you heal your trauma, has to be a passive on-looker. Far from it; he or she must be very active in listening carefully to you, ask you probing questions about the cause and history of your trauma, help you clarifying your healing intentions, provide you with healing tools and options like these innovative Trauma Healing Protocols, suggest creative and targeted interventions, help you overcome your internal resistance and fear, being empathetic and compassionate with your struggles and pain, and help you evaluate your healing progress. Your Therapist must be a caring teacher and a courageous supporter of your trauma healing work. To this end I have provided a case demonstration to model how to do this in the early chapters of this handbook.

Why I Focus So Much Attention in This Handbook on Helping Clients Like You Heal Their Childhood Trauma

I have found childhood trauma is invariably the root cause of my clients' depression, anxiety, relationship problems, debilitating work issues, suicide ideation, passivity, and other serious emotional and mental illness complaints.

When we think or hear of child trauma, we tend to equate it to physical abuse, emotional and mental abuse, and sexual abuse as well as the child having a serious accident, a major illness, losing a parent or loved one, surviving a natural disaster, and being caught in the middle of a war or shooting. However, there is another serious kind of childhood trauma that tends to fly under the radar for most folks. It is child trauma caused by their caretakers' interference with their children's natural stage development. This can take various forms such as caretaker rejection of the child, over-control of the child, exploitation of the child, neglect of the child, and threats to the child's existence. Since caretaker interference lies at the heart of creating childhood trauma and thus results in later adult depression, emotional disturbance, serious illness, and other post-trauma stress behaviors, clients' childhood trauma must be uncovered and addressed.

But There is a Big Problem Here

The problem is in our culture, we do not much concern ourselves with childhood trauma caused by caretaker interference in children's natural stage development. It is simply overlooked and neglected. This is a huge mistake. Childhood is the foundation of adulthood. If the child's foundation is weakened, then the adult life is built on this weak foundation is also weak and unstable. It is a well researched and documented fact that children who are interfered with in their natural stage development suffer trauma. It is a trauma that often goes unrecognized especially if the child does not exhibit overt trauma symptoms such as autism, serious anxiety, or debilitating depression, for example. But this unseen trauma is there none the less weakening the child's immune system, body flexibility, endurance, bright outlook on life, energy level, emotional stability, and spirit. This weakening of the child's foundation will cause it as an adult to develop a compromised immune system making it vulnerable to dangerous viruses, antibiotic resistant bacteria, and stress related illnesses. Its weakened childhood foundation will cause it as an adult to have a lower energy level, less endurance, less emotional stability, a less bright outlook on life, and less spirit which can over time lead to serious depression, anxiety, unstable relationships, alcohol & drug addiction, suicide ideation, and other serious health issues. This is the reason why psychotherapy and all types of counseling efforts—from treating depression and anxiety to dealing with relationship issues—must seek to correct and strengthen the clients' childhood foundation by healing this early caretaker's interference trauma and restructuring the limiting Energetic Holding Defenses that it produces. When psychotherapy and counseling practices as well as clients do not do this, it is a huge mistake of being penny-wise and dollar-foolish.

Many errant caretakers do not think they interfere with their children's natural stage development by using the same child rearing methods they were raised with or that such child rearing tactics can cause trauma in their children. They often think they know what is best for their children with ideas like, "Just let her cry it out," or, "Don't spoil him by giving him too much attention," or, "Spare the rod and spoil the child," or "She's just too cute to keep my hands off her," or, "Going to bed hungry will teach him a lesson," and so on. Their attitude is often, "Oh, they are just children who will get over it." These are just a few examples of how caretakers interfere in their children's natural stage development. But as Fred Rogers, on his long running PBS show, *Won't You Be My Neighbor*, demonstrated over and over again, children's needs and feelings must be taken very seriously and responded to with respect, caring, and unconditional love, just as caretakers would respond to adult family members and friends who they love with respect, caring, and unconditional love.

What's in this Handbook

This Innovations in Healing Trauma Vol. II handbook presents a large number of new Energetic Trauma Healing Protocols for use in almost any kind of trauma healing approach. Each protocol is designed to help you heal both acute and chronic trauma. In addition, this handbook presents an Energetic Trauma Healing Approach that does away with the medical model of diagnosis and prescription which is the framework most trauma healing approaches employ.

Thus the innovative Client-directed Energetic Therapy approach presented here is designed to help you direct your own trauma healing, with the guidance of your Therapist, by relying on your own spontaneous movements, internal resources, and rich body wisdom as well as the increased flow of energy in your body. Your own spontaneous movement allows you to uncover and heal deeply buried trauma memories and feelings that may have caused post-trauma stress responses and reactivity in your body and mind. Then the approach moves on to help you restructure your Energetic Holding Defenses, work through your fears and internal resistance that block forward movement, and release the muscular tensions in your body that keep your resistance and Energetic Holding Defense trauma in place.

The aim of this Client-directed Energetic Trauma Healing approach is to help you completely recover your physical and emotional health by restructuring your body to function as it was originally designed to do before your caretakers interfered with your natural child growth & development and/or you were physically and/or sexually abused as an adult by your adult perpetrators.

Using Energetic Peer Co-Counseling to Great Advantage

One of the drawbacks of clients like you doing in-person, full-on Client-directed Energetic Therapy to heal their trauma is it can be expensive. Consulting with Energetic Therapists, who use the Energetic Trauma Healing approach presented here, is far more productive than talk therapy or other forms of medical-model psychotherapy. This makes it very cost effective. Yet, clients who are in for the long haul can spend a lot of money on their healing which my colleagues and I as well as our clients believe is totally worth it. However, there is another very cost effective and productive approach to doing Client-directed Energetic Therapy. It uses peer co-counseling to great advantage. In his approach, as a client, you do your trauma healing work in peer-trios using the Energetic Peer Co-counseling Protocol. Using this protocol, trio members take turns being the Focus Person (who does the trauma healing work), the Assist Person (who helps the Focus Person do the work), and the Monitor-Safety Person (who helps keep the work on track and done safely). While clients learn to use this protocol, a Coach Person is added to guide the process.

I and my colleagues have used this Energetic Peer Co-counseling approach on a Zoom platform as well as in In-Person settings with great results. In fact, we have developed an organization and training to further the approach. It is called The Fire Circle Project. For more on this, see Using The Energetic Peer Co-counseling Protocol later in this handbook, or *Innovations In Healing Trauma Vol. I*. Additional information on using this protocol also appears on our website, innovationsinhealingtrauma.com.

Who is the Innovations In Healing Trauma Handbook Written for?

I want to reach several audiences who might be interested in this client-centered, Client-directed Energetic Therapy approach to healing trauma, so I have written this handbook to address Therapists, clients, researchers, and lay persons. In this regard, I have written most of the introductory and explanatory material directly to both clients and Therapists. I have also written the Client-directed Energetic Therapy Protocols in the way I have used them. My hope is clients who read this handbook will ask their Therapists to use these Client-directed Energetic Therapy Protocols to help them heal their trauma. I have also included a section on our Client-directed Energetic Therapy Outcomes which research psychologists, as well as graduate students who are interested in doing a thesis on Client-directed Energetic Therapy outcomes, may find of interest.

Case Demonstration on How to Use the Client-directed Energetic Therapy Protocols

I want to share a demonstration case which illustrates how I use the many Client-directed Energetic Therapy Protocols presented in this handbook in my Client-centered, Client-directed Energetic Therapy Trauma Healing practice as well as in my Energetic Peer Co-counseling Therapy training seminars and workshops.

I was invited to do this demonstration by a colleague for his Golden Shadow Training Class which was composed of experienced psychotherapists and healing practitioners. During the presentation I demonstrated a full range of my favorite Innovative Trauma Healing Protocols which are designed to help psychotherapists and healing practitioners move their clients' trauma healing therapy forward at a rapid pace. This included demonstrating how to use the Spontaneous Movement Protocol—my Mega Star Client-directed Energetic Therapy Protocol—to help clients direct their Trauma Healing Therapy under the guidance of their Therapists, and the Energetic Grounding Protocols—my Backup Stars—to help clients work through their internal resistance and keep their Trauma Healing Therapy on track and grounded, as well as additional Backup Energetic Trauma Healing Protocols designed to help clients resolve specific trauma healing issues on an as needed basis. Finally, it included a culminating demonstration on how to use the Energetic Peer Co-counseling Protocol—another Mega Star Protocol—to help clients take full responsibility for directing their Energetic Trauma Healing Therapy using a Zoom-type, online platform.

Demonstrating and using this many trauma healing interventions is not my usual procedure during a training class or regular trauma healing session with clients or in my on-going therapy groups. Normally I would use far fewer Energetic Trauma Healing Therapy Protocols during a training class or to help my clients direct their Energetic Trauma Healing work during a therapy session. In fact, I mostly rely on using the Spontaneous Movement Protocol and several Energetic Grounding Protocols to help my clients direct and realize the healing intentions which they set for their therapy sessions and to help them work through the internal resistance which they encounter during their trauma healing work as well as identify and deal with the rigid, compressed, flaccid, and/or frozen musculature and fascia in their bodies that keeps their Energetic Holding Defenses in place. However, since the case I present below was intended to help prepare the training class of healing practitioners on how to use my Client-centered, Client-directed Energetic Therapy approach in their own back home therapy settings, my host felt his training class needed to see the full range of Innovative Client-directed Energetic Therapy Protocols offered in this handbook, Thus, I used and demonstrated many of them in the presentation. Fortunately, it turned out to be very beneficial for the demonstration volunteer as well as to the training class members who attended.

My plan for demonstrating these Innovations in Healing Trauma Protocols was to the training class was to use several volunteers over the course of my presentation. However, as it turned out, the first volunteer's trauma healing work allowed me to do the demonstration without having to use additional volunteers. Part I of the demonstration to the training class was peppered with numerous breaks and practice sessions during the course of the presentation. However, for reading continuity, I have written the case report below as if it was done in one go without these interruptions. Part II, presented in the next chapter, was aimed at teaching the class members how to use the Toxic Shame Busting Protocol to help clients move past their toxic shame. This protocol is a formidable "show stopper"! The remainder of the demonstration focused on teaching the class members how to use the Energetic Peer Co-counseling Protocol to help their clients fully direct their trauma healing process.

The Introduction to My Innovations in Healing Trauma Presentation and Demonstration

The following introduction preceded my demonstration of the Innovations in Healing Trauma Protocols with a volunteer from the training class. My introductory remarks are in italics below.

Face to Face with Trauma

When we come face to face with a hidden part of ourselves—a part of our past—that we most likely do not want to see and do not want to face, it can shake us to the core of our being. But it is also an opportunity for us to heal our past trauma—trauma which has held us back for our entire life. The problem is until we come face to face with our past childhood and/or adult trauma that has been repressed and therefore buried and hidden in our unconscious mind and by our Energetic Holding Defenses (which protect us from emotional whiplash, overwhelm, and pain, especially as a child), we often do not even know we suffer from such trauma—although we may well know we suffer from something. However, when our trauma finally breaks through our protective Energetic Holding Defenses to become conscious, which it invariably will do, and we find the courage to face and the means to heal it, then our life will turn for the better as we become fully alive in our body, fully alive in the present moment, fully alive in our spirit, and fully on point as we live our life.

Everyone of us, with few exceptions, suffers from parental and societal interference during the ages and stages of our child development—birth to six years—and possible sexual and/or physical abuse on top of this—from age 6 onward. This early interference and possible later abuse causes us trauma which is often repressed and thus buried and hidden in our body musculature and unconscious mind. This early interference often happens due to the negative impact of our cultural values and flawed child-rearing beliefs and sayings such as, "spare the rod and spoil the child", or "a busy child is a good child", or "children should be seen and not heard", or "stop crying or I'll give you something to cry about", for example, or through more direct caretaker interference such as neglect, threats of annihilation, a chaotic and unstable child-rearing environment, exploitation, over-controlling child rearing behavior, rejection, and rigid-severely strict child rearing rules and discipline, for example. This developmental interference will limit us as children in ways which have profound life long negative effects unless we heal the trauma that this interference has caused us.

Helping Clients' Overcome Their Fears & Internal Resistance During Their Client-directed Energetic Therapy

Now let's turn to the therapeutic process of helping trauma victims heal from their childhood caretaker interference with their natural age and stage development as well as any physical and sexual abuse they may suffer. This can be a very difficult and daunting undertaking without the right Client-directed Energetic Therapy tools. During the therapeutic trauma healing process, these trauma clients usually encounter enormous emotional and energetic resistance as they revisit their painful childhood and adult trauma. This often prevents them from successfully working though and healing their trauma. Fortunately, trauma victims have within them a strong internal dive to heal their trauma. In addition, there are a number of powerful Energetic Trauma Healing Protocols that can be employed by clients, Therapists, and healing practitioners to help overcome their fears and internal resistance. In this presentation I will introduce these Energetic Trauma Healing Protocols and demonstrate how I use them in my own Energetic Trauma Healing Therapy practice. I describe these Client-directed Energetic Therapy Protocols as innovative because in my experience, very few psychotherapists and healing practitioners know about them or how to use them correctly.

The Client-directed Energetic Therapy Protocol I use most in my trauma healing practice is the Spontaneous Movement Protocol. It instructs clients to direct their own therapy by allowing spontaneous movements to arise from their bodies which helps them heal their trauma as their internal body wisdom points the way. I fondly call this Spontaneous Movement Protocol my "Mega Star Trauma Healing Protocol" because it really does the job of moving my clients' trauma healing forward at what I call "the speed of light" as compared to other trauma healing approaches I have used.

When I initially show my clients how to use this and other Client-directed Energetic Therapy Protocols, I necessarily have to teach them how to use the protocol. Thus, in my demonstration of these innovative Client-directed Energetic Therapy Protocols here with our volunteers, the first of whom you will meet shortly, I will do most of the directing as I teach them and each of you how to use them. This might appear to contradict my stated commitment to use a Client-centered, Client-directed Therapy approach. However, I assure you it is not a contradiction because one of the central roles of a Client-directed Energetic Therapist is to teach clients how to use the Client-directed Energetic Therapy Protocols they need to fully direct their own trauma healing process. So, please see my demonstration today as, not only helping my volunteers heal their trauma, but most importantly preparing each of you how to use a Client-centered, Client-directed, Energetic Peer Co-counseling Protocol which I will present in Part II of my demonstration tomorrow. Thus, today I will demonstrate and teach you how to use the Energetic Trauma Healing Protocols that your clients will need in order successfully direct their Energetic Trauma Healing Therapy—that is, how to use The Spontaneous Movement Protocol which is the main Energetic Trauma Healing Protocol designed to help client direct their therapy, the Energetic Grounding Protocols which they will need to keep their therapy on track and grounded, and some of the Backup Trauma Healing Protocols which they may need in order to resolve specific trauma healing issues that they are likely to encounter. I also want to add that should you choose to use a medical-model, diagnostic-prescriptive therapeutic approach rather than my Client-directed Energetic Therapy approach, most of the protocols which I will demonstrate can be used successfully in a conventional Therapist-directed approach as well.

A Case Presentation and Demonstration Illustrating How I Use of the Energetic Trauma Healing Therapy Protocols

The female volunteer for my Part I case demonstration was a class member of the Golden Shadow training group to which the presentation was aimed. (I was informed the focus of this training group was on, "Finding the Gold in Your Shadow", based on the work of Carl Jung.) She had spent a considerable amount of time with a prior psychotherapist trying to heal her childhood trauma but with little success. This woman, in her early thirties, volunteered to do the demonstration because she was desperate to move beyond the stuck place in her personal trauma healing work. We met prior to doing the demonstration so I could do a brief intake interview. I noted she was tall, fairly well proportioned, but with a stiff, rigid back, tight jaw, deep set penetrating eyes, and a slightly uplifted head with a hint of stubbornness in her attitude. Her hands, arms, and feet were cold to the touch and her legs had very tightly wrapped musculature. Her mouth and lips appeared to lack energy. She was guarded in sharing her childhood and adult history. She said she had a difficult childhood which she declined to elaborate on, nor did she want to talk about her childhood family members. She reported she loved to read historical fiction and murder mystery novels and lived inside her books. She had a young teenage daughter who she said was her best friend.

My brief and mostly intuitive energetic and psychological assessment was that she had adopted a primary Holding Back Defense. I based my energetic assessment on the observation of her rigid back and guarded attitude which she presented during my intake interview, both of which are characteristics of the Holding Back Defense (This defense is designed to protect trauma victims from emotionally reaching out to others for fear of being rejected thus giving rise to its name, "The Holding Back Defense".

It also appeared she may have adopted a Holding Out Defense as a very young child, but it was unclear to me, due to her reluctance to discuss her family of origin, the kind of childhood trauma she might have suffered which caused her to adopt this dissociated type of defense. I based this part of my brief assessment mostly on a sense that she was not fully present during the intake interview and her hands and feet were ice cold as well as the fact she reported spending so much time reading fiction and her statement that books were her life. Not being fully present, having ice cold extremities, and living in a fantasy world are all characteristics of the Holding Out Defense. However, I was hopeful that all of this might become more evident during her Energetic Trauma Healing work with me during the demonstration. I did not share my assessment during the intake interview because the Client-directed Energetic Therapy approach I use puts clients in charge of directing their therapy while I act as their guide by suggesting Energetic Healing Interventions and teaching them how to use these Client-directed Energetic Therapy Protocols.

A Note to More Conventional Oriented Psychotherapists

I want to note here that although I use a Client-centered, Client-directed Energetic Therapy approach in this demonstration, most of these Energetic Trauma Healing Protocols can also be used with good results in more conventional, Therapist-directed approaches to psychotherapy in which the Therapist uses the medical model of diagnosis and prescription to treat trauma clients.

Using The Hair-Pin Energetic Grounding Protocol to Begin the Demonstration

Following the introduction to my Energetic Trauma Healing Therapy Innovations presentation, I moved ahead with the demonstration by having the volunteer as well as the class members and myself do energetic grounding using the Hair-pin Protocol. It gets its name from the way the body resembles a Hair-pin when doing the Hair-pin Energetic Grounding Protocol.

Very briefly, this Energetic Grounding Protocol invites clients to remove their shoes, stand normally, and then bend forward at the waist letting their upper body hang down with their fingers nearly touching the floor. They are to soften their knees by bending them slightly, relaxing their neck muscles so their head hangs down freely, and then push their sacrum up toward the ceiling by straightening their knees slowly and then relaxing them several times. Doing this puts stress on their legs to create a vibratory movement allowing energy to flow into their lower body, legs, and feet which grounds them energetically and brings them more fully into the present moment. It is just one of a powerful set of Energetic Grounding Protocols I use in my demonstration. I call these Energetic Grounding Protocols my "Backup Mega Star Protocols" because they are so vital in helping clients move their Energetic Trauma Healing Therapy forward.

Using The Client In Charge Agreement Protocol

Then, I introduced my volunteer and asked her to read aloud, The Client In Charge Agreement, which I had previously handed out to the class members. When she finished reading aloud the agreement, I went over it again to stress the main points in the agreement. It states the client is in charge of her/his therapy process with the Therapist serving as a teacher, guide, and Assist Person. Next, I asked her if she understood the agreement, which she indicated she did, and then secured her acceptance of it by having her sign the agreement. As her Therapist for the demonstration, I followed by signing the agreement as well. I want to note here that this Client In Charge Agreement is critical for setting the stage to have clients direct their own Energetic Trauma Healing Therapy which is a central innovation in my client-centered approach.

Then, I asked her how she was feeling about volunteering to do the demonstration with me. "I am a bit scared," she answered in a barely audible voice while avoiding contact with my eyes. She looked pale, withdrawn, and energetically listless which was in sharp contrast to her more self-confident demeanor during her intake interview with me. "So, you are a little scared," I replied.

"Actually, I am terrified," she answered with a nervous laugh and looked like she might suddenly disappear from the room in a whiff of smoke. "What would help make you feel safer being here with me?" I asked. "I would feel safer if I was not on display," she said, moving a little behind me as if to shield herself from being seen.

Using the Healing Power of Group Energy Protocol

I then asked her if she would feel safer knowing the class members watching this demonstration were there to support her and were on her side. She answered that this might help but looked skeptical. In response, I asked the class members to move their chairs into a circle around us, leaving the volunteer and me in the center of the group so she could see the faces of everyone. She nodded that this change in seating was better but she still felt uncomfortable and frightened. This prompted me to further use the healing power of the group energy as follows.

Using the Validation Protocol to Help My Volunteer Gain More Energy and Strength to Move on with Her Trauma Healing Work

I asked her if it would help to know what the group members were thinking. She answered affirmatively, so I asked several group members to share their thoughts and feelings. She received validating answers such as, "I think you are very brave and courageous," and, "I appreciate your willingness to share your story," for example. Upon hearing these validating comments, her face brightened and she stood more erect with less of a look of wanting to disappear.

An Important Note on Using the Healing Power of the Group

I am a great believer in the healing power of group therapy. For one thing, doing Client-directed Energetic Therapy in a group setting can be very motivating for clients. They get to witness other clients as they work on healing trauma that is similar to their own. This gives them a feeling that they are not alone—that others are struggling with problems that are very familiar and similar to their own problems. In addition, they also get to see how others are working to resolve their problems and trauma which then gives them ideas and motivation to work on their own problems and trauma. Furthermore, there simply is a lot of energy in the room in a group setting which often helps clients push through and overcome their fear and resistance in moving forward with their healing. This is why I offer at least one ongoing therapy group which my clients can join at any time. If clients have mental health insurance, and therefore, can afford to do individual and group therapy at the same time, I often recommend they do so because they are able to make greater and faster progress by doing both kinds of Client-directed Energetic Therapy. When clients are struggling financially to pay for their therapy, and therefore must make a choice between doing individual therapy only two times a month, for example, and doing group therapy every week, I recommend they opt for doing the group therapy on a regular weekly basis. I also offer Client-directed Energetic Therapy workshops at least a couple of times a year which is another option for my clients to get the benefits of doing group therapy.

Back to My Volunteer: Using Energetic Grounding to Help Her Become More Embodied and Empowered

I followed up by asking if she was willing to do some Energetic Grounding to reduce her anxiety by bringing her more into her body and the present moment. She indicated her willingness but was still a bit reluctant. (I want to note here, doing Energetic Grounding often helps clients who are fearful or reluctant to move ahead with their therapy, overcome their fear or reluctance as the Energetic Grounding helps them feel stronger—this is literally true because doing Energetic Grounding strengthens their legs and feet by getting more energy to come into their lower body and thus their legs and feet.)

Using the Assisted Hair-pin Energetic Grounding Protocol

At that point, I reasoned it might be a good idea to have everyone in the room, including my volunteer, do some Energetic Grounding. In doing this, it could help the volunteer relax and not feel like she was on exhibition. I asked everyone to remove their shoes and socks to work in their bare feet before choosing a partner to do Assisted Hair-pin Energetic Grounding within a pair. This required each pair to take turns being the Focus Person who did the Energetic Grounding while their partner acted as the Assist Person to help them ground by putting more stress on their legs. I explained the Focus Persons' task was to bend forward at the waist, letting their head and arms hang down toward the floor while slightly bending and softening their knees. The Assist Person was then to place his or her forearms across the Focus Person's sacrum and push down on it slowly using the weight of their upper body to put increased stress on the Focus Persons' legs which would help them become more grounded.

I demonstrated this by asking the host to be the Focus Person. I instructed him to bend at his waist and let his head, upper body, and arms hang down while I acted as his Assist Person. My job as his Assist Person, I explained, was to stand beside him, and with his permission, place my forearms across his sacrum and push down slightly as he pushed up against my weight by straightening his knees. I further explained this pushing down on his sacrum would help to amplify the energetic grounding effect. The host agreed this was acceptable and so we proceeded with the demonstration of the Assisted Energetic Grounding Protocol. As we did so, I explained the goal of the Assisted Energetic Grounding was for the host as the Focus Person to feel more energy move into the lower half of his body which created increased warmth and heat in his lower body as well as a vibratory movement and energy streaming in his legs and a feeling of having his feet planted on the floor. This increased a feeling of strength in his lower body, especially in his legs and feet. When his legs began to tire I asked the host to come up into an upright standing position and report on the effects of doing the grounding exercise. He reported he felt much more in contact with his body, more present, and much more energetically grounded.

We then, as a group, proceeded to do the Assisted Hair-pin Energetic Grounding in this manner. Then, I asked the pairs to reverse roles so everyone had a turn being the Focus Person. When we finished the Assisted Energetic Grounding exercise, everyone reported feeling a difference in the room, and numerous class members commented they not only felt more grounded but also felt more present in their bodies with a clearer mind.

Using the Downhill Ski Energetic Grounding Protocol

When we finished the Assisted Hair-pin Energetic Grounding exercise, I asked the volunteer how she felt. She replied, "I feel more grounded...." She paused and did not finish her sentence. I could hear her unspoken "but" as she looked like she still wanted to disappear from being on display, so I decided to have her do more Energetic Grounding to strengthen her self-confidence. I suggested she use the Downhill Ski Energetic Grounding Protocol since she had told me prior to this she loved skiing. I thought perhaps having her do a simulated downhill ski run might be fun for her, thus allowing her to let down in a novel way. I explained my reason for wanting her to do the Downhill Ski Energetic Grounding exercise and asked if she was willing to give it a go. She agreed with a bit more enthusiasm, but it was clear she still harbored some reluctance to being on center stage.

I handed her two 36-inch-long dowel rod 'ski poles', and asked her to take a downhill ski stance by bending her knees to move her weight slightly forward as she held onto the dowel ski poles for balance. I then asked her to imagine she was on a downhill ski run and to alternately lean to one side and then the other as if she was making wide ski turns. The goal, I said, was to create a vibratory movement and streaming of energy in her legs. As she did so, a big smile appeared on her face. She was clearly having fun doing it. When her legs were tired, I suggested she rest by standing upright in a normal standing position. When she was rested, I asked her to repeat the imaginary downhill ski run once more.

"How was that?" I asked when she finished. She answered it was great and she looked a lot more present, self-confident, and ready to move on with the demonstration. At that point, I suggested she take her downhill ski stance once more, bend her knees, and lean as far forward as she was able. I asked her how that felt.

"I have a lot of stiffness in my ankles," she replied. I nodded and told her I had also noticed the stiffness in her ankles. I added it appeared she had high arches in her feet. I then asked her if she would like to do some release work on her calves to help loosen her stiff ankles as well as do some footwork to release the contracted muscles in the arches of her feet, both of which would help her become better energetically grounded. She agreed.

Using a Small Pressure Roller Protocol to Help Release the Muscle Holding in Her Calves

Tightness and tension in the calf muscles is often the cause of ankle stiffness, so to help her remedy this, I suggested she use a small 6-inch diameter by 18-inch-long foam pressure roller to help release this tension. (This foam roller is available on Amazon.com in various sizes and lengths.) I also mentioned as an alternative, I use a Yamuna Body Rolling ball about the size of a grapefruit to help release muscle holding in the calves and hamstrings. (The Yamuna Body Rolling Ball is also available in a set of three different sized balls on Amazon.com.) I gave her instructions as follows: "Lay on the floor backside down with both legs together and flat on the floor. Place the 6 inch foam roller under the calf of your right leg starting at the ankle end of your calf muscle and then place your left leg over the top of your right leg directly above the roller. Use your left leg to put pressure on your right calf muscle by pressing down with your left leg. Maintain this position for 15 to 30 seconds to help release the tension there. Then move the roller up an inch or two on your right calf muscle and hold for 15 to 30 seconds. Repeat this procedure until you reach the upper end of your right calf muscle." When she finished, I instructed her to repeat the same procedure on her left calf muscle. When she finished, I suggested she stand and ground once again using the downhill ski position. When she finished grounding, she reported her ankles felt less stiff.

(I want to note here that holding the above positions for 60 to 120 seconds or longer can be even more helpful depending on the painfulness of doing so. If placing the left leg on top of the right, for example, is too painful, then this step can be skipped by simply placing the right leg on the roller without the additional pressure of the left leg. Also, this same procedure can be used to help release tension in the hamstring muscles which may be contributing to the holding in the calf muscles.)

Using the Foot Saver Protocol to Help Release the Muscle Holding in the Arches of Her Feet

To help the volunteer release the contracted muscles in the arches of her feet, I took out two Foot Savers from my equipment bag. (Foot Savers resemble a moderately firm rubber ball about fist size which is cut in half with the flat sides placed on the floor. (These can be found on Amazon.com. A Pinky Ball, also found on Amazon.com, works well for this purpose and when cut in half is a cheaper alternative to the Foot Savers.) I placed the Foot Savers flat side down on the floor in front of a chair. I asked the volunteer to stand holding onto the back of the chair and place her feet on them with the Foot Savers in the center of her high arches. "Now just stand on the Foot Savers without putting a lot of pressure on them with your feet," I instructed her. She did so, and exclaimed, "Wow, these bite into my feet!" I followed up by encouraging her to play with the Foot Savers by putting a little less pressure on them by using the chair back to help her do so and to move her feet around when it became uncomfortable, so they put pressure on other parts of her feet." After a couple of minutes of using the Foot Savers in this way which still looked like it was not going well for her, I suggested she use only one Foot Saver at a time so she could better control the amount of pressure placed on the Foot Saver. She reported she liked standing on one Foot Saver at a time better. After several minutes of playing with the Foot Savers one at a time on both feet, I asked her to stand normally and report on how her feet felt. "I definitely feel my feet making better contact with the floor, " she replied, "and I'm also getting the idea of what it means to be more energetically grounded."

An Important Note on Using Energetic Grounding

Although I do not include every instance of having my volunteer's use of energetic grounding here, I often used energetic grounding not only with the volunteer but also the class members, and myself to keep us all energetically well grounded and in the present moment. Specifically I used the Hair-pin Protocol, Assisted Hair-pin Protocol, and the Downhill Ski Protocol as my favorite go to Energetic Grounding exercises when I began each demonstration session as well as at the end of each session. I also used these Energetic Grounding Protocols when the volunteer was about to do an intervention activity and at the completion of the activity as well as during the activity when it was needed. I do not always indicate this in the demonstration write-up here due to the fact it becomes very repetitive to do so. However, I do not want this to diminish the importance of doing energetic grounding continually as I did so with the volunteer, the class members, and myself to keep us all energetically grounded, in our bodies, and in the present moment.

Back to the Volunteer

"Are you now ready to proceed ahead with your trauma healing work?" I asked. "Yes, I am raring to go," she replied with a big smile. The group applauded this with shouts of, "Bravo!" and "Go get 'em girl!" This had the effect of bringing out her inner bravado as she raised her fists into the air above her head which brought even more applause and louder shouts of encouragement.

Using The Spontaneous Movement Protocol to Help the Volunteer Direct Her Client-directed Energetic Therapy and Move Her Trauma Healing Work Forward

To begin addressing her trauma healing work more directly, I asked her to stand facing me in the center of the group. Rather than provide some history about the issue she wanted to focus on, I suggested she begin by setting an intention for her healing work. She said she wanted to "get unstuck" in her therapy. I then instructed her to simply go to a still point in her body and let a spontaneous movement arise from her body that would help her realize her stated intention of getting unstuck and move her trauma healing and personal empowerment forward.

I explained to the volunteer that the use of the Spontaneous Movement Protocol is the main Client-directed Energetic Therapy Protocol that I use to help clients direct their trauma healing process. "Movement is connected to every part of the human brain," I said, "so when you set your healing intention and then allow a spontaneous movement to arise from your body to help you realize your healing intention, it will likely elicit buried and hidden trauma memories, feelings, emotions, thoughts, and new spontaneous movements. Your task is to express the elicited memories, feelings, and thoughts, and follow them wherever your spontaneous movements point. If you do so, it will advance your trauma healing therapy forward."

She did as I instructed, closing her eyes and becoming very still for several moments. Then she made a fist with her right hand and began to lightly pound her thigh. As she did so, I asked if there were any thoughts, feelings, words, sounds, or memories went with her spontaneous movement. "Yes, I feel sad and angry, but I don't like to feel this way," she said, glancing at the exit door. "So, are you feeling resistant about being sad and angry?" I asked. "Yes, I feel very resistant and actually quite fearful," she answered.

Giving a Mini Lecture on How Our Brain Alarm Signals Danger Ahead and Thus Creates Internal Resistance

I stopped the demonstration at that point and gave a mini-lecture on how our emotional brain alarm triggers our internal resistance and fear due to a sense of danger when our current experience begins to be similar to our past trauma experience. I explained this alarm response is designed to protect us from further harm, pain, and trauma—that is to say, when we perceive sensory information that might mean danger ahead, this information is sent directly to our brain's emotional alarm center which instantly compares the current situation to any stored memories of past danger and if there are any similarities, then the emotional alarm triggers a bodily response which prepares us to flee, fight, or freeze. When our flight or fight response is not available or cut off, our freeze response kicks in.

Back to the Volunteer

I then turned to the volunteer and suggested she was probably processing information around her sadness and anger which then triggered an alarm in her emotional brain forewarning her of danger ahead. I further suggested this must have prepared her to flee as she glanced at the exit door when she was about to begin her trauma healing work. I explained it certainly did not prepare her to fight because, as a trauma victim, she had been left without the internal resources needed to fight and do battle. She agreed with my assessment, indicating that initially she did have the urge to run from the room. However, she added that she also really wanted to solve her trauma problem because running from her sadness and anger in the past had only made her feel more of a victim.

I suggested that since fighting and fleeing from her sadness and anger were thus not an option in her mind, her emotional brain alarm's only alternative to protect her was to freeze and prepare her to resist moving ahead with what it perceived as dangerous work. She agreed with my assessment. I then suggested she now let a spontaneous movement arise from her body that would help her overcome her fear and freeze response.

Using The Spontaneous Movement Protocol to Overcome Fear and Internal Resistance

For the second time she closed her eyes and let her body be still. After a few moments, she spontaneously brought her left hand to her forehead, nearly covering her eyes. She indicated she felt very alone and did not want to see where her trauma work was headed.

Using The Personal Support Protocol

In response, I asked her if she would like someone from the training group to come forward to support her while doing her trauma healing work. "Yes," she said. "I feel very alone and vulnerable out here in front of all of you." She then chose an older woman from the group who had befriended her to serve as her Assist Person during her Energetic Trauma Healing work. As the older woman joined her, she visibly relaxed.

Using The Energetic Amplifying Equipment Protocols to Help Move the Trauma Healing Work Forward

However, I noted the volunteer was not breathing normally. Her chest looked tight and constricted as did her belly, with almost no movement in her diaphragm.

Using The Pressure Roller Protocol

As a result of this observation, I suggested she do some deep breathing exercise using a large pressure roller which I had on hand. This pressure roller is 14 inches in diameter and 24 inches long, made from a round fiberboard construction form and is covered with carpet over a 1 inch layer of foam. It is used to put pressure on the back and chest to release muscle tension and help deepen breathing. (Similar foam rollers are available on Amazon.com.) I suggested she lay on her back over the roller, which was placed on the floor, so her shoulder blades made contact with the roller while her legs extended out from it with her knees bent and her feet placed flat on the floor. I gave her a set of 2 lb. Dumbbells which she held in her hands to provide more pressure on her back and chest by extending them fully backward at a level a little below her head. Then I instructed her to roll back and forth on the roller very slowly. This put stress on her back and chest and helped open and deepen her breathing while at the same time increasing her energetic grounding to some extent.

After a couple of minutes of rolling, I asked if it was alright to have the older woman who joined use her hands to put some more pressure on her chest. The volunteer agreed to this modification and then proceeded ahead. After several moments of enduring the pressure on her chest, she began to breathe with a much fuller respiration so I suggested if any thoughts, feelings, words, or sounds came to mind she should voice them aloud. She immediately began to sob and voiced the words, "Mom and dad, where were you? I needed you! I can't do this alone." She continued in this vein for a time while still rolling on the pressure roller with the older woman still applying pressure on her chest; then she dropped her butt to the floor in exhaustion and rested with her back against the roller. She was now breathing very deeply while her body and face looked more energetically charged. She was also making full eye contact with the older woman and had a look of gratitude and affection on her face and in her demeanor.

While the volunteer rested, I asked her how it was going in the demonstration and if she had any suggestions or feedback for me so far. She replied everything was going fine so far but she was surprised by her statement that she needed her parents. "They were never there for me so why should I need them," she said.

Doing More Spontaneous Movement Protocol Work

When she had rested, I asked her to resume doing the Spontaneous Movement work, which I explained, might help her take the next step toward healing and finding her way forward. I also instructed her to use the Spontaneous Movement Protocol at any point in the work ahead if she felt stuck or more resistance and fear surfaced. I said I would still be there to help manage the process when needed but I wanted her to take direct ownership of it so she felt fully in charge of her healing. I indicated I would help her be aware of her spontaneous movements as they arose to direct her since these movements could be subtle and easily overlooked or ignored as her emotional brain alarm and internal resistance tried to interfere and protect her from further perceived healing danger.

The volunteer then moved on with her trauma healing work by closing her eyes and letting her body become still. Ever so slightly and slowly she began to open and close her hands. I pointed this movement out and asked her what her hands wanted to say. "I want to reach out for love and let it in," she said, "but I am terrified to do so. I don't know why I am so afraid to love, but I am." She lowered her head and stood silently for a while refusing to look at me and meet my eyes. It was as if she was very disappointed in herself for being so fearful. I broke the silence by asking if she felt stuck and resistant to continue the healing work. She nodded yes. I then asked her if she would be willing to play a part in a heroic story which might help her get unstuck. She said she was game for anything that could help her move forward.

Using The Heroic Story Protocol to Continue Moving Her Trauma Healing Work Forward

I suggested she imagine being the Sovereign or Queen of her Personal Realm, and as Queen, one of her roles was to protect her realm from the bad characters and transgressors that tried to invade and infiltrate it. I followed up by saying, "You are to summon all of your warriors—your energy, your courage, your intelligence, your spirit, your determination, and your perseverance—to do battle against these invaders who want to imprison you in a trauma trap. It is up to you," I said, "to lead this heroic fight and rid your Personal Realm of these bad characters and transgressors." I then asked her if she could imagine herself being this Queen who is up to taking on this task. She immediately squared her shoulders, and replied, "I am up to it!"

At this point she remembered my suggestion to use the Spontaneous Movement Protocol if she felt stuck and resistant in order to move her trauma healing forward. "I know what to do," she said. She immediately went to a still point in her body, and then her right hand moved spontaneously to cover her mouth. She was aware of the movement and indicated the thought that arose with it was, "As Queen of my Personal Realm, I cannot reach out for love and let it in because if I did so, I would be betrayed by someone close to me." I repeated her words back to help her realize their significance.

"Yes," she said. "My mother was jealous of me as a little girl. She acted as if she did not love or want me. She appeared to only care about my older brothers. I recall my father reading to me at bedtime and singing songs while playing his guitar, so I know he loved me. He would bring me little presents once in a while. Whenever he did so, I knew I would pay a price, however. My mother would tie me up the next day and whip me with a big willow stick she kept in the coat closet. I would try to hide from her on those days but she always found me. Then, when I was about eight years old, my father got a promotion which required him to work even longer hours at his job, so I saw even less of him after that. He would still bring me presents every now and then. I would hide them but my mother always found them and made me pay with her whippings. This change in our family life made my mother very unhappy and upset. As a result, my father began going to the bar after work so he did not have to face her wrath. As a result, my mother began to drink alcohol heavily and was drunk and raging all night at my absent father for leaving her alone to raise us children without his help and support. When I was about twelve years old, my drunk mother shot and killed my father one night when he arrived home and then turned the gun on herself to end her life. My oldest brother and his wife stepped in to raise me after our parents died. I thought things would be better after that because I knew my older brother and his wife loved me...." With her incomplete sentence, she moved her hands and shoulders slightly as if to shrug them and say, 'I don't know'.

Using The Identifying The Inner Judge Protocol

With this last statement and movement, she stopped talking and dropped her head to stare at the floor in silence. I let the silence continue for a little while. As she continued to stare at the floor, my sense was that an inner resistance was causing her silence and preventing her from moving forward with her trauma healing work. I raised this by asking her if she was feeling blocked. She nodded her head "yes", but continued to stare at the floor in silence. I then pointed out the movement of her hands and shoulders at the end of her last statement as if she was shrugging and saying non-verbally, "I don't know".

"I don't know," she said. I followed up by asking her what was going on in her mind. "Are you hearing a voice in your head speaking to you?" She looked at me startled, as if I was somehow reading her mind. "Yes," she said. "I'm hearing a voice in my mind say, 'Shut up and stop talking.'"

I explained my sense was that this inner voice was her brain alarm causing her to sense danger which thus produced in her a fear and resistance to moving forward with her work, and it was probably connected to her last unfinished statement about knowing her older brother and his wife loved her. I called this inner voice in her mind "The Inner Judge" which, I explained, was probably coming online in her head to say "Don't proceed ahead because it is dangerous". I also explained that if this was true, her Inner Judge was not her friend; in fact, the opposite was true, it was probably the introjected voice of her brother, or her mother, or someone connected to her childhood who wanted to control her and keep her from speaking the truth.

She listened to my explanation without much reaction. I continued by asking if she would be willing to talk to this Inner Judge voice. She agreed. I then asked her to choose a volunteer from the class who would act as her Inner Judge in a role-play drama. She chose a tall man from the class who had a stern looking face. I asked her to face the man while he spoke the words, 'Shut up, it's too dangerous'. "Yes," she said, "it does feel too dangerous to go on with this!"

Using The Just Be in Your Body Protocol

I asked her to just be in her body—to be aware of how her body felt. I let her sit with this for several moments. I then continued by suggesting, "Just be in various parts of your body". For instance, I said, "I want you to just be in your chest." A moment later, I said, "I want you to just be in your breathing." A moment later, I said, "I want you to just be in your back bone." I continued in this way, asking her to just be in various parts of her body until she began to visibly relax. As she did so, she looked to the older woman and beckoned her to come stand beside her. After several moments of just being in her body, she was breathing more fully and appeared more at ease and present.

Using The Defending Against the Inner Judge Protocol in a Role-play Enactment Drama

I asked her if she was willing to continue, and if so, to tell off the man acting as her Inner Judge by saying things like, "You are not my friend! You are just trying to control me, and I won't have it!" She faced the man acting as her Inner Judge and used the words I had suggested to her. "You are not my friend! You are my enemy. You are trying to control me, and I won't stand for it!" she yelled. As she did so, a posture of strength appeared to come into her body as she straightened her shoulders and stiffened her back. She was about to speak again when a terrified look came into her eyes and shut her down. She grabbed the older woman's hand and held onto it strongly for a moment; then she let go to cover her eyes with her hands. She stood in silence with her hands over her eyes. "Is there something you don't want to see?" I asked. She nodded slightly but did not speak as she pursed her lips as if forbidding herself to speak.

Using The Subtle Energy Protocol to Release the Energetic Holding in the Eyes

"I now want you to keep your eyes closed and just be in them for a few moments," I said. "Now, use your hands to lightly brush away the energy veil that is clouding your eyes and preventing you from seeing what you fear," I continued. She did as I suggested. "Now, just be in your body, open your eyes, and let yourself see clearly," I said.

She moved her hands away from her eyes, opened them, and blurted out, "I know my older brother loved me because he invited me to join him and his wife in bed at night." With this statement, she abruptly stopped speaking with a stricken look on her face. A long silence ensued.

Using The Tune-in For Resonance Protocol

"Your brother invited you to join him and his wife in bed," I repeated in a flat, non-emotional tone. "Yes," she said, "that is how I know he cared about me." I nodded, paused, and then said, "I'd like you to close your eyes, place your right hand on your heart, and go inside to the part of you that knows the truth because it resonates or does not resonate in your chest." She did so. "Now, I want you to say the words silently to yourself, "I know that is how he cared about me." She did so silently mouthing the words. "Now, ask yourself if your statement, 'I know that is how he cared about me,' resonates as the truth for you."

A moment later, she began to weep. I asked her what was making her sad. She shook her head without looking up. "No, it does not resonate and is not the truth," she said, "because when I joined my brother and his wife in bed, he made me be part of their sexual pleasuring, and I did not want to do that." With this admission she stood silent as if struck dumb, numb, and without further emotion or words. The older woman moved to embrace her and give comfort, but the volunteer ignored the older woman's embrace. I let this stand for a bit as I reflected on what the volunteer had just revealed.

As I thought about the volunteer's story, it was quite possible she might be feeling shame around having joined her brother in his sexual pleasuring as well as revealing this fact publicly to me and her training class members, and this could be shutting her down. I was well aware shame can be a major block to healing trauma. However, my intuitive sense was this was not the case, at least not in that setting where her class members were treating her as a hero. I decided to check in with her to ask if she was feeling shame. Her answer was "No", so I decided not to pursue it at that point. I reasoned I could raise it later if it appeared to me that shame was the roadblock to her moving forward. Instead, I pursued another idea.

"So, your brother betrayed you, and thus, in your mind and memory, love carries a very big price tag of betrayal," I said. "As a result, faced with reaching out for love now and letting it in, no matter how much you want and long for it, your emotional brain alarm gets triggered and mobilizes you to freeze, or at times flee, and not reach out for the love that is now staring you in the face for fear of being betrayed again even though it is not the same situation you faced as a child with your mother and father, and your brother and his wife. Is that right?" I asked. She affirmed my assessment was correct.

"But I don't know what to do," she lamented. "I feel totally helpless." At this point she looked completely dejected and defeated. The older woman turned to me with a sad, helpless look on her face as if to say, "I don't know what to do." I nodded and said to the volunteer, "I know things look hopeless right now, but I want to help you build a stronger energetic charge in your body and then do some more Energetic Grounding exercise. Things might look brighter afterward."

Using The Building a Strong Energetic Charge in The Body Protocol to Help Her Overcome Her Helplessness

I pulled out a small trampoline and asked the volunteer to bounce on it until she was breathing deeply, and the blood was rushing through her body. I explained by doing so, she was creating a much stronger energetic charge in her body and that an increased energetic charge can often help clients who have stalled in their therapy move forward again, or in her case, move past her feelings of helplessness. When she stopped bouncing, she appeared much more alive and much less helpless.

However, when I have clients create a stronger energetic charge in their body, I want them to ground that charge so that it moves down into their lower body, especially into their legs and feet; otherwise, the increased energetic charge can move upward into their head and cause their mind to become overactive and over reactive which can send them off in the wrong direction or create other problems such as a lack of concentration, unclear thinking, and a racing mind. To ground her increased body charge, I suggested the volunteer do an Energetic Grounding exercise which would also help her overcome her feelings of helplessness by pitting her ego against her body.

Using The Wall-sit Energetic Grounding Protocol to Help Her Ground the Strong Energetic Charge in Her Body

The Energetic Grounding exercise I suggested took the form of a Wall-sit. I instructed everyone in the class, including the volunteer and myself, to move to a wall, and then lean our backs against it. Next, I instructed everyone to side down the wall into a sitting position as if sitting in a chair. Our feet were spaced about eight inches apart with our heels sixteen inches or so from the wall. My further instructions were to stay in this Wall-sit stress position for as long as possible until it became too uncomfortable to maintain, and then to slide down the wall to a sitting position on the floor to rest. I also explained we must slide down the wall to avoid the temptation to slide up the wall into a standing position. "Sliding down the wall will bring our bodies into a resting, relaxed sitting position on our buttocks which will also help ground us," I said. I further explained the purpose of this Wall-sit Energetic Grounding Protocol was to get heat and a vibratory movement going in our legs which would fully energize them and thus increase the feeling of strength in our body, especially in our lower half—especially in our legs and feet. I encouraged everyone to avoid staying in the pain of the Wall-sit stress position as this would defeat its purpose. We all did the Wall-sit rest on the floor, and then repeated doing the Wall-sit two more times.

Following the completion of the Wall-sit Energetic Grounding Protocol exercise there was a noticeable shift in the class and in the volunteer. The whole room became more energized and there was a sense of determination in everyone, including the volunteer, to see things through. It was as if the whole class moved in unison, breathing fully as one being. I checked in with the volunteer to ask if she was ready to proceed ahead with her healing work which she had so courageously started. "I'm just raring to go," she said with a laugh and somewhat of a joke with a good deal of reluctance in her voice.

At that point, I reconsidered my decision to move forward with the demonstration. Instead, I decided it might be a good time to take a coffee break as well as a break from the intense drama the volunteer's story and trauma healing work had engendered. When I announced the break, the entire training class moved to embrace the volunteer with love and a sweetness that was very touching. Then, following the coffee break, we went back to work.

Using The Wall-sit Protocol to Pit Her Inner-Judge Against Her Body

"My guess is your Inner Judge is holding your body hostage," I said to the volunteer. "What I mean by this is that your Inner Judge has caused you to identify with it. Thus, in this way, it may have captured you and may now call the shots in your mind and body," I said. "Do you mean it has tricked me?" she asked. "This is exactly what I mean," I replied. "Your Inner Judge is full of trickery and will do anything to keep running the show rather than allow you to direct things. There are a couple of ways to stop it dead in its tracks. One way is to pit your Inner Judge against your body. The other way is to dis-identify with your Inner Judge."

I suggested she first use the Wall-sit Protocol to pit her Inner Judge against her body which would cause her captured ego to fail. To do this, she followed my instructions which was to do the Wall-sit and refuse to give in and go down to the floor nor stand up to relieve the enormous stress it would cause on her body. While doing the Wall-sit, she used words like, "I am not going down to the floor. I will win this one!" When her legs could no longer handle the stress, she collapsed to the floor where she found relief and could relax. I explained when she pitted her Inner Judge captured ego against her body, her body would win every time. In this way, her Inner Judge would suffer a defeat. She repeated the Wall-sit two more times, refusing to go down each time until her body forced her to do so. This left her totally spent as she rested after each defeated bout. She reported she felt clearer in her mind as if a dark cloud had been lifted from her mind and body. Thus, her Inner Judge was on the way out. But to insure this was the case, I suggested she do one more exercise.

Using The Dis-identifying with The Inner Judge Protocol

I then explained it looked like she had defeated her Inner Judge, but this may have now left it in only a weakened condition. "You are now in a position to deliver the final knockout punch to your Inner Judge," I said. To deliver the knockout punch, I asked her to dis-identify with her Inner Judge. I explained when someone says they are totally helpless, for example—also implying they are a total failure and bad as a result of being helpless and failing—they are identifying with their Inner Judge and speaking its words rather than their own truth. "The truth is," I emphasized, "no one, including you, is totally helpless, a total failure, and therefore bad. The truth is they may have been helpless and failed at things, but their whole being is not helpless and a failure. The truth is there is always some good and empowerment in every person no matter how helpless they feel or how much they have failed. Their TRUE SELF is never totally helpless, a total failure, nor totally bad and worthless. This applies to you as well.

"So, how do I dis-identify with my Inner Judge?" she asked. I replied that dis-identifying with her Inner Judge was a simple matter of saying, "My Inner Judge, NOT MY TRUE SELF, is telling me I am totally helpless, a complete failure, and therefore a bad and worthless person. However, I—My true self—am not totally helpless even though it feels like it. And, I am not a total failure nor a bad and worthless person. My Inner Judge is telling me this, not ME!" She repeated my words. Then I asked her to continue by speaking directly to her weakened Inner Judge by saying, "You are talking nonsense! Just because I feel helpless does not mean I am helpless, nor a failure, nor bad, nor worthless! So get off my back and get lost! I am done with you!" Again, she repeated my words speaking directly to her weakened Inner Judge. When she finished, she exclaimed, "Wow, it feels like a burden has been lifted from my back!"

Using The Advocate Protocol to End Her Inner Judge Voice

I suggested I act as her advocate to do some work to end her Inner Judge voice for good. I used the analogy that I would act as her advocate much as if I was her attorney to act as her Defender by going on the attack against her Inner Judge as if we were in a courtroom trial. She was a little apprehensive but agreed to my suggestion. I then said her Inner Judge did not take up residence in her mind without coming from somewhere—that is, it did not simply appear out of thin air. "Where did it originate?" I asked. She shrugged her shoulders and shook her head in bewilderment. "Who during your childhood treated you as a failure, as bad, and as worthless?" I asked. "That was my mother," she answered. "And, who used and exploited you?" I asked. "My older brother used me when he invited me into his bed to be sexual with him and his wife," she responded a little shamefaced. "So, it sounds like your childhood mother and your older brother were the originators of your Inner Judge voice which you introjected by taking in their negative treatment and exploitation of you," I said. "Yes, it certainly looks that way," she replied.

I then asked her to choose volunteers to come forward to role play her mother, older brother and his wife. When they were in place, I proceeded by having the volunteer stand behind me as I faced the stand-in mother, brother, and wife. I further instructed her to place her hands on my shoulders so she could feel the substance of me being there to advocate for her. I then told the stand-in mother, brother, and wife in very strong language and forceful tone that what they had done to her as a child was cruel, heartless, and beyond comprehension. "You tried to destroy that innocent, wonderful child by your thoughtless, betraying behavior, and you nearly succeeded but you did not reckon with her inner strength. Your unforgivable actions made her feel helpless, bad, and worthless as a child, and which still plague her as a woman today as her Inner Judge, which you created in her mind, continually turns against her. What you did was abusive and very traumatizing. You should be ashamed of your dastardly deeds! Yet, in spite of all your betraying behavior, she survived as a strong, loving woman who is doing good in the world as a caring mother and a talented Therapist. So, get out of her life and mind, and take her Inner Judge, which you created, with you!"

Using The Take-It-In Protocol

I then turned to face the volunteer and asked her if she was able to take in my advocacy words. She replied she was having difficulty taking in the idea that she was innocent. To counter this, I suggested the older woman speak to her, assuring her she had indeed been a young, innocent, loving daughter, and sister. Again, I asked her if she was able to take in the validating words of the older woman. She responded by saying she was still having difficulty. I then said, "Of course at age twelve, having lost your parents, you needed your brother's love, and because you were so young, vulnerable, and innocent, your brother used all of this to trick you into his bed and exploit you." I then asked her if my words resonated. She replied that they did. So, I asked her to repeat my words that her brother had taken advantage of her young inexperience, innocence, and need for his love to use and exploit her. She was able to do so. I followed up by asking her if she was able to take in her own words. "Yes, they do help me feel more empowered," she said. "But something is still holding me back." I replied by saying, "I have a couple of ideas about why something is still holding you back." She indicated hearing my suggestions might be helpful.

Using The Toxic Waste Dump Protocol

I retrieved a box of medical tongue depressors from my equipment bag and took one for me to use later. Them. I asked her to take one. I introduced The Toxic Waste Dump Protocol by saying as a child she had been forced to swallow a lot of toxic waste—"shit"—from her mother and older brother. I then told her that using the tongue depressor each morning for a while could help her get rid of that toxic waste. "This exercise is designed to activate your gag reflex," I explained. "Tomorrow morning, when you awake with an empty stomach, I want you to drink a glass full of water. Then, I want you to use the tongue depressor to activate your gag reflex by sticking it into the back of your throat. As you do so, I want you to imagine you are ridding yourself of all the toxic waste you were forced to swallow as a child as you throw up the water into the toilet. However, right now I want you to drink some water from your water bottle and then use the tongue depressor to activate your gag reflex only enough, so you do not actually throw up the water here." I placed a waste basket in front of her just in case she did vomit. She was very reluctant to do the exercise so I demonstrated how to do it by drinking some water and then activating my own gag reflex with my tongue depressor. With some encouragement she agreed to do the exercise. After completing the toxic waste dump exercise, she reported that her whole body felt fully alive. Her appearance confirmed she was more energetically activated and present. I finished by suggesting she do The Toxic Waste Dump Protocol each morning for several weeks. "Doing this will fully activate your gag reflex and stop you from holding in all the toxic waste and shit you were forced to swallow as a child," I said. "It will also help you set boundaries that will keep you from taking in the toxic waste that others try to get you to swallow."

Using A Spiritual Bridge Protocol to Help Her Connect with a Higher Power and Dispel Her Feeling of Being All Alone

Next, I suggested my second idea of what might be holding her back. I asked her if she believed in God or a Higher Power. She answered, "Not really any more. I used to believe in Jesus but that was when I was a child." I responded by saying, "I think you may have lost your faith in Jesus because you were angry at God for allowing your mother to be so cruel to you and for your brother's betrayal of you." She thought about my words for a moment. "That resonates," she responded.

Using The Take Your Anger at God to God Protocol

I grabbed a tennis racket from my equipment bag and handed it to her. I placed a large pillow on a chair in front of her with instructions to hit it with the tennis racket repeatedly using as much force as she could muster. While hitting, I told her to yell and keep repeating the words, "God, you did not protect me! You let my mother and brother abuse me! I am angry with you God!" or, some variation of this theme.

The volunteer hit the pillow with real force while voicing her anger at God and Jesus for not protecting her as a child. Finally she stopped in exhaustion to rest. "How was that?" I asked. "That was good," she said with a grin. "But, I hope God and Jesus are not angry with me for yelling at them," she said as she looked skyward. I answered, "I think God and Jesus are big enough to handle your anger. Besides, not expressing your anger to God and Jesus has separated you from them. You might even feel closer to God and Jesus again now that you have taken your anger at God and Jesus to them." She nodded and replied, "I do feel a bit closer to Jesus and God. But I hope that God and Jesus can forgive me for hating my mother and my brother for what they did to me," she repeated.

Using The God Has Already Forgiven Me Protocol

"I can understand this," I said. "However, I want you to consider that God has already forgiven you." She looked at me with a very skeptical look on her face. "Are you willing to try another Spiritual Bridge Protocol?" I asked. She shrugged her shoulders with a question mark in her demeanor. "Let me explain," I replied. "When I have transgressed against someone, I say to myself, God has already forgiven me for my transgression. This does not mean I am free to continue transgressing but it does help me forgive myself for what I have done, and therefore, not be burdened down with guilt and shame for my transgression. Does this make sense to you?" I asked. She replied that it did make sense. Then I encouraged her to speak the words, "God and Jesus have already forgiven me" in relation to her anger at her mother and older brother. After doing so, she reported speaking those words did lift her feeling of guilt from her shoulders somewhat. I also added she might need to hang onto some of her anger for a while longer because it could serve to empower her in moving forward with her therapy.

Using The God Has Already Forgiven Them Protocol

I added as an addendum I use a similar procedure when someone has transgressed against me by saying, "God has already forgiven them for their transgression." Doing this," I explained, "helps me let go of my anger as well as my wish to seek revenge on my transgressor. However, my sense is it may be premature for you to try forgiving your mother for her cruelty and your brother for betraying you for the same reason that it could serve to empower you in moving forward with your therapy.".

Asking a Delicate Question

"I want to change the subject by asking you a very delicate question," I said. "I do so, because to ignore this question will not help you gain your full empowerment as a woman." I paused for a moment to draw attention to the serious nature of the question I was about to ask. "This may not be the place to ask this question," I said, "so if you feel it invades your personal privacy, please say so, and you can address it, if you wish, in a less public venue such as an individual therapy session. I also want to remind you are in charge of your therapy and signed an agreement with me which stated this." With this disclaimer, I asked my question as follows. "Is it not the case that being forced to participate in your brother's sexual play as a twelve-year-old surely must have negatively affected your own sexual life as a grown woman?"

The volunteer blushed at my asking this question, but she did not back away from answering it which I found very refreshing. "Yes, it has caused some problems for me in my sexual relationships with my husband," she replied. "My pelvic area is frozen to some extent which prevents me from having much pleasure during sexual intercourse," she said, pausing for a moment to reflect on her statement. Then, she continued by saying, "Do you think there is something I could do about this?" she asked.

Using The Scissors Kicking Protocol

I responded by saying there was a good deal she could do about the problem. I explained one of my go-to energetic exercises for unfreezing the pelvis is using The Scissors Kicking Protocol to release the tension and holding in the abductor muscles. "This protocol gets its name from the way the kicking is done which makes your legs look like the blades of scissors as you kick while laying back side down on the floor," I explained. "If you wish to do this exercise, I will place a large pillow under your heels so you won't hurt them," I further explained as she made the decision to lay backside down on a mat on the floor. I instructed her to kick by alternately raising each leg off the floor and then bringing her heels down on the pillow in rapid succession and to do so one hundred times. When she finished kicking, I instructed her to rest and then repeat the scissors kicking two more times. When she finished kicking, she reported her pelvis did not feel so tight.

Using The Air-Hammer Protocol

"My second go-to protocol for releasing muscle holding in the pelvis resembles the action of an air hammer as you slam your butt repeatedly on a folded blanket," I said. I instructed the volunteer to stay laying backside down on the mat, bend her knees so her feet were placed flat on the floor, and place a folded blanket, which I handed to her, under her butt. Then I instructed her to raise her pelvis off the floor into a good stretch followed by slamming her butt down on the blanket with force to be repeated rapidly until she tired. When she finished, she reported having a good deal more feeling in her pelvis.

Using The Large Pressure Roller Protocol to Help the Volunteer Release the Holding In Her Pelvis

My third go-to protocol was to have her lay over a large pressure roller (14 inches in diameter) with her butt placed directly on the roller. "This will create a stretch in your pelvic muscles which will help to release the tense holding there," I said. "As this happens, it will allow more energy and feeling to come into your pelvis," I explained. I asked her if she would like to try using the pressure roller for this purpose. She readily agreed, so I brought out my large pressure roller once again. I instructed her to lay over it with her butt placed directly on top of the pressure roller. This created a bit of difficulty for her as she struggled to achieve the desired position. Then, I suggested she slowly roll back and forth on the pressure roller.

When she was tired from doing the rolling, I asked her to roll downward on the pressure roller until she was in a sitting position on the floor with her back resting against it. When she was rested, I suggested she stand in a normal position and check out whether she had more flexibility and feeling in her pelvis. She indicated this was indeed the case, and as if to confirm her statement, she looked more fully alive and present in her body. This prompted her to say, "I know what I must do now," she said. "I am not a helpless victim of my mother's rage and beatings, nor am I a victim any longer of my brother's past sexual abuse, betrayal, and lack of real concern and love for me. Now that I am no longer a victim, I can continue my healing and go on to find a new life filled with the love I want." As she stated this, she began to tremble as a wave of fear washed over her. When the trembling did not subside, she looked to me with alarm.

Using The Shake-Rattle-&-Roll Trauma Healing Protocol

To help lighten her alarm, I asked her if she recalled that old rock and roll song, Shake, Rattle & Roll," She nodded as she continued to shake. "Your body has just gone into Shake-Rattle-And-Roll-Mode," I said, "so let your frozen fear and trauma shake itself out of your body. It is your body's natural way of spontaneously healing the trauma you suffered as a child. I suggest you stay with the shaking and let it grow stronger if it wants to do so." With my words of encouragement, she closed her eyes and let the shaking and trembling continue until it eventually subsided of its own accord. (This natural trauma healing process is described in Waking The Tiger: Healing Trauma by Peter A. Levine [1997]. I let the volunteer be with her healing process until she slowly opened her eyes and came back to us free of some of her frozen childhood trauma. As she did so, she reached out to embrace the older woman at her side.

"What do you see in this woman's eyes," I asked. She gazed into the older woman's eyes for several moments. She then replied, "I see love." Next, I asked, "Can you let the love you see in this woman's eyes into your heart?" She paused for a bit before replying, "I can begin to let it in, but it frightens me." Her body began to tremble again. She let the trembling grow while continuing to hold the older woman's hands and look into her eyes. "Yes, I can do this," she said with a sense of grit in her voice. With this affirmation of her courage and strength to heal, the class members broke into spontaneous applause.

Taking a Break to Read Four Important Handouts

Following this, I suggested the class take an extended break to read and study four handouts which I provided entitled, The Energetic Holding Defenses Checklist Protocol, The Energetic

Holding Defenses Descriptions Protocol, The Start-Up Protocol, and Restructuring The Energetic Holding Defenses Protocol. (These handouts and protocols can be found in *Innovations In Healing Trauma Vol. I* which contains case examples of how I use them in my Energetic Trauma Healing Therapy practice.)

Using The Start-Up Protocol to Help My Volunteer Self-diagnose And Begin Restructuring Her Primary Holding Back Defense

When I resumed the demonstration, my focus was on how to use The Start-Up Protocol to help my clients self-diagnose and begin restructuring their Energetic Holding Defenses which they automatically adopted as children to protect themselves from the trauma caused by their caretakers' interference in their natural growth and development. I introduced this next segment of the demonstration by saying, "The Start-up Protocol gets its name from the way a computer window starts up with a number of programs ready to go if you click on them. In a similar way, trauma clients have an Energetic Holding Defense Start-up configuration which shows up in their body posture, facial expression, physical stance, attitude, and certain character behaviors that come online when they find themselves in a perilous environment where they can be hurt and suffer trauma again. When this happens, their 'on-guard' reactive brain alarm gets activated and they automatically put up a shield of protective behaviors which I call their Energetic Holding Defense Start-up. This Energetic Holding Defense Start-up is designed to protect them from re-experiencing the pain of their past trauma as well as defend them from experiencing similar future trauma." Following this, I asked the volunteer, and the rest of the training class members, to review two of the Energetic Holding Defenses handouts which I had provided earlier.

I normally do not have clients use the Energetic Holding Defenses Checklist and the Description of The Energetic Holding Defenses until they are well along in their Client-directed Energetic Therapy, or they hit what I call "The Great Wall of Resistance" when their trauma therapy stalls or slows to a crawl. The reason for this is because I do not want clients to stress over trying to identify what their primary and secondary Energetic Holding Defenses are before they are ready to do so. However, here I wanted to introduce this powerful innovation because the Start-up Protocol is one of the core protocols for helping clients direct their Energetic Trauma Healing Therapy to a successful conclusion. As well, I knew the volunteer had done a good deal of previous trauma healing therapy which had recently stalled, so it appeared very timely for her to do this work. In addition, the class members, including the volunteer, were certainly all well trained and experienced psychotherapists so there was no reason to believe they could not handle this core work without personally stressing over it.

To demonstrate the use of the Start-Up Protocol with the volunteer to help her self-diagnose and begin restructuring her Primary Energetic Holding Defense, I asked her to review the two Energetic Holding Defenses handouts and choose the Energetic Holding Defense which most closely aligned with her own sense of her Primary Energetic Holding Defense. She obviously had been reflecting on this question during the break because she immediately chose the Holding Back Defense, and then quickly indicated that the Holding Out Defense also applied to her. I told her I agreed with her self-assessment. I then asked her to step into the Holding Back Defense to show us the behaviors, attitude, and body posturing that mirrored her Holding Back Defense.

She was a very bright woman, so it did not take long for her to assume the classic Holding Back Defense pose she presented in any precarious and dangerous situation she encountered. She held her head high in defensive pride with a clenched jaw as if to say, "I don't need you," and, "I will go it alone." She stood with locked knees and a rigid back conveying her stubborn, untrusting, unyielding attitude toward others. Her weight was back on her heels as if expecting a blow of rejection, and her chest barely moved as she breathed with a minimum of exertion which indicated an armoring to protect her heart from being broken again. Her eyes were guarded as if to say, "I won't allow you to get close to me." Her shoulders were stiff, and her arms and hands hung passively at her sides indicating she was not able to reach out directly for what she wanted from others.

I suggested the older woman stand beside me and asked the volunteer, "What are you saying to us with your Holding Back Defense?" She reflected on my question and then replied, "In a nutshell, I am saying, I don't need you. I won't allow you to break my heart again. And, I won't reach out for your love or give you my love." When she finished speaking, I asked her how she felt. "It feels normal," she replied.

Next, I suggested she create a new, more functional, healthier Start-up to replace her Holding Back Defense Start-up. She used the Spontaneous Movement Protocol to tease out the replacement posture, attitude, and behaviors which consisted of shifting her weight forward onto the balls of her feet, unlocking her knees, softening her guarded eyes and rigid backbone, deepening her breathing, softening her chest to open her heart, and reaching out with her arms and hands to convey, "I am ready to live life fully; I will reach out directly for what I want; and I will open myself and my heart to love and receive love." She used the Pressure Roller to help release the tension in her rigid backbone and armored chest and I had the older woman use her hands and thumbs to put pressure on the bones and tissue beneath her eyes to help soften them.

Following this energetic work, I suggested when she returned home that evening, she practiced being in her new Start-up stance while standing in front of a mirror and saying the words, "I am ready to live life fully. I am ready to reach out for what I want. I am open to love and receiving love." I then asked her how she felt. "I feel wonderful," she replied. "I feel really empowered!" With that, the class erupted in cheers and applause.

Using The Energetic Holding Defenses Restructuring Protocol to Help the Volunteer Transform Her Holding Back Defense

"Now, you are ready to begin the work of restructuring your Holding Back Defense," I said. I went on to explain that it is the chronic muscle tension, freezing, and holding in various parts of her body as well as her on-guard brain alarm and buried feelings, emotions, and negative attitudes that keep these Energetic Holding Defenses active and ready to protect her. I then asked her if she would like to begin working to restructure her Holding Back Defense. She indicated she was ready to do so.

I explained she needed to identify the areas of her body's musculature that were causing her the most difficulty—pain, lack of mobility, tightness, tension, and rigidity, for example—connected to her Holding Back Defense. She replied she suffered from extreme tightness and tension in her back. "Can we start there?" she asked. I responded by saying, "The Holding Back Defense is all about holding in the back," and indicated that I thought this was a good place to begin the muscular restructuring work.

Using The Energetic Vibration Protocols to Help Release and Restructure the Muscular Holding in Her Arms, Shoulders, Legs, Back, and Jaw

"If you are up to doing some energetic muscular release work in order to begin restructuring your Holding Back Defense," I said, "I want you to start by releasing the muscle holding in your legs so you can become better energetically grounded. This will help give you a foundation to do the energetic restructuring work that is needed to allow you to reach out for the love and life that you want." I then explained I wanted her to use a small personal trampoline, which I had on hand, to help release the muscle holding in her legs. I instructed her to first bounce on it to get a good energetic charge in her body. Then I asked her to stand on it while holding the older woman's hands to help keep her balance. I explained her task on the trampoline was to bend her knees slightly, raise up on the balls and toes of her feet, and hold that position while she made an elongated 'Oh' sound with her voice. I further explained the goal was to get a vibratory movement going in her legs which the elongated 'Oh' sound of her voice as it resonated in her chest would help bring about.

She stood on the trampoline as I had instructed. After about 30 seconds, I asked her to shift her weight back on her heels and hold that position while she continued to make the 'Oh' sound. About 30 seconds later, I asked her to shift her weight to the right side as she continued to use her voice, hold the position for 30 seconds, followed by doing the same on her left side, and so on as she repeated the sequence of movements several times. When her legs began to tire, I asked her to simply stand on the trampoline, again with her slightly bent knees, and to allow a vibratory movement to develop in her legs and lower body while continuing to make the 'Oh' sound with her voice. As she did so, a vibratory movement developed in her legs which grew stronger and more visible. When it was clear she had reached the end of her endurance on the trampoline, I asked her to step off it, stand on the floor, and feel the difference in her legs. "Wow," she exclaimed, "do I ever feel them! They are vibrating like crazy and I feel so much more grounded. I also have pleasurable streaming up and down my body."

(I want to note here it is very unusual for clients to develop a vibratory movement in their legs so quickly by doing the trampoline work; nor do clients feel an energetic streaming in their body so easily. For most clients, the muscle vibration and body streaming will eventually come but it takes a good deal of energetic work for this to happen. However, clients who have also adopted a Holding Out Defense are an exception to this rule. For some reason which I do not fully understand, they can respond energetically very rapidly and learn new energetic concepts at lightning speeds. Since it appeared the volunteer had also adopted a secondary Holding Out Defense in addition to her primary Holding Back Defense, I believe this was the reason why she was able to get a vibration and streaming in her legs and body so quickly and easily.)

Using The Arm & Shoulder Pillow Lift Protocol

I let the volunteer enjoy the aliveness of her body for a time, and then handed her a medium size pillow. "I want you to stand holding a pillow in each hand and then raise your extended arms to shoulder height," I said. "Next, hold the pillows in this way until your arms tire and you can no longer maintain the position. When your arms tire, lower them." As she did this, I explained the purpose of this pillow lift. "As you stand holding the pillows in this way, it will put stress on your shoulders and back as well as your arms. The goal is to stimulate a vibratory movement in these body parts to begin releasing the tension and energetic holding in these muscles." When she lowered the pillows and had rested,

I suggested she repeat the pillow lift two more times. During her third go she burst into anger yelling, "I hate you! I hate you!" She threw the pillows on the floor and began to stomp on them. When she stopped, I let her be with her anger and bitterness for a bit. When I intervened to ask about what was going on, she said her mother had made her do cruel things like standing on her tiptoes for long periods of time to punish her for loving her father. I could see she was still holding in her anger which the pillow lift had engendered, so I suggested she give into her anger and let it out by kicking her 'childhood mother' around the room.

Using The Kicking Large Pillows Protocol

To do this kicking, I placed two large, heavy, oversize pillows at her feet and instructed her to kick them around the room as she screamed at her childhood mother, "I hate you!" She, then, did this pillow kicking with relish. When she was exhausted from the pillow kicking, she laid back down on the floor and rested. As she sat up, she grinned and said, "That was good!"

Using The Foam Hand Gripper Jaw Release Protocol

I nodded agreement and then retrieved a foam hand gripper from my equipment bag which I handed to her. "I can see you are still holding on to some feeling in your jaw which looks very tight," I said. "I suggest you place the foam hand gripper in your mouth and bite down on it as if you are trying to bite through it. This will help release some of the tightness and tension in your jaw."

When she finished the jaw work, I told her this was just a very small sample of the energetic work which she must do in order to free the muscular holding in her legs and other parts of her body, especially in her back, arms, shoulders, and jaw, in order to restructure her Holding Back Defense which she had adopted as a result of her childhood trauma of rejection by her mother and betrayal by her older brother. I briefly named and described several of the energetic protocols and tools that could be used to challenge and release the muscular holding in her body including the use of the pressure roller and stool as well as the Bongo Percussion Protocol described below to do so. (For more on the use of these protocols, see the chapter on Restructuring the Holding Defenses in Innovations In Healing Trauma Vol. I which contains case examples of how I use them in my Energetic Trauma Healing Therapy practice as well as the chapter in this handbook on Using Energetic Vibration & Slow Movement to Release Muscle Holding in the body.)

Using The Bonger Percussion Protocol to Help Release the Muscle Holding In Her Back

I introduced the Bonger Percussion Protocol by saying, "Muscle holding in the back is the main characteristic of the Holding Back Defense. One of my favorite ways, in addition to using the pressure roller and stool, to help clients release these tense back muscles is to use a Bonger Percussion Massager." (The Bonger Percussion Massager is available on Amazon.com.) It consists of a fist sized rubber which is attached to a spring steel band with a wood handle. A Bonger is held in one hand and used to lightly drum the clients' tense back muscles. The drumming helps soften and release their back muscle holding which will allow them to vibrate more easily and promote energetic streaming in them. The volunteer agreed to have me use it to help release the muscle holding in her back. Following my Bonger demonstration, she reported her back felt wonderfully alive.

Using The Wolf-bite Protocol to Help Loosen the Holding in Her Jaw

Muscle tension and holding in the jaw is another characteristic of the Holding Back Defense. My go-to exercise to help clients release the clamp-like holding in their jaw is to have them bite down on a folded washcloth and then pull on it in a tug-of-war as if to remove it from their mouth. This is the protocol I suggested the volunteer use to help further release the tightness in her jaw. I handed her a folded washcloth and instructed her to firmly bite down on one end of the two layers of washcloth.

Then, I asked her to pull on the other end of the washcloth that protruded from her mouth with her hands as if to remove it. "As you pull on the washcloth, I want you to imagine that the washcloth is a chunk of meat which another wolf is biting down on at the other end trying to take it away from you; however, you are not letting go as you growl through your teeth," I said. "I want you to engage in this tug-of-war until your jaw tires or it becomes painful, at which point, I want you to stop the exercise and rest your jaw.

She did as I instructed, biting down on the washcloth and trying to pull it from her mouth with her hands as she growled fiercely the whole time. After a minute of doing so, she stopped to report she felt pleasurable streaming running down her spine. After she had rested for a moment, she again clamped down on the washcloth with her teeth and began pulling on it again while growling. Within a few seconds, she began to weep, releasing the washcloth. She continued to weep for a bit with tears running down her cheeks. When she ceased weeping, I asked her why she was sad. "I don't know," she replied. "I am mystified by what is going on with me."

Using The If-I-Could-Let-Myself-See Protocol

To help her solve the puzzle of why she felt sad, I suggested she say the words, "If I could let myself see why I am sad, I am sad because...." and then finished the sentence with the first thought that came into her mind. She restated the sentence stem and finished it saying, "I am sad because I could never hold onto the things that I loved. I was always losing boyfriends and girlfriends that I loved and cared about for one reason or another. I was always losing precious jewelry and misplacing phone numbers, addresses, and important papers and documents," she lamented, throwing up her hands in frustration,

Using The Personal Tug-Of-War Protocol to Help Her Hang onto Things

To help empower her in the moment, I suggested she take the end of a towel which I handed her while the older woman was to take the other end and try to pull it away. The volunteer's task was to keep the towel by trying to take it back from the older woman. To create safety, I asked class members to stand behind each of the contestants to catch them in case there was an accidental letting go of the towel. While pulling on the towel to take it back, I suggested the volunteer image holding on to the relationships and important things she did not want to lose while yelling words such as, "I don't want to lose you! So, let's work it out!" and, "It is mine! I am not going to lose it!" When the volunteer and the older woman began to tire, I asked them to stop and rest. I then asked the volunteer how she felt after doing exercise. "I feel much stronger," she replied with a nod and a smile on her face.

Taking A Break for Questions & Answers

While the volunteer and the older woman were recovering from the tug-of-war exercise, I asked the training class members if they had anything they wanted to ask or was still unclear to them about the trauma healing work the volunteer had done during the demonstration. The main question had to do with what was left for the volunteer to do to fully heal. I responded by saying that, although the volunteer had made great progress during the demonstration, much more intensive restructuring of her Energetic Holding Defenses would be needed for the full healing of her childhood trauma and its limiting effects on her body, mind, and character. I indicated that helping her restructure her Holding Back Defense would require releasing the body musculature that kept it in place and this would take some intensive energetic work. I also noted she would need to address and restructure her Holding Out Defense as well. So yes, she had more work to do to fully heal her trauma and become truly empowered. However, I also added she had made a great start in achieving this outcome.

In my mind I was still left with the question as to whether the volunteer might have a latent Holding Up Defense due to her close relationship with her childhood father who may have treated her as 'daddy's little princess' which caused her mother to be jealous of the surrogate-spouse connection she had with her father. As well, she made a comment that her daughter was her best friend. One of the characteristics of the Holding Up Defense is clients who adopted it were made surrogate spouses as children by one of their parents, which in turn tends to give rise to them turning to one or more of their children and making them a surrogate spouse. And then, there was the issue of her brother using and exploiting her for his own sexual satisfaction.

Exploitation of a child is a sure fire way to cause the child to adopt a Holding Up Defense. However, I kept this question to myself as I knew such a latent Holding Up Defense would surface of its own accord when the time was right for her to heal it, and I wanted to respect the volunteer's right to be in charge of her own therapy process, especially with regard to privacy and personal disclosures.

In addition, I was well aware I had not demonstrated how to deal with the volunteer's possible toxic shame and Inner Victim identity which could significantly stall her trauma healing progress. However, I decided not to pursue the subject at that point as I sensed the volunteer and the training class might be on the verge of information overload. Furthermore, the volunteer had denied feeling any shame when I had asked her about it earlier, although I was rather confident that it was lurking below the surface of her consciousness, so this played into my decision not to pursue the matter at that time. In addition, helping trauma victims overcome their toxic shame around healing their trauma is not a quick fix, so given these facts, I decided to defer the subject and elected to present and demonstrate The Shame Busting Protocol in a later class session, possibly with another volunteer.

The Good News for the Volunteer and Some Trade-offs

At that point, I said there was good news as well as some trade-offs which the volunteer needed to consider in regard to fully healing her trauma. The good news, I explained, was two fold. One was that, once she had learned what she needed to do on an energetic level to restructure her Energetic Holding Defenses, much of this body work could be done on her own with some coaching guidance. Number two was her restructuring body work could be done very rapidly given how quickly and efficiently her Client-directed Energetic Therapy work with me had gone. However, there were also some trade-offs for her to consider, I further explained. One was that she needed to decide about what parts of her Energetic Holding Defenses she could live with because, although they were troublesome, they did not constitute a "must-address" situation, versus what parts were so problematic that they had to be addressed.

Her second consideration was whether to continue her Energetic Trauma Healing Therapy with the professional guidance of a client-centered Energetic Therapist doing individual and/or group therapy sessions, or doing Client-directed Energetic Therapy in a Peer-Co-counseling setting—using either an In-person or Zoom approach—which would reduce the cost of getting such guidance and still move her therapy progress forward at a rapid pace. My recommendation was that she continue her Energetic Trauma Healing Therapy in a group-community type setting for reasons which I present in a later Chapter entitled, "Trauma: The Elephant In The Room."

Using The Client-directed Energetic Therapy Journal Record Protocol

Before doing a group feedback whip to bring closure to the day's session, I suggested the volunteer keep an Energetic Journal Record of her trauma healing therapy and activity. "It should include the Client-directed Energetic Therapy work you do in your sessions and between sessions," I explained. "It might also include your insights, revelations, successes, challenges, and disappointments, for example." I explained the rationale for keeping this journal, which was, that over time, she might be able to see helpful patterns and connections in her trauma healing process. (See the chapter on Using the Support Protocols for this protocol)

Using The Group Feedback Whip Protocol And I-Learned-Statements Protocol to Elicit Personal "I Learned" & "I Realized" Statements from The Training Class Members

To help bring closure to this Part I of the presentation and demonstration, I asked the training class members and the volunteer to complete sentence stems such as, "I learned that I_____, I realized that I_____, "or "I discovered that I_____," and share them in a group feedback whip. This was a rapid voicing out loud of their completed personal sentence stem statements with everyone taking a turn in what I call a 'whip'. For example, one class member stated, "I realized that I have a Holding Back Defense." Another class member stated, "I learned that I have similar trauma shadow issues to those raised by our volunteer; I think that we all do." In response to these types of statements and many others like them, there was a lot of head nodding and whispered "Amen" and "I agree," affirmations.

Using The Session Rating & Feedback Evaluation Protocol

Next, I asked the volunteer and the training class members to rate my presentation and demonstration by completing an outcome & feedback evaluation form which I provided. It contained several rating scales focused on the presentation/demonstration content, approach, outcome satisfaction, and so on. I use this Session Rating & Feedback Protocol on a regular basis in my Energetic Trauma Healing Practice to help clients reflect on how their Client-directed Energetic Therapy is going as well as to provide me with feedback on what is happening for them in their therapy so I can make any necessary adjustments in their trauma healing process. I know most psychotherapists that I have been associated with do not solicit this kind of formal feedback from their clients on a regular basis, but I believe it is a serious mistake not to do so. For one thing, doing regular session outcome evaluations lets them know that I care about what is going on in their therapy and want to hear what they have to say. Second, I receive valuable feedback from them which keeps me on my toes as well as gives me ideas about how to improve the therapy I am doing with them. Third, by doing regular written session evaluations, it helps keep my clients and me completely invested in the therapy which we are engaged in doing together.

When I reviewed all of the class members' evaluations, I was appreciative of their positive responses and comments. However, there were two issues raised that got my attention. One comment indicated that, in effect, my commitment to helping my volunteer heal her trauma during the demonstration was strong and clear, but my desire to help her heal might have been felt by her as pressure to heal faster. This was important feedback I wanted to follow up with my volunteer. If it was true, then my desire to help her heal her at other than at her own speed was in conflict with my commitment and agreement to have her be in charge of her own trauma healing. Later, I checked in with the volunteer to ask if she felt pressured by me to heal during the demonstration. Her response was she had not felt such pressure. That was good to hear, however, I decided that in the future, I would check in with my volunteers periodically to ask if they were feeling pressure from me to heal in other than at their own speed, time, and way.

The second issue raised had to do with putting the privacy of the volunteer at risk by asking her a very personal question in the class setting rather than in a more private setting. This is a valid concern; however, in doing the class a demonstration with a volunteer client, such a risk is nearly unavoidable at times. To reduce the risk, I had asked the volunteer to sign The Client Is in Charge Agreement with an understanding she could say no to answering any question which I asked her or to any activity I suggested. Then, when I asked her a sensitive and possibly an invasion of privacy question, I reminded her she had a choice of whether to answer the question. It still leaves the question of, "Did I put undue pressure on the volunteer to deal with my sensitive question by simply being in an authority position as leader of the demonstration?" Thus, to avoid this, another way I could have dealt with the problem would have been to take a break, meet with the volunteer privately, and secure her permission to ask my sensitive question in the class demonstration setting.

My Instructions for Part II of My Demonstration for the Following Day

My instructions to the training class for the following day's demonstration were to bring a laptop computer or mobile device on which to access a Zoom meeting. This meeting would focus on how to use the Energetic Peer Co-counseling Protocol with clients online.

Using The Paired Energetic Grounding Protocol to End the Day's Session

Then I asked the class to end the session by doing Energetic Grounding. I explained when I end an Client-directed Energetic Therapy session, be it an individual or group session, I want to send my client(s) home energetically well grounded. I further explained doing Client-directed Energetic Therapy, especially in a group setting, generates a high energy charge in everyone. "If this high energy charge is not grounded, it will hang up in the clients' or participants' upper body and head creating a buzzed or high feeling which lacks Energetic Grounding," I said. "This high feeling and lack of Energetic Grounding creates in clients' minds, a lack of concentration, unclear thinking, and distracted attention. For example, when clients leave a therapy session in an ungrounded state, they can get into an auto accident, or become lost while driving home, or have to pull over because they are so distracted it is unsafe to drive. What I want is for this high energetic charge, which you all feel right now, to become grounded downward into your lower body, and especially into your legs and feet. This will clear your mind and allow you to drive home in a focused, attentive, and safe way. Thus, I cannot stress enough how important it is to do Energetic Grounding at the close of a session such as this."

To ensure these class members left the day's demonstration session feeling good and also energetically well grounded, I asked them to form pairs, and then for each pair to form a group of four. I instructed one pair in the group of four to do the paired Energetic Grounding while the other pair acted as Safety Persons by standing behind each person in the pair to catch them in case they accidentally fell backward. I instructed the pair doing the grounding to grasp each others' arms with their hands, so their arms were locked together. Then, I asked them to place their feet in a wide stance on the floor and slowly squat as if they were sitting in imaginary chairs while holding onto each other.

I demonstrated the paired energetic grounding position with the host of the shadow work training as my partner while two class members acted as Safety Persons by standing at our backs while we did the Paired Energetic Grounding exercise. Next, I gave the go ahead for the pairs to do the grounding. I then instructed the active pairs to maintain their squatting position and allow a vibratory movement to develop in their lower half which would help move their body's energy charge down into their legs and feet. When their legs were tired, I instructed them to come back into a standing position, let go of their partners' arms, and then hang forward to do the Hair-pin Energetic Grounding Protocol. Then, the active pairs switched places with the Safety Pairs and repeated the Paired and Hair-pin Energetic Grounding Protocols, so everyone completed the grounding exercises.

Using The Group Hug Protocol to Close the Session

To close the session, I suggested we give ourselves a group hug by putting our volunteer in the center of the group and then closing ranks to embrace her and each other in a massive, all-in-one hug. As I joined that happy group hug, my thoughts became poetic as I mused to myself, "What a beautiful Way, to end a glorious Day!"

This ended Part I of my presentation and demonstration. In the next chapter I share Part II in which I was offered a surprising challenge as the volunteer came face to face with her Toxic Shame Shroud when she returned home that evening.

A Case Demonstration on How to Use The Toxic Shame Busting Protocol

I had planned on using a new volunteer to demonstrate Part II of my Innovations In Healing Trauma presentation on using The Toxic Shame Busting and The Energetic Peer Co-counseling Therapy Protocols. However, things did not work out that way.

A Return to My Volunteer Demonstration Case Example

As you will recall in the previous chapter, the volunteer did not exhibit symptoms of toxic shame nor admit to feeling shame when I asked her if she was feeling it during my Part I Demonstration. I was skeptical but did not press the issue with her. I believed, at the time, she was not feeling shame during the demonstration because her classmates were treating her as a hero for sharing her trauma story and doing her trauma healing work in front of them while they cheered her on. However, that suddenly changed when the volunteer phoned me the next morning to tell me she was in very bad shape and did not think she could continue with the training class. She did not want to tell me what had happened over the phone so I simply encouraged her to come in early to class, and I was certain that whatever was wrong could be straightened out. She reluctantly agreed to come in an hour early, telling me she trusted that I could help her. I immediately scrapped my plan of using a new volunteer to demonstrate how to use the Toxic Shame Busting Protocol and decided to continue with my Part I volunteer if she would consent to do so.

When the volunteer did not appear for our early meeting the next morning, I phoned her, but she did not answer. When she arrived and I did meet with her, it was just before the starting time for Part II of my demonstration. When she faced me she had shame written all over her body and behavior. She apologized for arriving late for our meeting but after no reason for doing so. I asked her how she was doing. She replied, "Not good." I then asked her if she was doing well enough to hang out with the older woman with whom she had a strong connection for a short period of time while I introduced and set up the next segment of my demonstration. I then promised I would return to help her move through her shame shutdown. With this reassurance, she agreed to do so. I then began my presentation to the training class by introducing The Toxic Shame Protocol. Here are my introductory remarks.

On Using The Toxic Shame Busting Protocol

"Feeling shame can be a useful thing. It tells us we have crossed a social barrier and we need to reconsider our actions. Toxic shame, on the other hand, is a disabling and crippling condition. It overtakes us with self-attacks which make us feel unworthy and unlovable. As well, it affects our behavior by making us withdraw and isolate from others.

For me, toxic shame was a shame shroud which I wore for many years. As a late adolescent and early teenager, I spent my time in a fantasy world dreaming about owning a large Hereford beef ranch, reading about the red and white cows, and looking after the ones I owned on our family farm. It was a totally unrealistic dream. As a young boy, I spent my time playing the cowboy hero, reading Zane Grey western novels, and listening to the Lone Ranger, Gene Autry, and Sky King on the radio while doing my farm chores, and hunting sparrows with my BB gun. Although I was not aware of it, I kept a low social profile in elementary through junior high school as well as the first two years of high school. My teachers and school classmates would have described me as shy, withdrawn, and somewhat of a loner. Due to my father's jealousy and constant anger at me for being my mother's favorite child and his steady berating of my farm work performance in addition to his periodic whippings and beatings for having my head in the clouds and breaking farm equipment, I saw myself as not measuring up to his high standards. When I now look back on those days, I realize that at an unconscious level I felt unworthy and unlovable.

Then in my sophomore year of high school, my English teacher took an interest in my prolific short story writing and the long poems I composed. During a school awards ceremony, she gave me a special award for a poem I wrote about the wonders of living in Michigan. That award seemed to suddenly break me free of my shame shroud as if some kind of magic had happened, although at the time I did not realize it. As a result, I broke out of my self imposed social isolation by trying out for the Junior and Senior plays and getting the starring roles. That was totally unlike me prior to that point in my life. "So, why?" I later asked myself. In addition, I took an intense interest in doing magic tricks after I found a book called Later Magic (Hoffman, 1904) in the school library and began performing big stage magic acts to appreciative audiences. I even performed my magic act to a packed audience of The Future Farmers of America in the Michigan State University Auditorium. Again this was completely out of character considering my prior social history. I also started a Combo Orks dance band in which I acted as the leader, recruiting talented musicians in the community to join it as we strutted our stuff for local dances wearing white tux jackets. As I look back at all this, I cannot believe I was so socially isolated for all of my early years until that English Award somehow broke through and set me free. "So, what happened," I found myself pondering this question years later. "Why was I suddenly liberated by such a seemingly nominal event that lasted all of two minutes?" I will give my studied answer to this important question following a brief look at the key features of toxic shame.

A Brief Look at The Landscape of Toxic Shame

The key features of being afflicted with toxic shame are living in social isolation, feelings of being unworthy, seeing oneself as bad, feelings of being inferior, extreme defensiveness for making even minor mistakes, existing in a fantasy world, harboring a desire for revenge, acting out aggression on others, poor emotional boundaries with others, compulsive behaviors such as substance abuse or an eating disorder, a feeling of being flawed, and a feeling of extreme guilt. These are either debilitating behaviors or behaviors that have negative repercussions. Fortunately, there is a cure for the affliction of toxic shame.

Using The Toxic Shame Busting Protocol

At this point in the presentation, I decided to do double duty by demonstrating how to use the two protocols at the same time—that is, how to use the Energetic Peer Co-counseling Protocol to help the volunteer resolve her toxic shame shutdown using The Toxic Shame Busting Protocol, if she was willing to do so.

Using The Energetic Peer Co-Counseling Protocol as a Framework to Demonstrate How to Use the Toxic Shame Busting Protocol

I explained to the class that I wanted to use the Energetic Peer Co-counseling Protocol as a framework to demonstrate how to use the Toxic Shame Busting Protocol with a toxic shame afflicted client. To do this, I needed to first teach them how to use the Energetic Peer Co-counseling Protocol.

Using The Energetic Peer Co-Counseling Protocol

The basic working unit for doing Energetic Peer Co-counseling is the Co-counseling Trio. It consists of the Focus Person who does the energetic healing work, an Assist Person who helps the Focus Person do her/his healing work, and a Monitor & Safety Person who helps keep the healing work on track and done safely. When the healing work time is up for the first Focus Person, these roles are rotated so each trio member serves as the Focus Person, Assist Person, and Monitor & Safety Person. During the period of teaching clients how to use the Energetic Co-counseling process, a Coach Person is added to help do this.

The Energetic Peer Co-Counseling Protocol can be used in ether an in-person format, where the co-counseling trios engage with each other face-to- face, in an online format, where the co-counseling trios remain at home and engage with each other using a personal computer or phone on a Zoom type platform. Even though the class members were able to use an in-person format, I wanted them to experience using the online format.

To demonstrate how to use the Energetic Peer Co-Counseling Protocol online, I formed a Co-counseling Trio with my Part I demonstration volunteer who had consented to serve as the first Focus Person and the older woman to whom she was strongly connected, to serve as her Assist Person. A volunteer from the training class agreed to serve as the trio's Monitor & Safety Person and a second volunteer agreed to serve as the Coach Person directly under my tutelage since she had no experience in doing Energetic Peer Co-counseling.

I then asked everyone to fire up their laptops or mobile devices and log on to the Zoom meeting which I had previously set up. I also asked the volunteer Focus Person and Assist Person to sit together on the stage and use only one of their computers while the volunteer Monitor & Safety Person and Coach Person sat with me near the front of the class but separated from the stage and used their computers to carry out their roles as the co-counseling work proceeded. This was my attempt to replicate how Energetic Peer Co-counseling is done on an online, Zoom type platform since I recommend the Focus Person have an in-person Assist Person at his/her side when doing the co-counseling work online. The reason for this is that it can be difficult for the Assist Person to see the Focus Person's work, such as her/his spontaneous movements, when viewing the co-counseling work on a laptop screen, for example. Next, I handed a brief set of instructions for starting the co-counseling work to The trio members and trio Coach Person as well as copies for the class members. Here is that set of instructions:

1. As trio members, Jump Start a strong energy charge in your bodies by doing 1 or 2 minutes of vigorous physical exercise such as taking turns kicking a large pillow back and forth between you, for example. This is followed by doing Energetic Grounding using one or more of the Energetic Grounding Protocols such as the Downhill Ski Energetic Grounding Protocol, or Hair-pin Energetic Grounding Protocol, for example.

2. When it is your turn to be the Focus Person, state a healing intention for doing your energetic healing work.

3. Then, use the Spontaneous Movement Protocol to direct your Client-directed Energetic Therapy in order to realize your stated intention and move your energetic healing work forward.

4. Use the Energetic Grounding Protocols as needed, especially to work through any fear or anxiety connected to hidden-buried trauma memories that surface, for example, or resolve any internal resistance issues that may pop up—such as your inner-judge-voice-alarm in your head/mind voicing or screaming, "Stop! Danger ahead!" or, some other dire warning, for instance.

5. When the Focus Person appears to finish his/her work, the Assist Person is to check in with her/him to ask if he/she feels complete or needs to do more co-counseling work in order to realize her/his healing intention,

6. When the Focus Person feels complete, his/her Assist Person is to remind her/him to do Energetic Grounding.

When the class members fully understood the instructions, I gave the signal for the Energetic Peer Co-counseling work to begin. Thus, the volunteer, as the Focus Person, and her Assist Person jump started a strong energy charge in their bodies by kicking a large pillow back and forth between them for a couple of minutes. They followed up by taking turns doing the Assisted Hair-pin Energetic Grounding Protocol. Next, the volunteer stated her healing intention of getting unstuck and not being shut down.

Using The Covering Shame Protocol

The first words out of her mouth were, "I just want to disappear," as she covered her face with her hands. Her Assist Person stood up and moved to embrace her but she pushed her Assist Person away and retreated further into a slumped withdrawal. I suggested to her Coach Person that she relay (using the Zoom App) the suggestion that the Assist Person use The Covering Shame Protocol to help our Focus Person come out of her shutdown state. This protocol simply called for covering her with a sheet. The Assist Person retrieved a sheet from my equipment bag and secured permission to cover her with it. Under the sheet, she remained silent for a few moments, and then said, "Wow, I can relax." She remained silent for another few moments and then said, "It seems silly to sit here with a sheet over me like this but my shame shroud has lifted for the moment."

I suggested to her Coach Person that she relay a message for the Assist Person to crawl under the sheet with our Focus Person if she affirmed the move. When the Assist Person did so, our Focus Person exclaimed, "This is even better!" They remained hidden under the sheet for several moments and then our Focus Person removed the sheet from them and said, "Now, I can breathe." She looked at her Assist Person for several moments and then said, "I think I am ready to move on." She continued to look at her Assist Person for direction. With a little hesitation, her Assist Person suggested she stand and let a spontaneous movement arise from her body that would help her further realize her stated healing intention of getting unstuck. Her spontaneous movement was to lower her head toward the floor and crunch her shoulders slightly forward at the same moment. Her Assist Person suggested she exaggerate the movement which she did. Then her Assist Person asked if she had any feelings, thoughts, or memories connected to her spontaneous movement. She replied she again felt stuck.

Her Assist Person then, suggested she let another spontaneous movement arise from her body that might help her get unstuck if she continued to express any feelings, thoughts, or memories connected to it. She immediately covered her eyes with her hands and said, "I don't want to see it."

"What don't you want to see?" asked her Assist Person. She replied, "I don't know. I don't want to see it. I just feel stuck and completely shut down." Her Assist Person followed up by asking if she wanted to let another spontaneous movement direct her work or do some more Energetic Grounding to help get unstuck. She replied, "No, I don't have the energy or will to help myself get unstuck and stop being shut down." With that statement of giving up, she sat down in her chair and slumped forward in a state of resignation. Her Assist Person instantly looked at me with a look of helplessness on her face.

I turned to the Coach Person and suggested she have the Assist Person use a Bunker Busting Protocol with our Focus Person. I quickly explained how to use the Bunker Busting Protocol to the Coach Person, the trio members, and to the class.

Using The Bunker Busting Protocol to Help Break Through the Focus Person's Toxic Shame Shut Down

To help our volunteer Focus Person mobilize her aggression and get unstuck, I explained that having her build a giant, "bunker busting" energy charge in her body might help her break through her denial in order for her to get in touch with her toxic shame feelings. I suggested that in order to build such a large energy charge in her body, she uses a tennis racket to rapidly and repeatedly hit a large pillow placed in a chair, giving it everything she had in her. I also suggested she keep hitting the pillow until she was completely exhausted and could not possibly hit it one more time. The Trio Coach repeated these instructions to the Assist Person adding that all of her classmates were there to cheer her on. Her Assist Person, then repeated the instructions and then added, "I want you to look out at all the smiling faces of your classmates who stand with you and who will cheer you on." As our volunteer Focus Person did so, the whole class erupted into one big cheer. With that encouragement, our Focus Person agreed to give it a try. She then hit the pillow with all the force and energy she could muster while her classmates cheered her on. When she finally hit for the last time, she collapsed on the floor and began to sob in great heaving sobs while also sucking air into her oxygen starved lungs. Her Assist Person simply let her sob and then recover from her valiant effort of hitting the pillow.

When she recovered enough to speak, she began to tell the story of what had shut her down when she had returned home from the previous day's training class demonstration. She said she had suffered a crippling bout of shame as she reviewed what had happened in the demonstration. She said she became mortified that someone outside of the training class might hear she had participated in her brother's sexual escapades when she was a young girl. This, she stated, had completely shut her down. "I felt totally ashamed," she reported.

She continued to pour out the shame she felt, when as a child, she wished her mother would die. "Of course, my wish came true when my mother shot and killed my father and then turned the gun on herself to end her life," she blurted out. "I feel totally responsible for her death as well as the death of my father. My wish got fulfilled and, as a result, I feel ashamed for having ever made such a wish."

At that point she buried her face in her hands but continued to speak. "But the most damning and shameful thing I did was to get revenge on my brother for making me participate in his sexual play," she confessed. "I joined in because I was afraid if I refused, he would turn me out on the street with no way to survive." She went on to also admit she had fantasized about getting revenge on her brother by whacking him on the head with a baseball bat while he slept. She immediately stopped speaking and was still for several moments as if trying to hold back a dam in herself that was ready to burst and flood us with the shame she could no longer contain. Then, the dam inside her broke, "One morning my desire for revenge overpowered me," she revealed. "While my brother's wife was away, I crept into my brother's bedroom while he slept and hit him on the head with a baseball bat causing him to lose consciousness. I was immediately overcome with fear and guilt. I was afraid I had killed him, so I instantly concocted a plan to make it all look like an accident." She went on to divulge she quickly removed the heavy glass framed picture from the wall above his bed and hit it with the bat to make it look like it had been damaged when it dropped from above to hit his head. She then banged the hook which had held the picture on the wall with the bat knocking it loose from the wall to make it look like it had failed to hold the heavy framed picture above the bed. When her brother regained consciousness, he was not seriously hurt by the incident. He simply assumed the picture hook had failed and the heavy frame had done the damage to his head, none the wiser for what had really happened.

However, our Focus Person revealed she was surprised she had actually taken revenge on her brother and confessed she could not forgive herself for such a cruel act. She kept repeating over and over, "What if I had killed him? What if I had killed him? " Then she fell silent and remained so for a minute or so. Then, her Assist Person asked her how she was doing. "I feel relieved," she replied. "I no longer feel stuck and shut down."

After another long pause, the Monitor & Safety Person intervened (using the Zoom App) to remind the Assist Person to check in to see if our Focus Person felt complete with her co-counseling work. She did so. Our Focus Person replied she still felt some shame and guilt but she no longer felt so shutdown. With that, the Coach Person suggested that our Focus Person and her Assist Person do Energetic Grounding. When they finished doing The Assisted Hair-pin grounding again, I suggested that the whole class do some Energetic Grounding using the Downhill Ski Protocol.

Before taking a coffee break, I briefly spoke to the training class about the problem of self-inflicted toxic shame. Here is what I said:

The Trauma of Self-inflicted Toxic Shame

I want to speak to you about self-inflicted toxic shame. It is hard enough to face and deal with the devastating, life crippling trauma that gets heaped upon innocent persons in which they have no say, choice, and are certainly not willing participants in their trauma. That is bad enough. But what is even harder and worse for traumatized victims to face and deal with is the toxic shame that envelops them due to what they did or did not do in response to their trauma—that is, for their own participation, denial, and vengeful actions in response to having been traumatized. This kind of self-inflicted trauma is often the hardest for them to forgive and heal. It can be tough for trauma victims to forgive their aggressors and move beyond the shame of being assaulted, but it can be even tougher when trauma victims become the aggressors as a result of being abused and thus act out their aggressors' abusive behaviors by assaulting others who may or may not have been the perpetrators of their abuse. This can, for them, be completely unforgivable.

The victimized part of clients, which I call their 'victim identity' or 'assailed child identity', interacts with their internalized 'inner judge' to create all kinds of inner dramas and problems for them. Their victim identity and inner judge interact in their minds to keep them wrapped in a shame shroud of unworthiness. The way out of this toxic shame shroud is to have them get rid of their victim identity by being extolled by others—that is to say, by receiving and taking in others' high praise, validation, and personal blessing. This extolling can completely remove their victim identity of being unworthy and unlovable, and rip their toxic shame shroud into shreds. As a result, their 'inner judge' has no 'victim identity' to attack and thus shrinks away as those unused inner judge neural pathways in their brain wither away. The result is they get rid of both their paralyzing 'inner victim identity' and their self-attacking 'inner judge identity' to boot.

Using The Extolling Protocol

When the class returned from their break, I suggested we shift gears to do some Toxic Shame Busting work with our Focus Person volunteer using the Extolling Protocol if she was willing to do so. The steps for using the Toxic Shame Busting Protocol and its Big Brother, the Extolling Protocol, were quite simple. I outlined them as follows:

Step 1. Introduce the Toxic Shame Busting exercise to the training class members.

Step 2. Have the training class members extol our volunteer—that is, to give her high praise for her strengths, talents, abilities, accomplishments, values, character traits. Especially as these related to her trauma story.

Step 3. Check in with our volunteer to see if she was able to take in the high praise she received.

Step 4. Do any needed therapeutic work with our volunteer, if she was unable to fully take in the extolling statements given her, and to help her remove any internal resistance and inner judge obstacle which prevented her from doing so.

I further explained that the ground rules for The Extolling Protocol were as follows:

1. Those giving the high praise to our volunteer were to refrain from using qualifying words like, "sometimes", "mostly", or "usually," and, "on-the-other-hand," for example.

2. Our volunteer was not to respond to the training class members' high praise statements except to say, "thank you." Otherwise, she was to refrain from commenting on the high praise she received or by diminishing, down playing, and/or explaining it away.

Our volunteer, after a good deal of encouragement from her classmates, reluctantly agreed to receive their extolling words. To carry out the mission, her classmates formed a circle with her in the center, and one by one, shared their extolling statements with her. After each class member did so, she was asked if she was able to take in the extolling words she received. The good thing was she was able to do so with only a little difficulty which she quickly overcame.

Examples of the High Praise which Our Volunteer Received from the Training Class Members

Here are some examples of the high praise and extolling statements given:

1. Regarding the Client-directed Energetic Therapy work she did during my Part I demonstration sessions as well

as serving as the first Focus Person in the co-counseling demonstration, the training class members gave her high marks for her bravery in opening the intimate details of her struggle to heal her trauma with high praise like, "I am inspired by your fearlessness in sharing your healing journey so openly."

2. In terms of doing the Toxic Shame Busting work, she received high praise for her courage confronting her shame with remarks like, "Your courage in dealing with your shame issue was truly admirable."

3. She received praise for the way she was raising her daughter with comments like, "I love the way you are raising your daughter with such loving care."

4. She received high praise for way she was able to overcome the enormous pain of her difficult childhood years, especially regarding her mother's cruelty toward her with statements like, "I am in awe of the strength you had as a young girl in surviving such a horrible and cruel mother who turned on you at every chance she could find."

5. There was high praise for her dealing with the emotional blow of losing her father in such a dreadful way with comments such as, "I am so sorry you lost your father in such an odious way, but I am awe-inspired by your resiliency in moving on with your life in such a remarkable way."

6. She was applauded for the backbone she displayed in standing up to her brother's betrayal of her love for him by whacking him with a baseball bat with statements like, "I feel empathy for your feeling of betrayal when your brother invited you into his sex play, and I completely understand and sympathize with your desire to get

revenge on him. Furthermore, I do not judge you for hitting him with a baseball bat. In fact, I applaud you for doing it because he truly deserved it."

7. There was lots of high praise for the admirable character traits she exhibited during her trauma healing work with words like, "I respect and admire the honesty, forthrightness, directness, and clarity which you have displayed during your healing work here with us,"

8. Her classmates gave her high praise for her willingness to talk openly about having a frozen pelvis which interfered with her sexual life. They acknowledged her painful story by saying things like, "Thank you for being so open about how your frozen pelvis is creating problems for you because you are not alone in having to deal with this issue. I too, have difficulty in my sexual life due to holding in my pelvis so I greatly appreciate your courage and willingness to share your pain and story."

9. She received rave reviews regarding her Shadow Work psychotherapy practice with comments like, "I recently conducted a Shadow Work Seminar which several of your clients attended. They gave high praise for your Shadow Work Therapy skills in helping them move forward with their trauma healing and personal growth. They obviously hold you in very high esteem."

The Toxic Shame Busting Protocol Outcome for Our Volunteer

When I checked in with our volunteer early during the Extolling Process, she admitted it was difficult to hear such lavish praise and that a voice in her head, which she labeled as her, 'Inner Judge,' kept trying to diminish what she was hearing. However, she quickly added, "I told her to shut up and that I was not going to listen to her crap!" With that defiant statement, the training class burst into applause.

After the last extolling statements were given, I asked our volunteer again if she was able to take in all of the validation given to her. She faced me with a big smile, "Yes!" she replied. "My Inner Judge is silent with nothing to say. That is remarkable because she has always had something negative to say!" she exclaimed with delight. "Yes," I said. "Your inner judge is silent for a good reason. That is because of all the high praise you received. That high praise has caused your inner victim voice to go silent and become non-existent. Thus, your inner judge has no where to hang its hat. Its existence totally depends on your inner victim voice which your inner judge could hook with its constant negative judgments. Without it, your inner judge is nothing."

She contemplated my words, mulling over and digesting them, to see if they resonated for her as the truth. Moments later, she nodded with a big smile returning to her face. She voiced a soft ,"Wow!" As she did so, she turned to face her classmates with tears in her eyes and her arms open as if to embrace them all. "My tears are tears of joy and my heart is filled with gratitude!" she said. Upon seeing her tears and wide open arms, her classmates quickly surrounded her and gave her and themselves hugs. It was clear to me that her Toxic Shame Shroud was busted, gone, and that it may never return again. I can testify that as of this date, her Toxic Shame has, indeed, not returned.

Completing The Energetic Peer Co-Counseling Demonstration

We then returned to complete the Energetic Co-counseling Demonstration. The co-counseling trio switched roles, so the remaining two trio members took turns being the Focus Person to complete their co-counseling trauma healing work. Following this, the class divided into co-counseling trios, so each class member had a chance to practice using Energetic Peer Co-counseling Protocol.

Taking a Break to Have the Class Members Complete a Written Session Rating & Feedback Evaluation Form

Before closing my demonstration, I suggested the class members take a break to complete a written rating & feedback evaluation for the session. I wanted to do this before using my favorite closing activity which is The Shower of Light Protocol because it allowed the class members to fill out their evaluation forms without the pressure of rushing the task so they could leave the class to head for home. When I reviewed their written feedback, the thing that really stood out was summed up by one of the written statements which was, "High praise gets rid of one's Inner Judge because it gets rid of one's Inner Victim." This let me know they got it!

Closing Using The Shower Of Golden Light Protocol

To close my final presentation and demonstration session, I proposed we encircle our volunteer, raise our arms in the air above her, and shower her with golden light from our fingertips as we wiggled then above her. We honored her by doing so, and then turned our shower of golden light on each other. The real golden light was on everyone's face as we all beamed with love and joy. My session received high marks and the feedback was positive without any serious issues being raised.

Other Methods of Helping Clients Lift Their Toxic Shame Shrouds

There are a few other methods of helping toxic shame victims get out from under their crippling shame shrouds, at least on a temporary basis. My experience is that beginning clients are often not ready to embrace the Toxic Shame Busting Protocol with its intense validating & extolling process. For one thing, receiving validation and high praise from others can bring up buried and painful emotional feelings that may be overwhelming even for seasoned trauma clients. For another, there can be a prohibition on the part of some clients about receiving high praise. Parental statements like, "Don't get too full of yourself," and, "I don't let praise give you a big head," are examples When this kind of internal resistance is encountered, there are some alternative methods of helping clients alleviate and deal with their toxic shame. Below, I cite several resources that contain ideas and methods that I have used successfully with toxic shame filled clients prior to using The Toxic Shame Busting Protocol, or with trauma clients who were reluctant to engage in its intense validating & extolling process.

Instructions For Using the Energetic Peer Co-counseling Protocol and The Toxic Shame Busting Protocol

Below, you will find detailed instructions for using The Toxic Shame Busting Protocol and The Energetic Peer Co-counseling Protocol along with additional resources.

The Toxic Shame Busting Protocol

Part I: Helping Clients Recognize Their Toxic Shame Shutdown

Before clients can heal their toxic shame, they must become aware that it is shutting them down. The first step in doing this is to help them recognize the signs and symptoms of how toxic shame is disabling them. Here are a few signs and symptoms that signal a client is suffering from toxic shame:

1. The client feels flawed and inferior to others.
2. The client struggles with feelings of being worthless.
3. The client has excessive negative self-talk.
4. The client is fearful of intimacy and afraid of exposing himself/herself with others.
5. The client feels extremely defensive or humiliated when confronted with having made a mistake or when given negative feedback.
6. The client cannot say 'no' to others or tries to set emotional boundaries by isolating from others, trying to please others, or raging at others, for example.
7. The client covers her/his feelings of shame by adopting compulsive behaviors like substance abuse, an eating disorder, and becoming a workaholic, for example.
8. The client is extremely lonely and feels like an outsider with others.
9. The client feels extremely guilty, and shame filled about making the most trivial mistake and continually apologizes for his/her behavior.

Talking with clients about their toxic shame feelings and behaviors can help them recognize their toxic shame. In addition, there are numerous Energetic Trauma Healing Protocols that can be used with clients to help them recognize the signs and symptoms of toxic shame, and in some cases, begin to heal it. Here is a list of the trauma healing protocols which can be found in the Chapter on The Backup Support Protocol later in this Innovations in Healing Trauma handbook.

Chapter 3: How to Use the Toxic Shame Busting Protocols • 91

1. Using The Just Be with Your Feelings Protocol with clients can help them identify their toxic shame feelings.

2. Using The Advocate Protocol with clients can help them recognize their toxic shame feelings and behaviors when their Advocate confronts their abusers in a psychodrama/role-play situation.

3. Using The Silencing Your Inner Judge Protocol, The Dis-identifying With Your Inner Judge Protocol, and The Defending Against Your Inner Judge Protocol with clients can help them identify and deal with their toxic shame self-talk and the negative inner voice that puts them down, self-attacks them for making mistakes, or calls them nasty names like, 'You worthless piece of crap!'

4. Using The Validation Protocol with clients can help them identify their inner victim voice and its negative self-talk like, 'I will never be any good,' or, 'I am totally worthless.'

5. Using The Change A Core Belief Protocol with clients can help them recognize and get rid of toxic core beliefs like, 'I am bad,' or, 'I will never amount to anything.'

6. Using the Toxic Energy Waste Dump Protocol with clients can help them get in touch with as well as get rid of their toxic shame feelings.

7. Using the Claiming Your Boundaries Protocol and the Heroic Story Protocol with clients can help them recognize their poor boundary setting behavior which is connected to their toxic shame.

8. Using The My Ideal Vision of My Life Protocol with clients can help them get in touch with their current toxic shame based life feelings and behaviors.

9. Using The Energetic Holding Defenses Descriptions Protocol and The Energetic Holding Defenses Checklist Protocol with clients can help them learn about how their childhood caretakers traumatized and instilled toxic shame into them.

10. Using The Bunker Busting Protocol with clients can help them break through their denial and get in touch with their toxic shame feelings and behavior.

Part II: Covering the Toxic Shame Filled Client

When trauma clients say things like, "I just want to disappear," indicating they are indirectly aware of their toxic shame or are more directly in touch with their toxic shame which is overwhelming them, suggest they allow themselves to be covered with a sheet or blanket during their trauma healing work. If they agree, simply place the sheet or blanket gently over their head so the top half of their body is completely covered. Then, allow them to experience being under this covering. Often shame filled clients who are covered in this way will visibly let down and relax as well as comment on how good it feels to not be seen, both of which confirm the benefits of the covering. If these clients do not relax, or find the covering not to their liking, check in with them to ask about what is going on for them. Then, simply respond to their feedback as appropriate. At some point, the clients who like the covering will want the covering removed and can then proceed forward with their trauma healing work. If they do not ask to have the covering removed, again check in with them to ask how they want to proceed. One possibility is to ask if you can join them under the covering and do the validating & extolling in Part III. Whatever their response is, take your cue from them. Go to Part III when and if they are ready.

Part III: Validating & Extolling the Toxic Shame Filled Client

Using this validating & extolling Part III of the Toxic Shame Busting Protocol requires the Therapist, group members, and/or family members have a close and familiar connection with the client/Focus Person who is to be validated and extolled. If this is not the case, then the Therapist, group members, or family members will need to do a fair amount of research into the client's life to learn the strengths, abilities, and accomplishments of the client in order for this to work.

The validating & extolling steps are quite simple.

Step 1. The client/Focus Person is to agree to receive the validating & extolling statements—that is to say, to receive high praise from the Therapist, family members, and/or group members.

Step 2: The Therapist, family member(s) and/or group members validate & extol the client—that is to give the client high praise and validation for his/her strengths, talents, abilities, accomplishments, values, and character traits. If this protocol is used in a family or group setting, then all of the family or group members are to validate & extol the Focus Person by giving her/him their high praise and validation.

Step 3. The Therapist checks in with the Focus Person to see if he/she was able to take in the high praise and validation. If the client was unable to take in the extolling and validation, then some therapeutic work has to be done with the client to remove the block(s) that prevents him/her from taking it in.

The ground rules for this part of the client validating & extolling exercise are as follows:

1. In a group or family setting, those giving the high praise to the Focus Person are to each take a turn doing so and to not use qualifying words like, "sometimes, mostly, usually," and, "on-the-other-hand," for example.

2. The Focus Person receiving the high praise is to simply take it in and refrain from commenting on it by diminishing it, down playing it, and explaining it away, for example.

The Energetic Peer Co-Counseling Protocol

To use this protocol, simply follow the steps outlined below:

1. Form a co-counseling trio.

2. In your co-counseling trio, decide who will be the Focus Person to do her/his Energetic Trauma Healing work, who will be the Assist Person to help the Focus Person work, and who will be the Monitor & Safety Person to help keep the energetic healing work on track and safe.

3. Next, Jump Start a strong energy charge in your bodies by doing a few minutes of vigorous physical exercise such as doing Jumping Jacks or kicking a large pillow back and forth between trio members, for example. Follow this by doing Energetic Grounding using one or more of the Energetic Grounding Protocols such as the Downhill Ski Energetic Grounding Protocol, or the Hair-pin Energetic Grounding Protocol, for example.

4. When it is your turn to be the Focus Person, state a healing intention for doing your trauma healing work.

5. Then, use the Spontaneous Movement Protocol to direct your Client-directed Energetic Therapy in order to realize

your stated intention and move your trauma healing work forward.

6. Use the Energetic Grounding Protocols as needed, especially to work through any fear or anxiety connected to hidden-buried trauma memories that surface, for example, or resolve any internal resistance issues that may pop up—such as your inner-judge-voice-alarm screaming, "Stop! Danger ahead!" or, some other dire warning, for instance.

7. As needed, use the Start-up Protocol to self-diagnose your Primary or Secondary Energetic Holding Defense(s), and use The Restructuring of the Energetic Holding Defenses Protocol to restructure your Energetic Holding Defense(s).

8. When you finish your Client-directed Energetic Therapy work, or your time is up as the Focus Person, switch roles so each trio member takes a turn being the Focus Person, Assist Person, and Safety & Monitor Person.

9. When each trio member has taken a turn at being the Focus Person, end the trio co-counseling session by doing Energetic Grounding.

Additional Resources for Healing Toxic Shame

Byron Brown, in his handbook *Soul Without Shame*, describes a number of practical strategies for dealing with the workings of the mind which cause people to go into shame and to unwittingly perpetuate it in their lives. (Brown, 1999.)

Bernard Golden in his April 22, 2017, *Psychology Today* article, "Overcoming the Paralysis of Toxic Shame", identifies a number of key strategies for overcoming toxic shame.

Ineffable Living presents a very useful article, as well as ready made materials, to help the reader understand and deal with toxic shame. See: *The Top Signs of Toxic Shame In A Person* at www.ineffableliving.com. (October 9, 2022.)

Michael Lewis has written a very informative and helpful book on dealing with shame entitled, *Shame: The Exposed Self* (1995), New York: Simon & Schuster.

The Elephant in the Room

There is an obvious but largely ignored problem which we face with regard to preventing and healing trauma in our families, communities, and culture. It is the proverbial elephant in the room. This problem has been obvious for years but rarely mentioned by psychologists, sociologists, and health care practitioners because it is personally, socially, politically, and professionally uncomfortable, embarrassing, and controversial. For example, Teju Ravilochan in his GatherFor post entitled, "Could the Blackfoot Wisdom that Inspired Maslow Guide Us Now?" (2021), explains the noted psychologist, Abraham Maslow visited the native Blackfoot Nation in the late 1930s to do research on his theory of self-actualization. He wanted to test the universality of his theory that social hierarchies are maintained by dominance of some people over others. However, he was surprised to find there was no quest for dominance in Blackfoot society. In fact, he was shocked to find the Blackfoot people had astonishing high levels of cooperation with minimal inequality and high levels of life satisfaction.

He estimated 80-90% of the Blackfoot people had a quality of self-esteem that was far greater than found in his own population back home—which he estimated to be 5-10% —thus making self-actualization among the Blackfoot as the norm. (Maslow defined self-actualization as the individual becoming everything that he or she is capable of becoming, or in the Blackfeet language, niita' pitan, meaning someone who is completely developed.)

As Maslow explored this striking difference between the Blackfoot population and his back home US research subjects, the explanation appeared to be three-fold. One, the Blackfoot saw their children as inherently sacred, wise beings and therefore treated them as important members of the community to whom they gave great freedom and space to express themselves as opposed to tightly governing them with the strict, disciplinary approach found in his own back home US culture. Two, the Blackfoot eliminated wealth disparity in their community by holding Giveaway ceremonies in which the wealthiest members gave away their possessions to those in greater need. This was in sharp contrast with Maslow's back home US culture which allowed the top 0.1 of wealthy individuals to make 196 times as much as the bottom 90% of society's members while also permitting one in four families to suffer food insecurity, and furthermore, consented to the richest 20% of US society members contributing only 1.3% of their income to charity. Three, the Blackfoot treated negative deviants who disrupted the community with wrongdoing and conflict, for example, with understanding and compassion, allowing them to redeem themselves if they left their negative deviant behavior behind and contributed to the community. Again, this was in sharp contrast to Maslow's back home US culture which blamed, shamed, and/or punished deviant wrongdoing behavior with prison time, or simply ignored it when the wrongdoing was only hurtful within families

Similar findings apply to many other First Nation peoples. For example, Dana Arviso, a member of the Navajo tribe and the Executive Director of the Pot-latch Fund, asked the Natives in the Cheyenne River territory about poverty there. They told her they don't have a word for poverty. They said the closest words for poverty were "to be without family". However, they added, for someone in their tribal community to be so isolated that they had no family, kinsmen, or other tribal members to help provide for them if required, was simply unheard of since the tribal community was always there to take care of them if needed. In other words, the tribal community is there to insure when tribal members are born, their needs for love, care, belonging, food, housing, clothing, safety, education, purpose, and protection are fully met. A similar explanation for poverty as well as a total tribal commitment to ensure community members' needs are fully met are the founding values of First Nation societies in North America. This First Nation approach to caring for their tribal members' needs is in striking contrast to the US approach of expecting each family, or each individual, rather than the community to meet society members' needs for love, care, belonging, food, housing, clothing, safety, education, purpose, and protection.

What About Trauma in First Nation Societies?

Maslow does not report on trauma in the Blackfoot society. However, we can safely assume the type of individual trauma resulting from the deviant behavior of society members—that is to say, physical abuse, sexual abuse, emotional abuse, which is so highly prevalent that it affects one in four families in the US, as well as childhood developmental interference abuse which affects nearly every family in the US—was undoubtedly non-existent at that time in the Blackfoot culture. This was because the tribal community in the 1930s and before would have immediately stepped in to stop such deviant abusive behavior if it existed. Of course, we know the Blackfoot and other First Nation peoples had suffered trauma but at that time it was due largely to historical, intergenerational, and racial trauma, for example, that affected all of the tribal members as whole rather than being limited to individual members and due to the wrongdoing behavior of deviant society members, or the errant child-rearing practices of misguided caretakers, as was the case in the US. Of course this historical, intergenerational, and racial trauma is now being recognized, addressed, and slowly healed. However later, as First Nation tribes became Westernized, alcoholism became a serious problem and along with it, the appearance and rise of individual abuse and trauma of a physical and sexual nature as well as trauma caused by caretaker interference in children's stage growth and development.

Here is the Central Trauma Question

Let's say the US moved away from its individualistic, mostly hands-off approach to dealing with physical, sexual, emotional, and developmental trauma and instead, adopted a full-out community response like that of the pre-Westernized Blackfoot society to deal with this kind of trauma. As a result, would individual physical, sexual, emotional, and childhood developmental trauma in the US drop from its current level of one in four people (mostly women and children) being afflicted to near zero of individuals being impacted (which was the pee-Westernized Blackfoot norm)? I hypothesize that the answer to this question has to be, "YES!" That based on the Blackfoot norm, the level of this kind of abuse and trauma in the US would similarly drop dramatically to near zero. This would happen because family members, neighbors, church groups, community development organizations, women's rights groups, child protective agencies, law enforcement, and local government offices would immediately mobilize (as the Blackfoot did) to stop this kind of abuse and trauma, and then institute measures to prevent it from happening again in the future. Thus, we can imagine that not only would the physical-sexual-emotional abuse to children stop if this community caring approach was adopted but the trauma caused by misguided and ignorant parents and child caretakers—teachers, religious workers, and babysitters—interfering with children's natural child-development stages would also be eliminated. For example, here is how this community care approach might work at various child development stages:

1. Parents and caretakers who are unwelcoming or extremely rigid when their child is born, for example, and thus threaten their child's existence at that early stage of development when their child needs to feel safe, secure, and wanted, cause their child extreme trauma which will cause it to adopt a Holding Out Defense. In this defense, the child dissociates from its body so as to not feel the pain of being unwanted and/or the terror-threat to its existence. However, this threat to its existence will not be allowed to continue since the community care approach would welcome the child and make it safe by removing the threat to its existence.

2. Parents/caretakers who neglect their child's basic needs for nurturing at this early critical developmental stage when their child needs to be secure in its needing will cause their child trauma and thus lead it to adopt a Holding On Defense. In this defense, the child clings to its parents/caretakers in a desperate attempt to gain any vestige of nurturance from them. However, using a community care approach, the community would immediately intervene to help the neglectful caretakers meet their child's needs or remove the child from the neglectful situation and help meet its basic needs for love, care, and nurturing.

3. Parents/caretakers who exploit their child for their own purpose at this critical stage when their child needs to develop a sense of autonomy will cause their child trauma and thus lead it to adopt a Holding Up Defense. In this defense, the child cuts off from feeling its body and therefore the pain of being used and exploited. However, with a community caring approach, the community would immediately step in to stop the exploitation of this child and provide the conditions to help it develop autonomy.

4. Parents/caretakers who over-control their child at this critical stage when their child needs to develop independence will cause their child trauma and thus lead it to adopt a Holding In Defense. In this defense, the child hardens its body so it won't feel the pain of being over-controlled as well as withdraws energy from its expressive organs to keep from showing its anger and outrage which would result in even more parental/caretaker control. However, with a community caring approach, the community would immediately intervene to prevent this child from being over-controlled and help it develop independence.

5. Parents/caretakers who manipulate their child to keep their child from directly reaching out for what it wants as opposed to what the parents/caretakers want for it at this critical stage when their child needs to develop the confidence and freedom to pursue its own interests and wants unimpeded by outside imposition will cause their child trauma and thus lead it to adopt a Holding Back Defense. In this defense, the child stiffens its resolve—by literally stiffening its back and jaw—in a stubborn attempt to hold back from reaching out directly for what

it wants, and instead, moving indirectly to gain what it wants. However, with the community caring approach, the community would immediately intervene to prevent this child from being manipulated and help it develop the freedom to reach out directly for what it wants.

Using The Pre-Westernized Blackfoot Community Caring Approach Model to Help Heal Trauma

The pre-Westernized Blackfoot community caring approach to dealing with disruptive wrongdoing, deviant behavior as well as other critical problems that confront the tribe—such as dealing with health issues, for example—was to 'mobilize all hands to the front' so to speak. The question is, "How could we use this Pr-Westernized Blackfoot community response model to help heal trauma in our US communities?" One simple way is for Therapists and clients to do trauma healing in on-going groups—that is to say, in "community-caring" settings. When I was a full time Energetic Trauma Therapist before becoming Director of The Center For Innovations In Healing Trauma, I offered a number of on-going trauma healing groups—family groups, couples groups, women's groups, men's groups, and mixed gender groups, workshops & training seminars—as did my colleagues, which formed a caring community approach to support our trauma healing work. Of course, these efforts were not a total, full community wide response by our city or region to healing trauma but at least it was a move in that direction. The next step is for each of us who share such a caring community response to healing trauma vision, to begin moving toward realizing it. Here is the vision spelled out in a Caring Community Response Approach To Healing Trauma Protocol presented below.

The Caring Community Response Approach to Healing Trauma Protocol

1. If you are a client, do your trauma healing in an ongoing trauma healing group-community-oriented setting.

2. If you are a psychotherapist, offer an ongoing trauma healing therapy group and encourage clients to join it.

3. If you are a parent, raise your children employing an approach like the one offered by Rudolf Dreikurs in Children: The Challenge (1991) which uses encouragement and natural & logical consequences as the central child-rearing methods.

4. If you are a policy maker, agency leader, or local government official, design and use family and community interventions to bring negative deviant behavior back into alignment with community values without resorting to punishment, blame, and shame. This especially applies to parents and child caretakers who threaten their child's existence, neglect their child, use and exploit their child, over control their child, or manipulate their child to keep it in line, all of which cause the child trauma and lead it to adopt various Energetic Holding Defenses. (Google "How to Do Family & Community Interventions," for resources on this topic.)

5. Speak up for and elect representatives, policy makers, and local administrators who can create avenues for the less fortunate in our society to become food-income-wealth secure, as well as level the playing field so there is greater equity between the wealthy and the less wealthy/have-nots.

The Body Knows Best

There are a number of ways to help clients tap into and use their own body wisdom to direct their trauma healing therapy. Here are three that I have used with great success with my Client-directed Energetic Therapy clients. One way is to help clients use The Spontaneous Movement Protocol which is the Mega Star of my Energetic Trauma Healing Therapy approach. It can be used in doing individual Client-directed Energetic Therapy as well as in couples and family Client-directed Energetic Therapy. A second way is to teach clients how to follow their body impulses in order to help heal themselves. This was the precursor to my Spontaneous Movement Protocol. A third way is to help clients tune into their intuition in order to navigate their healing journey.

Using The Spontaneous Movement Protocol with Couples to Help Them Heal Their Relationship Trauma

I mainly use the Spontaneous Movement Protocol to help client couples and families work through their trauma, problems, and difficulties. It is very similar to using the Spontaneous Movement Protocol to work with individuals except that the couple or family members alternate doing the work. In working with couples, first

I ask the couple to do Energetic Grounding. (See the Chapter on Helping Clients Jump Start A Strong Energy Charge In Their Body To Move Their Trauma Healing Therapy Forward for some of these Energetic Grounding Protocols.) Next, I ask the couple to each set an intention for their Energetic Healing work. Then I have the couple face each other and take turns letting a spontaneous movement arise from their bodies that will help them realize their healing intentions. I start working with the partner who makes the first move, pointing out his/her spontaneous movement. I ask her/him to amplify it and express any feelings, thoughts, and memories connected to the movement, and so on. (See below for a description of the Spontaneous Movement Protocol.) Then at an appropriate point, I will turn to the other partner and work with him/her in the same way. I simply keep alternating between the couple partners, using the Spontaneous Movement Protocol to do their healing work until they have realized their healing intentions or they have run out of time for the session. Once the couple has learned how to use this Spontaneous Movement Protocol, they can often assist each other in their work. Here are two examples of this kind of couples Client-directed Energetic Therapy.

Hand Play

This couple came to see me seeking a better, closer relationship. During one of their early sessions, after doing some Energetic Grounding work and intention setting, I asked the couple to stand facing each other and let a spontaneous movement arise from their bodies. He made the first spontaneous movement by holding out his hands, with palms up, to take her hands in his. She responded by placing her hands in his but then immediately reversed them with her palms up so he could place his hands in hers. He did so but then reversed his hands, palms up, so she could place her hands again in his. She once again placed her hands in his but then reversed them, palms up, so he could once again place his hands in hers which he did. This hand play happened very rapidly and spontaneously.

"What was that hand play all about?" I asked as they stood facing each other perplexed by what had just happened. "It was just natural for me to hold her hands, so that is what I initially tried to do," he said. "But I feel controlled when you do that," she replied.

"So, you feel less controlled when you hold his hands in yours?" I asked. "That's right," she said. "I feel safer when he places his hands in mine." I asked, "Did you feel controlled when you were a child?" She nodded. "For sure!" she said. "My father tried to control me in every way." I then asked her if she felt controlled in her everyday relationship with him. "Not like it was with my father," she replied. "But yes, sometimes I feel he is a bit controlling." She then raised her head slightly as she looked up at him since he was quite a bit taller than she. I pointed out her spontaneous movement of slightly raising her head looking up at him. She acknowledged the movement but had no response to my pointing it out. I then asked her to exaggerate the movement while looking in a full length mirror which hung on the wall in my office. She looked at herself raising her head higher and then instantly lowered her head to look at the floor and shuddered. "It is scary to see myself raising my head higher like that," she said. "It feels very dangerous, as if I will get punished for doing so." I suggested she again repeat and exaggerate the movement of raising her head several times while looking at the mirror and each time she withdrew into fear.

"Are there any words connected to the movement of raising your head?" I asked. She looked in the mirror and raised her head again. "I have a right to hold my head up high," she said. "Oh, that feels so defiant!" she said, cringing in fear. "But it looks so good," her partner said as he looked on. "You look in control and so proud when you hold your head up high." She looked at him in disbelief.

I then asked her to once again repeat the movement of holding her head higher and repeating her words, "I have a right to hold my head high." She did so and immediately said. "I'm beginning to leave my body." At that point, I asked her to do some Energetic Grounding work by hanging forward and doing the Hairpin Grounding Protocol exercise. This helped bring her back into her body. I then asked him to tell her that she had a right to hold her head up high. As he did so, it elicited more fear and she again reported she was leaving her body. I then had her repeat the grounding work followed by him telling her she had the right to hold her head high several times until she was able to hear his words without leaving her body. She then looked in the mirror, raised her head, and was able to say, "I have a right to hold my head high, without leaving my body.

I then turned to him. "What was happening with you as she did that work?" I asked. "I was feeling so much love for her," he replied, facing her. He then reached out for her hands but this time he placed one hand in hers and took her other hand in his. "I love you so much," he said, looking at her with mist in his eyes. "You are so courageous and brave when you let your feelings out." As he said this, he crossed their held hands, one set over the other, and then reversed the crossing a couple of times.

I pointed out the crossed hands movement and asked him what that was about. He thought for a moment and then said, looking at me, "I am using it to control my feelings." Then he turned back to look at her. "I love it when you express your deepest feelings," he said, "but don't expect me to do that. No way!" I responded by saying, "So, you feel resistant to express your feelings as she just did?" He replied, "You bet I do!" I asked,

"Is that where you want to be in your relationship with her?" He hesitated for a moment and then said, "No, it is not where I want to be. I do want to be able to express my deepest feelings with her, but there is something within me that won't allow me to do it."

I suggested he stay with his feelings of resistance and work with it by doing a Wall-sit Energetic Grounding Protocol exercise. "This is an exercise which pits your ego against your body to help you melt through your internal resistance," I said. It required him to sit against my office wall, as if he was sitting in a chair, and to do so for as long as he was able to maintain the position. He was to say, "I am never going to express my deepest feelings like she did!" a number of times while he maintained the wall sit position and resisted going down to the floor as the position became more difficult to maintain. He did so until his legs could no longer hold him up and then slid down the wall to the floor. Even then, he tensed himself as if he was still trying to hold himself off the floor. I encouraged him to give in to relaxation and let himself feel the comfort of having the floor support him rather than holding up to resist letting down and relaxing. It was difficult for him to do so. He then repeated the wall sit exercise two more times. When he slid to the floor the third time, he finally allowed himself to let down more but still resisted expressing his feelings. At that point he was able to say, "I'd like to express my deepest feelings," to his partner without choking on his fear of doing so.

I then asked him if he was up to doing a little more spontaneous movement work on his fear of expressing his deepest feelings. He agreed and after going to a still point in his body, his initial spontaneous movement was to slightly turn the left side of his mouth downward. I pointed out the movement but he was unsure as to what I meant. Thus, I suggested he look in the mirror and exaggerate the downward turn of his mouth several times.

He studied himself as he did the downward movement and then blurted out, "I hate that! It looks like I am sad. And it looks like I don't know who I am."

I then asked him how old he was when this downward turn of his mouth first occurred. Without hesitation he replied, "Maybe, I was three or four years old. I was not allowed to be sad at that age or any age. Mom could not have handled it. I had to keep a smile on my face around her. I've always had to keep a smile on my face since. I cannot show that I am sad around others."

"No wonder you don't know who you are if you cannot be sad when you feel like it," I said. "Yes, that's right!" he said, feeling validated. "And that makes me feel sad now." I suggested he go ahead and show a sad face if he felt like it. He did so while looking at himself in the mirror. "Wow!" he said, "That feels different and very strange. But I still don't like it." I asked, "So, do you think you should smile even when you feel sad?" He replied, "That is kind of stupid! No, I want to be able to express my sadness when I feel it." He turned back to the mirror and let his mouth turn downward. "I have the right to feel sad and express it around others," he said. "I do not have to keep a smile on my face all of the time when I don't feel like smiling." Then he addressed his imaginary mom in the mirror. "I don't have to smile when I don't feel like it mom, just because you cannot handle my sadness." His face lit up with a genuine smile. "Wow, that feels good to say." He then turned to his partner. "I can express my deepest feelings with you," he said. "I can let my sadness show when I feel it." Tears came to his eyes. "I feel sad right now because I have missed so much." With that he embraced his partner and let the tears flow. Then he turned to me. "There, I did it! And it feels great!"

We ended their couples counseling session on that bright note. As you can see, I simply alternated working with each partner using the Spontaneous Movement Protocol. Notice I also asked each of them to respond to the spontaneous movement work that their partner did as it seemed appropriate.

The Stoic and The Innocent

Here is a follow up session with this same couple. In terms of setting an intention, he indicated he wanted to stop being so defensive with his partner when she triggered his fear alarm. She indicated she wanted to stop withdrawing and isolating from him when he got triggered. "When he gets triggered and becomes defensive, he often begins to attack and blame me," she said. "That's when I become defensive and withdraw. I want to stand up to him even in the face of his attacks and blaming."

To begin their work together, I asked them to do some Energetic Grounding work using the Downhill Ski Protocol. Next, I asked them to face each other and then let a spontaneous movement arise from their bodies that would help them realize their intentions by rewiring the neural pathways in their brain which triggered their emotional brain alarms thus causing them to become defensive with each other. His face and body immediately took on a stoic look—his initial spontaneous movement. He then began a discourse directed at her, telling her he thought their defensiveness would eventually fade away the more they loved each other which he felt was happening. As he continued the discourse, she looked at him with a wide eyed, childlike innocent expression on her face—her initial spontaneous movement.

I began working with him first. I pointed out his stoic look and he did not dispute it. Rather, he said he was very familiar with it and often used stoicism to keep from feeling vulnerable. I then asked him if he knew where his stoic defense had originated. He indicated it started with his mother when he was a very young boy. "My mother was very disappointed in my father while I was growing up because she received so little attention, support and love from him," he said. "Consequently, my mother turned to me to get the attention, support and love that she was so hungry for." In effect, his mother made him her little surrogate spouse. He indicated he had not liked being put in the position of feeling responsibility for her well being as a boy. "She was often very depressed and even tried to commit suicide at one point when I was about eight years old," he said. "My parents had divorced by that time, and she was a mess. There was really nothing I could do to help her but she still looked to me for emotional support. I didn't like it! I guess my way of dealing with my helpless, hopeless feelings was to become stoic and not feel my feelings at all."

I then turned to her and pointed out her spontaneous movement of looking wide eyed and innocent as he went on with his discourse about their defensiveness fading away the more they learned to love each other. She was a little surprised by my observation but did not dispute it. I then asked her what was going on inside her as she looked at him in her wide eyed, innocent way.

"I was really making a judgment about what he was saying," she said. "I was thinking his words were all bullshit." I said, "So, your wide eyed, innocent look was a cover for your judgment he was not speaking the truth," She replied, "Yes it was. I think I often do that when I'm judging what someone is saying or doing. I don't want to be seen making a judgment, so I cover it with my wide eyed, innocent look."

"Do you know where your need to cover up your judgments originated?" I asked. She answered, "As a child, if I told people the truth about what I was feeling, I got into big trouble with my parents. I would be sent to my room to think about how wrong I was to feel that way, or get punished by having to miss a meal, or be grounded in my room for a day. So, I learned to keep my judgments to myself and act very innocent as if I had no judgments at all about what went on in my family."

"So, you did not like what went on in your family?" I asked. "Are you kidding!" she responded. "I hated all of the fighting, physical abuse, and especially the sexual abuse that was happening to me. I often got blamed for it all, and that is where I learned to withdraw and isolate myself, especially when they started yelling at me—just like he does," nodding at her partner, "when he gets defensive and starts yelling at me."

I then asked them to face each other and let a spontaneous movement arise from their respective bodies that would help him stop triggering his defensiveness when he felt overly responsible for her and that would help her stop being defensive when she felt blamed by him because of it. His spontaneous movement was to smile and hers was to laugh out loud. I pointed out their respective spontaneous movements and asked them what their movements meant in terms of helping each become less defensive. "Well, I could just smile when I begin to feel defensive with her," he said. I replied by suggesting he say the words, "I have a choice to smile rather than become stoic or lash out at her when I feel responsible for her." He repeated those words several times and then acknowledged he could indeed make the choice of smiling rather than going stoic and lashing out. I explained the more he smiled when he felt defensive rather than going stoic and lashing out, the stronger this new smiling neural pathway would become thus allowing the old, disused stoic-lashing-out neural pathway to weaken and eventually fade away which would turn off his brain alarm trigger when he felt responsible for his partner.

I then turned to her. I suggested she say the words aloud, "I can choose to express my judgment that he is speaking bullshit by laughing out loud rather than trying to cover up what I feel by acting wide-eyed and innocent." She repeated my words and then immediately reported she was leaving her body. In response, I asked her to do some Energetic Grounding by stomping her feet on the floor which brought her back into her body. I followed this by saying, "So, it is very scary for you to let yourself be seen in your truth." She replied, "Yes! I never do that. It just feels too dangerous!"

"I then suggested she say the words, "It was very dangerous to tell the truth when I was a helpless child, but now it is no longer dangerous because I have power as an adult woman and therefore, I am no longer helpless to protect myself." She repeated those words several times and then reported she felt fully in her power. She added, "I don't know why I leave my body like that." In response, her partner chimed in. "I think I know why you leave your body," he said. "Didn't you have to leave your body when you were a child as a way to keep your sanity when your father was sexually molesting you?" he asked. "For sure!" she answered. After a moment of reflection, she added, "You are right. That is when leaving my body started, and then got reinforced when I tried to tell my mother about it and she accused me of making up the story." She then tilted her head as she looked at him. I pointed out her spontaneous movement of tilting her head and asked what it signified. She replied, "I really doubt he believes me. Rather, I think he believes I am making this all up about my father sexually abusing me just like my mother didn't believe me when I told her what was happening." I followed up by suggesting she look at him directly without tilting her head and ask him if he believed her. She did as I suggested. I then asked, "How was that?" She answered, "It feels good to be direct with him, but it also feels very scary to do so."

I then suggested she say to him, "I have the right to tell the truth and be believed, and not have to leave my body when I say my truth." She did so and reported it felt wonderful to say those words. "That is a big one for me!" she said. I explained the more she said those words and acted upon them, the stronger they would get wired into her brain as a new neural pathway of feeling safe to speak her truth instead of firing the old neural pathway of hiding her truth while feeling helpless and in danger. "This repetition will eventually weaken the old neural pathway from disuse and it will fade away." I added that as a result, "your emotional brain alarm will no longer get triggered by this issue." On this note, the couple's therapy session ended.

Cold And Distant

Here is a case example of a man who did relationship trauma healing work with me without his partner being present due to the fact she did not want to engage in relationship counseling. This is the way it went:

"My partner and I went to a movie last night," he said, "and we had a huge fight afterward. She got triggered by a scene in the movie and just fell apart. She became a complete mess. I can't stand it when she does that. I feel like I need to fix her, but really I don't know what to do, so I just get cold and non-responsive. When I did that, she got angry with me. Well, that really did it! So I became even more distant and withdrawn. We spent the rest of the evening in stony silence and went to bed without a word to each other. The next morning, she threw some things in a travel bag and left without saying goodbye. After she left I was completely miserable. I felt like I had lost her and there was nothing I could do."

"So, you felt completely helpless about the situation," I said. "Yes," he replied, "I felt totally helpless." I then asked, "Is this a pattern of behavior that you are familiar with, feeling totally helpless with your partner?" I asked. "Yes, it was the same in my previous marriage," he answered." I followed up by asking, "And, how about as a kid? Did you ever feel totally helpless with your mother or father?" He paused to reflect for a moment. "Yes," he said, "I felt completely helpless with my mother many times. I remember she got all emotional and a real mess when my dad was sent to prison for tax fraud when I was a young boy. She then tried to kill herself by taking an overdose of sleeping pills and had to be rushed to the hospital. There she just kept calling for me. It was as if I was supposed to save her. But there was nothing I could do! I felt totally helpless." I said, "So, when your partner gets all emotional, you feel like you need to save her but feel totally helpless because you don't know what to do to fix things just like you did with your mother." He replied, "Yes, that is the case, but what can I do about it?"

I then explained how his brain alarm was getting triggered by his partner's emotional behavior which closely resembled the emotional behavior of his mother that traumatized him as a boy. I suggested if he wanted a better relationship with his partner, he would need to do some trauma healing work around his issues with his childhood mother in order to turn off his overreactive brain alarm which caused him to withdraw when he felt helpless. I also added he would probably need to change some of his core beliefs about fixing his partner when she became over emotional. I indicated using the Spontaneous Movement Protocol might help him rewire his brain so he would not be triggered by his partner's over emotional behavior. I said I would be glad to assist him in such work, but it would be more effective if his partner joined him in doing it. He replied this was a non-starter since he was certain she would simply refuse to join him. I asked him if he wanted to go ahead without her and the risk of doing so was he might lose her as his partner. He agreed to move forward without her.

After having him do some Energetic Grounding using the Downhill Ski Protocol and then set a healing intention, I asked him to let a spontaneous movement arise from his body that would help him realize his healing intention. His spontaneous movement was to make a fist with his right hand. I pointed out his movement of making a fist and asked him if there were any feelings, thoughts, or memories connected to it. "I am very angry," he replied. "But I can't show it. That sets my partner off. It is better to keep my mouth shut, and that is what I do." I responded by asking him how that was working in his relationship with his partner. "It's not working well," he said, and then added, "I am damned if I do, and I am damned if I don't."

I let him sit with his helplessness for several moments. I then asked him if he wanted to change things, so he did not feel damned if he did and damned if he didn't. He answered he would jump at the chance of doing so but did not see how that was possible. I nodded and suggested that he let a spontaneous movement arise from his body that would help him solve the dilemma. His spontaneous movement was to make both hands into fists. I pointed this out and asked him to exaggerate making his hands into fists. He did so but quickly opened his hands and shook his head slightly from side to side. I again pointed out his spontaneous movements and asked him if there were any feelings, thoughts, or memories connected to them. He looked at me and said, "I don't want to see it."

I followed up by asking him what he did not want to see. He replied he did not know what it was that he did not want to see. I suggested his movement and words, "I don't want to see it," were important to his healing and encouraged him to let another spontaneous movement from his body help him find the answer. His spontaneous movement was to rub the 'third eye' area of his forehead with his left hand. I encouraged him to keep rubbing his forehead just above his eye brows. He did so, and then reported he did not want to see his childhood mother fawning over him as she lay helplessly in her bed. "I get sick to my stomach when I let myself see that image," he said. "I didn't want to see her lay there helpless, looking at me like I was supposed to fix things. That made me feel totally helpless." With those words, he curled his hands into fists.

"You were helpless to fix things as a boy, but you are a man now who has power," I said. "You were a victim as a boy, but you no longer have to be a victim as a man." I let my words sit with him in silence. Then, he looked at me and nodded. "You are right." he said, raising his fist to eye level. "I do have power as a man." With this realization, he was able to move forward with his Energetic Trauma Healing Therapy by restructuring his blinding Holding Up Defense and his guarded Holding Back Defense to recover his full power as a man. This required that he spend several sessions working to release the muscle tension and tightness in the occipital area at the base of his skull as well as his attitude of feeling stuck with his childhood mother and the sense of helplessness that this engendered in him.

When this tension released, he reported he no longer felt blinded about seeing clearly what was going on with his partner nor helpless in dealing with her. He also spent a good many sessions working to release the muscle tension in his back and jaw that kept him from reaching out to his partner with empathy and love. As a result he began to heal his relationship with his partner.

Instructions for Using the Spontaneous Movement Protocol

The Spontaneous Movement Protocol can be used to help clients direct their Energetic Trauma Healing Therapy in individual, group, family, and co-counseling sessions both in-person and on a Zoom platform. (Using it on Zoom is more challenging due to the lighting requirements needed to see clients' spontaneous movements and the muscle holding in their body. Also, clients' spontaneous movements and muscle holding are simply more difficult to see on camera than during in-person energetic work. This is why we suggest when doing Zoom sessions, both the Focus Person doing Client-directed Energetic Therapy work and his/her Assist Person be in-person in the same location which allows the Assist Person to directly observe the Focus Person's spontaneous movements and energetic muscle holding which then can be reported to the Coach who is located in a different Zoom location.)

Therapist/Assist Person Instructions:

Step 1: Before the client/focus person begins, do the following:

A. Ask the client/focus person to identify any physical or emotional limitations that need to be addressed before engaging in the healing work.

B. Ask the client/focus person to do Energetic Grounding. (See the various Energetic Grounding Protocols and instructions for using them in various chapters of this handbook, or on our website at www.innovationsinhealingtrauma.com.)

C. Ask the client/focus person to set a healing intention by answering the question, "What do I want to have happen here?"

D. Ask the client/focus person to get any support that is needed in order to feel safe and supported in the trauma healing work. This is especially important when doing the Spontaneous Movement Protocol work in a group setting.

E. Check to see if the client/focus person has a strong energetic charge in her/his body. If there is a weak energetic charge it will likely impede the client from making progress in the trauma healing work. If there is any doubt, have the client use one or more of the Energy Jump Start Protocols in this handbook—that is, doing physical exercise that increases the client's heart rate and deepens his/her breathing such as kicking a large pillow around the room, hitting a pillow placed in a chair with his/her fists, doing jumping jacks, or running in place, for example. Follow this up by having the client do more Energetic Grounding so that she/he is not over charged.

Step 2: Begin the Spontaneous Movement Protocol work by doing the following:

A. Have the client/focus person go to a 'still point' in his/her body and mind.

B. Then, ask the client/focus person to let a spontaneous movement or sequence of spontaneous movements arise from her/his body that will help her/him realize the answer to the question, "What do I want to have happen here?"

C. Mirror the client's/focus person's spontaneous movement or movement sequence, reflecting it back to the client/focus person by saying, "I noticed that you moved _____" with his/her spontaneous movement or movement sequence in the blank space. You can also have the client repeat the movement or movement sequence to help him/her become more aware of it.

D. Ask the client to repeat the spontaneous movement or movement sequence and then amplify it by exaggerating the movement or movement sequence.

E. Ask the client/focus person to get in touch with and express any memories, thoughts, feelings, emotions, sounds, and body sensations (or lack of sensation such as numbness) that are connected to her/his spontaneous movement or movement sequence.

F. Ask the client/focus person to continue letting any further spontaneous movements that might arise and expressing the memories, thoughts, feelings, emotions, sounds, and body sensations connected to them.

G. Ask the client/focus person to identify any internal resistance such as fear, energetic holding/tension/constriction in the body that is connected to the spontaneous movements and expressed memories, thoughts, feelings, emotion, sounds, and body sensations.

H. Ask the client/focus person questions that will help move the trauma healing work forward. (See our website for a list of these questions.)

Step 3: At appropriate places, as the client/focus person continues her/his Spontaneous Movement Protocol work, do the following:

A. Ask the client/focus person to identify any fear or internal mental-emotional-physical resistance to moving forward with his/her healing work.

B. Honor the client's/focus person's fear/resistance by saying something like, "I'll bet there is a good reason why your fear/resistance is appearing right now."

C. Ask the client/focus person if he/she wants to work through his/her fear/resistance, and if so, to make a choice of either,

1. letting a spontaneous movement or movement sequence arise and then expressing the memories,

thoughts, feelings, emotions, sounds, and body sensations tied to it that will help him/her work through the resistance, or

2. using one of the working through resistance protocols, and/or,

3. doing more Energetic Grounding work by using one of the Energetic Grounding Protocols presented in the Chapter on Using The Energy Jump Start & Energetic Grounding Protocols. The Energetic Grounding protocols often help internal resistance and fear melt away. If the client/focus person answers that she/he does not want to work through the resistance, or after doing more Energetic Grounding, for example, she/he decides not to continue working to resolve the resistance, ask, "Do you want to end your work?" If the answer is yes, then have the client end the work by skipping to Step 4. If the answer is no, then redirect the client by having him/her do more Energetic Grounding work, get more support by having a support person join her/him, do one or more of the Energetic Backup & Support Protocols such as a Backup Protocol to help the client feel and strengthen her/his backbone, or an Advocate Protocol to strengthen her/his self-confidence, for example.

D. Have the client/focus person continue his/her Spontaneous Movement Protocol work until he/she feels complete or the allotted time for the work has elapsed.

Step 4: To end the session:

A. Ask the client/focus person to energetically ground his/her healing work by using one of the Energetic Grounding Protocols

B. Ask the client/focus person if she/he needs anything else to end the session.

Helping Clients and Therapists Use Their Intuition to Move Clients' Energetic Trauma Healing Therapy Forward

Here is another very powerful way for Therapists to help clients direct their Client-directed Energetic Therapy. Helping clients learn to tap into their intuition to guide and direct their trauma healing efforts has the effect of not only moving their Client-directed Energetic Therapy forward at a rapid pace, but also gives them great self-confidence and trust in their own inner wisdom and self-empowerment. In addition, when Therapists also tap into their own intuition to help clients move their trauma healing therapy forward, doing so can often produce great results. My colleague, the Reverend Karen Arndorfer offers two case examples of helping clients learn to use their intuition, as well as how she uses her own intuition, to move their Client-directed Energetic Therapy forward.

Tapping into Intuition to Heal Trauma by Rev. Karen Arndorfer

The innovations in healing trauma that are presented in this handbook are nourished and intensified by tapping into our intuition as Therapists and encouraging our clients to do the same. In our work with clients, we believe it is critical to honor and call upon both the conscious and unconscious mind. The conscious mind is the expert at logic and the unconscious mind connects us and our clients with hunches and feelings at the gut level. Psychiatrist Carl Jung (2021) said that intuition is a psychic function that gives outlook and insight. For many people intuition is experienced as a gut instinct, a knowing, something they sense even if they can't always put their finger on it. Intuition plays a key role in not just our physical survival but also in our emotional and psychological well-being, assisting us to function better in the outside world.

In doing Client-directed Energetic Therapy, both the Therapist and the client need to tap into that gut feeling, that little something instinctual from within that tells us how we feel beneath the mental layers of knowing. The intuitive process bridges the gap between the conscious and unconscious parts of our mind. Working with the body provides a pathway for accessing the unconscious mind. The use of intuition complements the energetic protocols in this handbook. We honor and call upon the conscious and unconscious mind in the innovations in healing trauma work, seeking balance.

Helping individuals to develop a more conscious relationship with their intuition is a key component of our Energetic Trauma Healing work. When we tune into our intuition we are able to access a higher level of internal truth. It is what allows us to read the body and the energy of others more acutely. In helping clients to face and heal their trauma, it is important to ask them what their intuition is telling them, and to follow their intuitive impulses to heal.

When clients fully connect with the wisdom of their intuition, there is often a big shift in the way they view the circumstances that lead them to healing. In more fully connecting with their intuition they are able to see how their intuition is trying to guide them all along in making choices that fill them with a greater sense of peace, balance and acceptance.

Developing a healthy relationship with intuition is about learning to trust and work with our internal sensory system. It helps us to sense when something is off, can guide us to trust that feeling, and allow it to steer us on the right path. It is through being attuned to our bodies that this occurs. We have seen the Innovations in Healing trauma process and the energetic protocols help clients and Therapists connect to their intuition, trust it and more easily utilize it in their lives.

Life is a bodily experience, and the body is a source of wisdom that the mind alone cannot provide. We don't feel emotions in our brain, we feel them in our body. A body-centered therapy approach bridges the mind-body divide. Being healthy requires integrating all aspects of ourselves: mentally, emotionally, physically, and spiritually.

There was a point in my life where I had done talk therapy and a number of other things but still felt I wasn't really getting to the core issues, that there was a part of me that was not fully alive. These other modalities had definitely helped but I knew that my own mind got in the way – I talked around issues with my Therapists and easily fooled myself with my words! I wanted an experience that would by-pass my brain and this is when I discovered body-centered counseling. My own work changed my life drastically and I then knew that I wanted my counseling practice to be body centered.

Body-centered counseling is based on the belief that the body "armors" itself against painful and uncomfortable experiences. This armoring prevents free expression and causes chronic muscular tension. Patterns are created over time creating neural pathways that keep us locked into old feelings and actions. The counseling that I do in my Energetic Trauma Healing practice incorporates trusting the body wisdom, deep breathing, verbal processing, body-centered exercises plus using the inner wisdom of the higher self. All of this leads to a deeper knowledge and empowerment. Overtime, along with my colleague, Leland Howe, Spontaneous Movement Healing emerged from our work.

I look at the structure, movement and breathing patterns in a person's body. I also look at muscular patterns in the body and their relationship to movement, breath, posture and emotional expression. All of these tell a story of past experience, of past trauma. History is revealed in the form our bodies take and how our bodies move.

The healing process can be activated on a body level by listening to our bodies, deepening our breathing, tuning into the deeper knowledge the body holds and by releasing muscular tension in a variety of ways. When we bypass the intellectual mental processes for a while, the body will direct and guide the healing.

We start by learning about energetic grounding. Being grounded is to have a physically secure but flexible stance. It means to be fully present right now. When we are grounded with our feet firmly planted on the earth and our spirits being solidly in our bodies, we can deal with anything.

In my practice, I trust the wisdom of each individual's body and its cellular memories. Together we look to find the blocks or restrictions in their body. Then we explore what it would feel like to begin to release these patterns and recover some of the feelings that have been repressed. We come to understand how and why these patterns of constriction developed; how these Energetic Holding Defenses that get in the way today, allowed us to survive in an early environment that was not supportive of our being. As these defenses became chronic, so did the muscular patterns in the body. This process is illustrated with two of my client stories below. The clients' names have been changed to protect their confidentiality. Their stories are our stories too.

Trouble Getting Pregnant!

"Sara" came to me because she had been trying to get pregnant. She had been trying for a while and decided there was maybe something physically wrong with her or her husband. All the testing showed that physically everything was fine for both of them. Sara's doctor was tuned into complementary medicine and was well aware of how health involved all aspects of a person's being – mental, emotional, spiritual and physical. He was also well aware of body-centered counseling and felt that Sara's issues were related to old experiences that were being held in her body and were blocking the pregnancy. In working with Sara and the wisdom of her body, we soon uncovered memories that Sara had about her mother. Sara had always felt she did not have much of a childhood mother. Her mother was judgmental, did not spend much time with Sara, and was self-absorbed. As a child, Sara yearned for a mom that did things with her, encouraged her and really loved her.

One of the memories that was brought forth while working with her body was a time when her mother told Sara that she was just like herself. At that time, Sara remembered making a promise to herself that she would never have children because she didn't want them to experience what she had gone through as a child. This was stored away in her cellular memory and a neural pathway was created. In working with this memory and releasing the emotions from Sara's body, she felt a new openness and joy that had been missing in her life. About six months after our last session, Sara called me to say that she was pregnant and she strongly believed it was the work we had done together that had allowed this to finally happen. She now has three beautiful children and is a great mother.

He Was His Childhood Mother's Surrogate Husband

"Paul's" presenting problem had to do with a crisis in his marital relationship. In assessing his body in the initial appointment, some of what I observed was that his:

- Left arm hung out in front of his body more than his right arm.
- Left eye was more open than the right one.
- Upper body was more muscular and developed in comparison to his lower body that looked young with thin legs and calves that were small.
- Ankles collapsed inward.
- Right foot turned outward.
- Shoulders slumped forward with the left one higher than the right.
- Chest looked armored and closed; he said that his heart felt encased.
- Butt was tucked under and his pelvis thrust forward.
- Energy level was very low.
- Breathing was very shallow.
- Self did not look present.

Paul shared he had a wall up for protection and that it was very hard to break through it. He felt cut off from his feelings. He realized there was a part of him that was cut off from himself. Paul's mate felt rejected and abandoned by him. As we worked with his body wisdom over time by listening, allowing the spontaneous movement to lead us, the body released the following information:

- As a little child, he adored his childhood father but later felt intimidated, fearful of him and put down. His father used shame as a form of discipline. His parents fought a lot and divorced when he was in the third grade and the father moved out of state. Paul adored his childhood mother and after his father left, he was her surrogate husband. Over time he came to resent this and he felt she expected him to "save her". He made the connection that his wife also came from a wounded family and they seemed to potentiate each other's issues.

- Paul was not very grounded to the earth or present in the "Now". At an early age, he learned to leave his body as a way to survive all the intense energy/feelings around him that were too overwhelming and traumatic for his young self to deal with. He used his intellect as a way to stay somewhat connected, but was split off from his body and his emotions.

- He felt how much his heart was constricted. Paul wanted to expand and open his heart more but was stuck in fear—fear that if he kept his heart constricted that he would die from a heart attack but if he opened it, he would feel more pain and fear and be too vulnerable.

- Paul started realizing that when his heart opened more, there seemed to be a tendency for his pelvic area to close or lock. He was having sexual difficulties in his marriage and we linked all of this to his childhood mother's turning him into her surrogate husband. Even though there was no sexual contact between his mother and him, there were inappropriate emotions and expectations shared which were seductive and too much for a young boy to handle.

- As a child Paul was powerless and this was carried with him into adulthood.

Paul's body assisted him in moving through his anger, fear, anxiety, sadness and cutting the old cords which were energetically still attached to his parents. He became very aware of his body and more grounded. He learned to open his heart yet protect it when needed. Paul was able to come into alignment with his truth and his power. At the end of our time together, Paul and his wife separated and he felt more empowered. He also took a risk by leaving his job and going to a new job out of state. Paul said he would never have been able to do this in the past because of his fears. He stayed in touch to let me know that his life was more joyful, he was not as fearful, he felt alive and energized by the new connection to his body and heart.

I feel truly inspired and blessed by the people that come to me for body-centered work. It is an honor and privilege to be of assistance and a witness to their healing.

Through the physical and emotional release found through the Spontaneous Movement Protocol work and the experience of a safe, healthy, supportive environment in which to do the healing work, you can relate to yourself and others in new and more satisfying ways.

Using The Intuition Protocol

Here is a protocol that I, Leland Howe, have used as a Therapist to help me and my clients tap use our intuition to move trauma healing forward. To use this protocol simply follow the instructions.

The Intuition Protocol

Instructions:

1. Do some Energetic Grounding (using one of the Jump Start Energetic Grounding Protocols in the next chapter) to ensure you are energetically well grounded.

2. If you are a Therapist working with a client, say to yourself, "My intuition says that you need to _____ in order to move your healing forward," and fill in the blank with the first thought that comes to mind. If you are a client, say to yourself, "My intuition says that I need to _____ in order to move my healing forward," and fill in the blank with the first thought that comes to mind.

3. Then follow what your intuition says to do. Keep repeating step 2 above and this step 3 if needed.

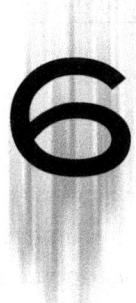

Jump Starting a Strong Energy Charge to Help Move Clients' Trauma Healing Therapy Forward

The most difficult time for helping clients heal their trauma is in the beginning of their Energetic Therapy. They inevitably arrive in my office depressed, anxious, fearful, shutdown, angry, hopeless, helpless, betrayed, lacking energy, and usually at the lowest ebb of their life. My challenge, as their Therapist at that point, is, of course, to listen empathically to them, and then help them jump start the free flow energy in their body which will start their trauma healing therapy moving forward. To help them get the free flow of energy moving in their body, I have them use the Energy Jump Start Protocols along with the Energetic Grounding Protocols presented below.

When energy moves freely in the body, it pulsates, vibrates, streams, and resonates. Trauma, of course, disrupts and shuts down the free movement of energy in the body. Trauma causes shock to the body which freezes and/or contracts against the trauma pain that trauma victims suffer. When caretakers interfere with their children causing them trauma, they automatically adopt various Energetic Holding Defenses, depending on their age and stage of development, to protect themselves against the trauma pain. If trauma happens at two or more critical child development stages, they adopt the types of Energetic Holding Defenses needed at those ages to protect them against the pain of the trauma as well to prevent the possibility of the same type of trauma occurring again in the future. Each type of adopted Energetic Holding Defense is located in various muscles of the body as dictated by the child's age and stage of development. These muscles freeze, contract, or fail to develop in direct response to the trauma which shuts down energy flow and thus feeling in the body.

How The Energetic Holding Defenses Prevent the Free Flow of Energy in The Body: A Quick Overview

Let me give you a thumbnail sketch of how this occurs.

1. **Holding Out:** When children are not welcomed at birth but rather are treated with hostility or extreme rigidity by their caretakers, for example, this threatens their existence and sends them into severe shock and trauma causing them to automatically adopt a Holding Out Defense in order to dissociate from the trauma pain—that is, they freeze their vital and expressive energy which is then held in their core organs thus preventing its free flow in their body, especially in the lower part, in order to insure survival. This severely reduces their energetic grounding.

2. **Holding On:** When children's basic needs for nurturing go unmet by their caretakers during the first year or so of their life, perhaps due to illness or death of a caretaker, or due to the caretaker suffering from drug addiction, for, example, they adopt a Clinging Holding On Defense as they literally cling to their caretakers trying desperately to get the sustenance which is so

vital to their early growth and development. A bit later, if their caretaker is insecure and needy, and as a result discourages or punishes them in order to prevent normally separating and individuating, then they will adopt a symbiotic relationship with their caretaker—or what is called a Joined-at-the-Hip a Holding On Defense. Both Holding On Defense subtypes result in diminished energy flow in their bodies which impedes further normal growth and development.

3. **Holding Up:** When children are exploited, at the stage of their development where they are trying to become autonomous, due to caretakers seducing them into becoming a special surrogate spouse, or preparing and bullying them into becoming the special son/daughter-and-heir, for example, they adopt a Holding Up Defense by cutting off from feeling the pain of their exploited body and manage their lives using only their mind without the wisdom of their body. This denial of their body has a profound effect on their energy flow which is misused to feed their inflated ego and upper body leaving their lower body deficient in energy and growth. They use their inflated ego and over-active mind to turn the tables on their caretakers by either power-manipulating them—resulting in the adoption of a bullying Power Controlling Holding Up Defense—or by seducing them—resulting in the adoption of a Seductive Controlling Holding Up Defense. These Holding Up Defenses help stop or reduce their caretakers' exploitation by gaining the upper hand and control of the relationship. Their energy flow is mainly restricted at the base of the skull

which prevents awareness of their trauma pain and also severely reduces their energetic grounding.

4. **Holding In:** When children are at the developmental stage of moving toward more independence with a caretaker who over controls them and restricts their development by withholding approval and love, they adopt a Holding In Defense This defense limits their independent expression as they try to please their caretaker in order to gain the caretaker's approval and conditional love. This attitude prevents energy from flowing into the organs of expression as well as to their energetic discharge outlets in their body thus creating an overcharged, overdeveloped torso while leaving their extremities and organs of expression—their arms, hands, legs, feet, pelvis, and head—undercharged and underdeveloped. Energy is mainly held in the core of their body with severe contractions in the muscles of the neck, torso, diaphragm, pelvis, and buttocks as well as holding in the jaw, shoulders, wrists, and feet to prevent its free flow and the expression of the pent-up negative feelings and rage, thus reducing feeling and trauma pain in their body.

5. **Holding Back:** When children's expression of love as well as their growing sexuality and sexual identity formation, at around five years of age, is rebuffed and rejected by their caretakers due to their discomfort, or jealousy and competition between their caretakers, for example, they adopt a Holding Back Defense in which they literally hold back and guard against any direct expression of love or reaching out for their caretakers' love. This limits their assertive energy and restricts their expressive energy as they hold back

such energy by reaching out indirectly and with great caution for what they want. Depending upon their caretaker's gambit, it will produce several variations of the Holding Back Defense—namely the Willful Determined sub-type (characterized by persistent pushing of themselves forward to achieve), the Stoic Rescuing sub-type (characterized by doing good deeds as they try to measure up and prove themselves), or the Designing Persona sub-type (characterized by a genuine but sometimes beguiling sweetness, when needed, and a rigid, underlying stubbornness). Energy flow in the body of these Holding Back sub-types is mainly contained and restricted by the long muscles of the back as well as by the tightness of the jaw muscles to keep them from reaching out directly for what they want as well preventing them from feeling the trauma pain of holding back their love and reaching out directly for love.

These Energetic Holding Defenses Continue to Limit the Free Flow of Energy in Adulthood

The problem is these childhood Energetic Holding Defenses are carried into adulthood where they continue to disrupt energy flow. They literally limit the ability of these adult trauma victims to manage and negotiate the challenges of living in their complex world of relationships and job stress. That is what brings them to my office as clients in such an anxious, confused, depressed, and debilitated energetic state. My immediate therapeutic task then, beyond initially listening to their complaints, is to help them develop a strong, grounded, energetic charge in their body to enliven them so they can move their trauma healing therapy forward.

The Power of Energy Movement in the Body

In this handbook, I often refer to the fact that energy movement in the body can help clients advance their Energetic Trauma Healing Therapy. I want to clarify what I mean by this.

Pulsation of Energy in the Body

As living beings, we are aware of the pulsation of our breathing and heartbeat. However, many of us may not be aware that pulsation is involved in every cell of our body. Just as our lungs pulsate by expanding to take a breath in and contract to expel a breath out, and our heart pulsates as it contracts to push nutrient rich blood out into our cells and expands to pull waste filled blood back into our cleansing organs, our cells also pulsate by expanding to take in the nutrients and contracting to push out waste. Those of us who do aerobic, fitness, and strenuous exercise are aware of how the pulsation that occurs as a result of such exercise makes our body stronger, feel more alive, and increases our energy level as every cell in our body seems to be, and is in fact, effected. In Energetic Therapy, increasing the pulsation in clients' bodies helps them move forward with their therapy by making them feel stronger and have more energy available to do the painful and difficult trauma healing work involved.

Vibration Energy in the Body

Some of us who do strenuous physical exercise may be aware of the vibratory movement of energy in our bodies if we are physically fit. When we are fit and do strenuous physical workouts, we can often feel our body become vibrantly alive. When we tune into our body's musculature, we can become aware of various muscles vibrating in different parts of our body. Muscles are designed to vibrate when they are toned. Each end of a muscle is attached to the bone, and when toned, the muscle vibrates much like a violin string vibrates when the tuning peg is turned to tighten or loosen a string just right and thus produce an in-tune tone. The problem is that trauma causes muscles in various parts of the body to become flaccid or so tense and rigid that they no longer vibrate as they should. This is especially true of the leg, feet, and pelvic muscles which are critical for standing and energetic grounding. When clients lack vibrant standing and energetic grounding, they are unable to adequately support themselves and move their trauma healing therapy forward. Thus, a good deal of energetic work must be done with clients' legs, feet, and pelvic muscles to either strengthen the flaccid muscles or release the rigid tightness in these muscles, so clients become more vibrantly, energetically grounded. The point here is that, in Energetic Therapy, increasing the vibration in clients' bodies helps them become stronger and thus move forward with their trauma healing.

Streaming Energy in the Body

Streaming energy in the body is even more of a mystery and lesser-known phenomena. However, many of us have experienced chills running up and down our spine when we are frightened or have experienced orgasmic release which produces pleasurable streaming sensations in our body during sexual intercourse or masturbation. But there is another pleasurable, Kundalini type of energy that can run up and down our spine and in our body when we have a strong sense of well-being and wholeness, or when we bask in a spiritual sense of togetherness with the Universe or a Higher Power. Trauma tends to shut down clients' ability to feel energetic streaming in their body as their muscles contract in order to reduce and shut off their trauma pain. However, if the natural trauma healing power of their body is allowed, supported, and encouraged to come back online, it can work wonders to restore their ability to feel pleasure again. With more energetic work designed to release holding in various parts of the body, especially in the back muscles, this Kundalini type, streaming energy can be freed up to provide more pleasure. Since pleasure helps heal trauma, increasing the streaming in clients' bodies helps them move forward with their trauma healing.

Resonating Energy in the Body

Empathy, compassion, and truth are strong human characteristics that are highly valued in our close relationships with family and friends as well as in our job and other interpersonal relationships. Trauma, however, can impede clients' ability to feel empathy and compassion for others as well as to resonate and know the truth in their interactions with loved ones as well as strangers. The internal processes and interpersonal dynamics involved in empathy, compassion, and truth resonance are not fully understood but there are some hints about how it works on an energetic level. The chest and heart appear to be directly involved. A person's chest is like a drum in that it can resonate much like the skin that is stretched over the head of a drum and its hollow shell filled with air below. In a similar way, a person's chest muscle-skin-covering, and the air-filled lungs underneath can resonate in such a way that a person can feel the pain and joy exuded from others in his/her own chest and heart just as if there is a direct connection between them. The same principle apparently applies to a person's truth knowing. When a person tunes into her/his chest and heart, he/she can feel truth resonate while falsehoods and lies will fail to resonate.

Trauma can impede clients' ability to resonate with others due to the muscle freezing and/or armoring in their chest which protects their heart from pain and heartbreak thus stopping them from having empathy and compassion or knowing truths from falsehoods. This condition can be remedied by applying pressure to the chest to release clients' frozen state and/or muscle-armor-holding and once again resonate which allows them to regain their ability to be empathetic, have compassion, and know the truth with others. Thus, in Energetic Therapy, increasing the resonance in clients' bodies helps them move forward with their trauma healing.

Jump Starting Energy Movement in the Body

So, the real question in Energetic Therapy is, "How can we help clients increase the beneficial pulsatory, vibratory, streaming, and resonating energies in their bodies?"

My answer is to help trauma clients build a strong, grounded energy charge in their body which they can then use in their therapy to get their pulsatory, and eventually their vibratory, streaming, and resonating energies moving more freely in the underdeveloped or rigid/frozen holding musculature of their body. The pulsatory energy movement in their body is relatively easy to get going. The vibratory, streaming, and resonating energy movement will come as they move forward with their Energetic Therapy. I begin by securing clients' agreement and then instruct them in how to jump start energy pulsation in their body and then energetically ground it. The great thing about these Energy Jump Start Protocols, as I will refer to them, is that they can be used, at any point in clients' trauma healing therapy with very good effect, to move their trauma healing forward. They do need to be followed up with energetic grounding, but I will get to that later in this chapter.

One of the main ways that trauma and the resulting Energetic Holding Defenses shutdown the free flow of energy in trauma victims' bodies is by reducing their respiration—that is, they breathe paradoxically which means that their chest wall and abdominal wall move inward instead of outward when taking a breath, or their chest wall and abdominal wall move in opposite directions with each breath. As a result, they do not take a full, deep breath which limits the energetic charge and available energy in their body. The reason for their paradoxical breathing may be twofold. One is that it reduces feeling in the body which dampens or stops the trauma pain. Second, it may be the result of a suspended fear reaction to the trauma that continues to persist in their body in a frozen, unending way. This reduction in their energetic charge and available energy often keeps them from moving forward in their trauma healing therapy. Therefore, I suggest that new trauma clients start their therapy by building a strong, grounded energy charge in their body which forces them to breathe more deeply. This is accomplished by having them engage in doing a number different Energy Jump Start Protocols over the course of their initial therapy.

The Energy Jump Start Protocols described below must be used with sensitivity by taking account of clients' likes and dislikes. For example, some clients may have an aversion to hitting, or they may dislike laying back side down on the floor. Turning a Jump Start Protocol into a fun, game-like activity such as having them use the Whack-A-Mole Protocol below, may help clients overcome such aversions and dislikes. Also, giving them a detailed explanation of how and why the suggested protocol will jump start energy movement in their body, and thus move their trauma healing forward, may be helpful in this regard.

These Energy Jump Start Protocols must be followed by having clients use an Energetic Grounding Protocol for a very good reason. Whenever I have clients build a strong energetic charge in their body, which these Energy Jump Start Protocols will do, I want them to energetically ground the charge so it does not hang up in their upper body causing their head to become overcharged which can be quite disorienting and uncomfortable.

When this happens, it can result in clients operating solely from their overactive mind rather than from the wisdom of their full energetic body. It can also be so disorienting that it is unsafe to drive a car, for example.

With beginning clients, I have them do energetic grounding using the Hair-pin Protocol described below, which is one of the least strenuous energetic grounding exercises. Or, if clients can handle a little more strenuous energetic grounding activity, I have them use the Downhill Ski Run Energetic Grounding Protocol also described below.

The Energy Jump Start Protocols

Here are the Energy Jump Start Protocols which I use regularly to begin a trauma healing session or before doing a challenging trauma healing exercise, as well as when needed with clients who encounter inhibiting or overwhelming fear, or begin to flag as their session drags on, for example. When clients use an Energy Jump Start Protocol, it must be followed up by having them use an Energetic Grounding Protocol. (See the Energetic Grounding Protocols presented below.)

Using the Whack-A-Judge Energy Jump Start Protocol

My go to Energy Jump Start Protocol is The Whack-a-Judge Protocol which gets its name from the Whack-a-Mole Game as well as the colloquial use of the term to depict a situation characterized by repetitive hitting of a negative target. I like to use the Whack-A-Judge hitting exercise with beginning clients because it is a fun way to help them build a strong energetic charge in their body as well as mobilize their aggression which is often sorely lacking. To use the protocol, I ask them to get in touch with their Inner Judge voice which is not their friend because it is constantly judging everything they do and putting them down with inner thoughts like, "You are so stupid!" or, "Can't you do better than that!" or, "You are so bad!", for example. Then, I place a thick pillow in a chair and hand them a tennis rack or plastic bat with which to hit the pillow with. I ask them to imagine their Inner Judge repeatedly pops up from out of the pillow to verbally judge and attack them. Their task, I inform them, is to hit a thick pillow vigorously and rapidly in a chair with the tennis racket or bat to stop their Inner Judge's attacks. As they hit the pillow, they can alternately imagine they are whacking all the repeated attempts their caretakers made to stifle and drive underground their move toward autonomy and independence as well as their reaching out for love and affection, for example. Having clients yell "No!" while hitting increases their energy charge and aggression.

(Note: Don't forget to have your clients follow up after using these Energy Jump Start Protocols by using one of the Energetic Grounding Protocols below.)

Using The Bouncing Jump Start Protocol

For beginning clients who lack lower body strength, I like to have them bounce on a small trampoline while holding onto a pole or chair back for balance. Most beginning clients find the bouncing fun and it distracts them from what they see as the serious business of doing therapy. Having them hold their breath while bouncing, and then take in a big breath after each holding of their breath, increases the energy charge in their body.

Using the Hammer Heels Kicking Energy Jump Start Protocol

Another favorite energy jump start exercise for beginning clients who lack both upper and lower body strength is to have them do vigorous kicking while lying prone on their backside. The idea for this protocol comes from the pneumatic hammer, also called an air hammer. This type of kicking is reminiscent of the pneumatic hammer's rapid percussion movement. I suggest clients imagine their heels as air hammers which makes the exercise fun. To use the protocol, I instruct clients to lay back down on the floor and place a thick, heavy pillow or foam pad under their heels to protect them as they kick. Then, keeping their legs straight, they kick very rapidly and vigorously on the pillow or pad as if their legs and heels are air hammers. They can imagine they are hammering the stone or concrete edifices of their abusive caretakers to crush and pulverize them, for example. They are to kick in this way at least 200 times or until their legs tire, rest, and resume the air hammer kicking. This is repeated three to four times followed by energetic grounding. This exercise gets them breathing deeply and greatly increases the blood flow and energy movement in their body. It also is good for releasing tension and holding in their pelvis.

Using the Team or One-On-One Tug of War Energy Jump Start Protocol

This is a great protocol to use in a group therapy setting. It gets its name from the Tug of War game in which two teams, or individuals, at opposite ends of a rope, try to pull and drag each other across a center line. Clients love it because it is fun and generates lively action between the two teams or participants doing the Team or One-On-One Tug of War exercise. To use the protocol in a group, divide the group members into two teams and each team is to hang onto their end of a rope or bedsheet and try to pull the other team across a center line. To use it on an individual level, hand the two participating individuals a towel which they are to take away from each other as each holds onto an end of the towel. As the teams or individuals do so, they yell, "Give it to me! It is mine!" and so on while imagining they are taking back their independence or getting the nurturing they missed, for example. It also increases the participating clients' aggression. Safety is a concern here so to make the exercise safe, a Safety Person must stand behind each team or individual participant to catch them in case one of the Tug of War teams or pairs let go of the towel, thus keeping them from falling to the floor. Also, remind the Tug of War team or pair to place their feet underneath them in such a way as to keep their balance in case one of teams or pairs let go of the rope/bed sheet or towel.

In an individual therapy session, the Therapist and client can do the Tug of War exercise by each pulling on the towel with chairs placed behind them for safety so they can fall back into them if either person let's go of the towel.

Using The Energetic Grounding Protocols

Here are the Energetic Grounding Protocols. I always have clients use these protocols as a follow up to jump start a strong energy charge in their body at the beginning of a session, before doing a challenging trauma healing exercise, and at the end of doing their trauma healing work. They are my favorites to use with beginning clients to help them ground after using the Energy Jump Start Protocols presented above.

(Note: These Energetic Grounding Protocols can also build a good amount of energy charge in clients' bodies. Thus, they can be used as standalone protocols for this purpose. I use them when clients present in my trauma healing practice with an overcharged body or a hyper-active body to help them ground their high energy charge. This is especially the case with clients who have a supercharged Holding In Defense. I also use them with clients who have a disability that keeps them from doing the kind of vigorous physical activity called for in using the Energy Jump Start Protocols.)

Using The Hair-pin Energetic Grounding Protocol

To use this protocol, I have clients bend at their waist to hang forward with their knees flexed slightly so their fingers touch or nearly touch the floor. Then, they straighten their knees and slowly push their butt up toward the ceiling several times which puts stress on their hamstring muscles. Then they are to maintain this Hair-pin position in order to get a vibratory movement, and eventually energetic streaming, in their lower body. (Clients may take a while and a number of goes of using this protocol before they report feeling vibratory and streaming movement of energy.)

Using The Downhill Ski Energetic Grounding Protocol

This protocol gets its name from the downhill ski racing position in which skiers go into a semi-crouch by flexing their knees and lean forward with their body weight on the balls of the feet, This position puts stress on the calf and hamstring muscles thus leading eventually to a vibratory movement and energy streaming in the lower body and later in the upper body as well. This is my favorite energetic grounding position which I have used for years to quickly induce pleasurable streaming sensations in my lower body and upper body. This leaves me feeling extremely grounded, relaxed, and ready for activity or sleep. I use it regularly, especially when I have difficulty letting down before sleeping or giving a speech, for example. To use the Downhill Ski Energetic Grounding Protocol with clients, I ask them to take a normal stance with their feet placed on the floor about 6 to 10 inches apart. Then I ask them to imagine they are on skis doing a downhill ski run. They are to lean forward, flex their knees and lower their butt so they are in a crouch with their weight mostly on the balls of their feet. They are to extend their arms outward as if holding ski poles. (I like to hand them two 36-48-inch-long dowel rods, which they can hold, one in each hand, as if they are ski poles, to help them keep their balance.) They are to stay in this downhill ski position, moving slowly from side to side and up and down as if making wide turns, until a vibratory movement and eventually energy streaming develops in their lower body. With beginning clients, this may require quite a few repetitions and rest periods for the vibratory movement, and eventual streaming movement, to develop strongly. However, if clients' legs are very rigid, it takes even more repetitions and quite a bit of time for the vibratory, and, especially, the energy streaming movement to develop.

(Note: When I first began doing Energetic Therapy, my legs were extremely rigid, so it took a long time for a vibratory and streaming movement to develop. Now, when I use the Downhill Ski Protocol, most of this rigid holding is gone from my legs so I get a vibration and pleasurable streaming in my lower body almost immediately as I move slowly from side to side as if making wide turns on my imaginary skis. It is a wonderful experience and brings me quickly into a down-to-earth energetic grounded stance that is very enlivening and yet relaxing as it helps me let down.)

Using the Get-A-Leg-Up Energetic Grounding Protocol

For clients who have difficulty doing energetic grounding while standing, this protocol is a great alternative. It gets its name from the idiom, "to get a leg up on the competition," which means to gain an advantage over someone or something. In the case of this protocol, it literally means to get a leg up on doing the task of becoming energetically well grounded. It can be difficult for beginning trauma clients to do energetic grounding work and realize its benefits in moving their trauma healing therapy forward. The major reason for this is that the muscles of their legs and feet are so tight and tense, or frozen, that they are unable to get a good vibration and any energy streaming going in them.

Muscles in the body are meant to vibrate. The ends of muscle fibers are attached to the bone and when the right muscle tone is reached, the muscle will vibrate much like a violin string vibrates at the right tone when strung correctly. I like to use a trampoline or 4-inch-thick foam pad such as a couch cushion to help clients get a good vibration going in their legs as they stand on the uneven, flexible surface of the trampoline or couch cushion which makes their leg muscles work harder. (See the chapter on Using Vibration and Slow Movement Stretching for this trampoline protocol.) However, beginning trauma clients often have difficulty doing energetic grounding when standing upright even on a trampoline due to the weakness of their rigid or frozen legs, so I use this 'Get-A-Leg-Up' Energetic Grounding Protocol which gets them off their feet to do the energetic grounding work.

To use this protocol, I have clients lay on the carpeted floor, or a thin mat, backside down with their knees in a raised position and their feet placed flat on the floor. Then they raise one leg into the air at a 45-to-90-degree angle, whatever is more comfortable, while still getting the job done, and point their heel toward the ceiling by pulling their toes downward toward their torso. The upward thrust of their raised leg must be strong enough to put stress on their hamstring and calf muscles. This position will usually get a vibratory movement going in the raised leg. They are to maintain the raised leg stress position for a count of ten and then relax the leg by lowering it to the floor. The exercise is then repeated with the other leg. Clients are to continue by alternating the exercise with each leg a number of times until the legs tire.

If clients are up to it, I have them raise both legs at the same time and push their heels toward the ceiling with their toes pointed downward. This will increase the stress on their legs, pelvis, and belly muscles producing a stronger energetic grounding effect. When clients do these leg-raised exercises over a period of time, they usually are able to develop a very strong vibration in their legs, feet, and pelvis. As they continue to do this protocol, they often report feeling pleasurable streaming sensations in their body which serve to release muscle tension and increase their energetic grounding. To strengthen the effect of the exercise, I suggest they imagine their raised leg(s) as a lightning rod(s) which attracts energy from the heavens to feed their body and spirit.

Using the Bridge Energetic Grounding Protocol

For beginning clients who have difficulty becoming energetically grounded, this protocol often works like magic. The protocol gets its name from the arched appearance of the body which resembles a bridge spanning the running water of a brook. It is literally a bridge to doing energetic grounding.

To use this protocol, I have clients lay back side down on a mat with their knees in a raised position and their feet placed flat on the floor. Then, they are to raise their pelvis off the floor into an arched stretch. Next, they are to lower their butt, so it is about an inch above the floor. They are to relax their pelvic floor by pushing outward as if having a bowel movement and maintain this position until they tire of doing it. As they do so, they usually develop a vibratory movement in their lower body which eventually will lead to pleasurable streaming in their musculature when repeatedly done over time. However, if their thigh and calf muscles are very tense and contracted, their lower body may spasm, jerk, or buck repeatedly as the energy flows downward and slams into these tense and contracted muscles. If this happens, they are to continue the exercise and eventually the jerking/bucking movement will become a vibratory one as the tense holding in these muscles begins to release allowing energy to flow more easily.

When clients tire of maintaining the bridge position, they are to lower their butt to the floor and relax. The exercise is then repeated several times. To strengthen the effect of the exercise, I suggest they imagine running water beneath their bridged body, feeding their energy and spirit. This bridge position will build an energy charge, vibration, and eventually streaming in their body which, with intention, can be moved downward into their legs and feet as well as upward into their belly and torso, and even into their chest, arms, hands, and face/head.

(Note: I use this Bridge Energetic Grounding Protocol while lying in my bed at night when I have difficulty letting down and falling asleep. Thus, I can do the energetic grounding to relax and let down without having to get out of bed to ground myself using standing energetic grounding exercises.)

Using the Backup Energetic Grounding Protocol

This is a great Energetic Grounding Protocol to use in a group therapy setting. It gets its name from the back-to-back position used to do the exercise which helps clients literally feel supported and backed up by an Assist Person. Energy streaming tends to move along the toned muscles of our spine. It is referred to as pleasurable Kundalini energy or feel-good orgasmic energy. It is also felt as chills running up and down the spine when we are frightened, for example. Helping beginning trauma clients feel pleasurable streaming in their spine is no easy task. However, I find that the Backup Energetic Grounding Protocol can do wonders in helping with this challenge.

I use the Backup Energetic Grounding Protocol in my therapy groups as well as in my individual sessions with clients. To use this protocol in a group setting, I have the group members pair off and then stand back-to-back with one person of the pair being the Focus Person and the other acting as the Assist Person. The

Focus Person is to stand in such a way that she/he feels supported when leaning back against the Assist Person's back. This can be done by having the Assist Person place one foot ahead of the other in a braced stance or by using a wall for bracing. The Focus Person is to lean back against the Assist Person's back, making full back to back contact.

I then have the back-to-back pairs check to see if the middle of their backs are making full contact. If one or both have an inward curve of the backbone, caused by muscular tension, then I have them insert a rolled-up towel of the right size to fill the space. They are then to move their feet outward, so they lean strongly on each other. This puts stress on their legs and will often cause a vibratory movement in them. I instruct the Focus Person to relax and rest in this position in order to take in the feeling of being supported and backed up by the Assist Person. As the Focus Person's tense back muscles release, the curvature of the spine will reverse, allowing the backbone to make contact with the Assist Person's back without using the towel (assuming the Assist Person and the Focus Person have a normal curvature of their spines). This position will build a strong energetically grounded charge in the Focus Person's body.

I instruct the Focus Person to take in the feeling of being supported and backed up, and simply be with any emotions that surface such as fear, sadness, anger, or joy. To strengthen the effect of this exercise, I suggest the Focus Person's picture in their mind of taking in the love and support they have always longed for from their childhood caretakers. I suggest they express any emotions, feelings, thoughts, and memories that surface. When they begin to tire in this back-to-back position, I have the pairs' reverse roles and do the exercise, so the Assist Person becomes the Focus Person, and the Focus Person becomes the Assist Person. The pairs can also repeat the exercise as needed. I then have them do energetic grounding as the final step. When clients do this exercise, they often report feeling their spine for the first time. It is also not unusual for them to report feeling pleasurable streaming in their spine for the first time.

To use the Backup Energetic Grounding Protocol in an individual therapy session, I act as my client's Assist Person or have the client invite a family member or friend to attend the session and assume the Assist Person role.

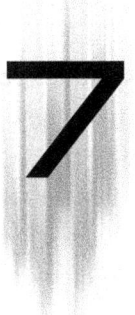

Using the Vibration & Slow Movement Stretching Protocols to Help Clients Restructure Their Energetic Holding Defenses

Helping clients restructure their Energetic Holding Defenses requires that they release the muscle holding in their body's defensive musculature. The Energetic Vibration Protocols help clients do this by using energetic exercises designed to create a vibratory movement in the various tight, tense parts of their body's musculature. The Slow Movement Stretching Protocols help clients release holding in the fascia that wraps around these tense muscles thus keeping the defensive holding in place. When clients have flaccid muscles, as they do with a Holding On Defense, these same vibratory and slow movement exercises help clients build and tone new body musculature that they must develop to restructure their Holding On Defense.

Vibration and Slow Movement Stretching Protocols can be used in two ways to help clients restructure their Energetic Holding Defenses: One, they can be used as stand-alone protocols by trauma clients. Their muscle holding can range from severe and debilitating to chronic and troublesome. Both types of holding can be painful. These protocols can help them with the muscle holding in their body which causes this pain. Of course, the long-term solution is to help clients heal the trauma that caused their muscle holding by using a coordinated and integrated restructuring of their Energetic Holding Defenses. To do this, I use a Client-centered, Client-directed Energetic Therapy approach featuring the use of The Spontaneous Movement Protocol to help my clients restructure their Energetic Holding Defenses. For detailed instructions and case examples of how to use this Client-centered, Client-directed Energetic Therapy approach see *Innovations in Healing Trauma Vol. I* (Howe, et. al., 2023.)

How Vibration and Slow Movement Stretching Help Release the Tension and Holding in Defensive Muscles

The important thing to understand, when working to help clients release the energetic muscle holding in their bodies, is that muscles are designed to vibrate to function properly. Each end of a muscle is attached to the bone. Thus, the muscle is like a violin string which is attached to the violin fretboard at both ends with pegs. When the top peg is turned to tighten the string, it produces a sound that can be toned to the right pitch. Likewise, a muscle can be toned with exercise and stretching by tighten it if it is flaccid or releasing the tightness if it is rigid and thus too tight or thawing the muscle if it is frozen—that is, in a state of shock—and thus too fixed or releasing the compression if it is too contracted and dense. When the muscle is well toned, it will vibrate with a fine oscillating movement that facilitates its proper functioning. When it has too much tension, as in the Holding Back Defense, it becomes rigid without the kind of movement that allows the muscle to work properly. When the muscle is flaccid, as in the Holding On Defense, it will not vibrate and must be strengthened to do so. When the muscle is frozen, as in the Holding Out Defense, it is too cold and fixed to vibrate and work properly. When the muscle is compressed, as in the Holding In Defense, it is too contracted and dense to work as it should. Or, when the muscle exhibits a combination of rigidity, compression, coldness, and/or flaccidity, as in the Holding Up Defense, it also will not function properly.

The aim of Energetic Trauma Healing Therapy is to help clients get their rigid, dense, frozen, and/or flaccid muscles to vibrate in a well-toned way. However, this is not an easy process since the body's Energetic Holding Defenses work to keep the current muscle state in place to protect the trauma victim from feeling the pain caused by the original trauma. Thus, when trauma clients attempt to restructure their Energetic Holding Defenses, they usually encounter stiff internal resistance to doing so.

Helping Clients Work Energetically to Release Their Rigid Muscle Holding

Clients who have a rigid body structure with tight, tense muscles resulting from childhood caretakers who were very rigid and withheld their love as a means to demand obedience. This occurred around five years of age just when these clients were developing their childhood sense of self and sexual identity. This caused them to adopt a Holding Back Defense to protect against the trauma pain of having to hold back reaching out directly for the love and close connection they wanted and needed. One of the most effective ways for these clients to release their rigid muscle tension is to jump start a vibration in their body. These clients have rigid holding in their long back muscles and tight jaw muscles as well as rigidity in their legs and pelvises. They often make good therapy progress using a small trampoline and/or a vibration plate (both of which are described below in more detail) to help release the rigid holding in these muscles by inducing a vibration in them. Another effective way to help clients overcome stiff, rigid muscle-fascia tension is for them to move and stretch these muscles very slowly and gently by using The Bow Protocol and The Pressure Roller/Stool Protocols (described below) to do so, for example. This can take considerable effort if the layers of fascia around their muscles are firmly glued and stuck together. If clients push too hard and fast into their tense muscle holding, it can rip and tear the muscles and fascia. Very slow, deliberate, and gentle muscle stretching movement will allow the layers of fascia around the muscle to slide by each other and thus facilitate rigid muscle tension to release. A do-it-yourself program I recommend to my clients to help them do this is Miranda Esmonde-White's Classical Stretch DVDs (2008-2022) which are available from Amazon. Each Season, of which there are now 14, provides 18-30 full body workouts of stretching that really help clients release their rigid muscle holding. Even if clients do not go on to fully restructure the tense muscles of their Holding Back Defense, working to release some muscular tension can reduce their pain level and bring about limited trauma healing recovery.

Helping Clients Work Energetically to Release Their Dense Muscle Compression Holding

The most effective way to help clients, with a Holding In Defense, release their muscle compression is to have them move and stretch their large contracted and compacted muscles very slowly and gently. One way to do this is to have them lay over a Pressure Roller and/or Pressure Stool and reach backward with their arms and hands holding dumbbell weights in their hands. This takes a lot of repetition and effort since the dense layers of compressed muscles and fascia of their Holding In Defense are so large and thick and are firmly glued and stuck together. Very slow, deliberate, and gentle muscle stretching movement on the Pressure Roller/Stool allows the layers of fascia around the dense muscles to slide by each other and thus facilitates their muscle compression to release. I also recommend clients with a Holding In Defense, do Miranda Esmonde-White's Classical Stretch. As with the above rigid muscle tension release work, clients who do not go on to fully restructure their Holding In Defense can achieve some limited trauma healing recovery by doing slow movement stretching.

Helping Clients Work Energetically to Build Up and Strengthen Their Flaccid Muscles

Clients who have an underdeveloped body with flaccid, weak muscles resulting from their childhood caretakers' neglect of their basic needs for nurturing at a very early age, adopted a Holding On Defense to protect themselves from this trauma pain. Their first energetic-therapeutic task is to build up and strengthen their weak, flaccid body musculature. I like to use a small trampoline or a vibration plate to help them do this. Simply standing on a trampoline repeatedly for 10 minutes at a time helps them build muscle by inducing a vibratory movement in their body. It works wonders to help these clients build up and strengthen their musculature if used on a regular daily basis for a period of several months. The same is true when they use a vibration plate for 10 minutes daily over the course of several months. It also helps clients with a Holding On Defense build up their flaccid, underdeveloped musculature by having them bounce on the trampoline while holding their breath and then stand on it for a couple of minutes in between each round of bouncing. This works well to strengthen the weak muscles of their body and forces them to increase their respiration. (See such a case example in *Innovations in Healing Trauma Vol I* (Howe, et.al.,

2023). In addition, I suggest they do Miranda Esmonde-White's Classical Stretch as homework to build up and strengthen their underdeveloped body musculature.

Helping Clients Work Energetically to Thaw Out Their Frozen Muscle Holding

Clients with a Holding Out Defense suffered the terror of having their childhood right to exist threatened—that is, they had childhood caretakers who did not want, nor welcome them when they were born, or were extremely insensitive, strict, and rigid with them, or were very chaotic, unstable, insecure, and non-present with them—so that the threat of annihilation was ever present and real. This threat to their existence caused them to go into trauma shock and dissociate from their body. The result was their energy was withdrawn from their peripheral organs and held in their core, life-supporting organs of their body. This left their peripheral organs—their face, hands, arms, shoulders, chest, pelvis, hips, legs, and feet—in a frozen-shock-like state.

Fortunately, clients with this Holding Out Defense have a natural healing process built into their body that can kick-in when it gets triggered to help them thaw out their frozen shock trauma. Peter A. Levine details this natural trauma recovery process that exists in human beings, as well as animals, in his best-selling book, *Waking the Tiger: Healing Trauma* (1997). This natural trauma healing process can be triggered when the right conditions are created so the trauma victim feels safe enough to let the trauma discharge from her/his shock-frozen body by trembling and shaking it out.

In my Energetic Trauma Healing Therapy practice, I have found that the right conditions to help trauma clients feel safe enough to trigger the necessary trembling and shaking process is best done in a caring, loving, supportive group setting. As this trembling and shaking process (see the Shake, Rattle & Roll Protocol below) is a vibratory one, having trauma clients do energetic grounding such as standing on a small trampoline, a firm foam pad, and/or a vibration plate in order to jump start a vibratory movement in their body—which in turn helps trigger the needed trembling and shaking discharge process—is very helpful. Also, having an Assist Person in the therapy group massage the bluish-cold feet, legs, hands, and arms of a client with a Holding Out Defense can be very beneficial.

Helping Clients with a Mix of Rigid, Compressed, Flaccid, and Frozen Muscles Work Energetically to Create A Healthy, Vibrantly Alive Musculature

The above vibratory and stretching protocols are all useful in helping clients with a Holding Up Defense, who are notable for having a mix of rigid, inflated, compressed, frozen, and/or flaccid body parts. Specifically, here are a couple of examples of how I have worked energetically to help them heal their childhood trauma which resulted from their childhood caretakers exploiting them.

To help clients who have adopted a Power Controlling type of Holding Up Defense due to their childhood caretakers using and bullying them as they were prepped to become their caretakers' special "son-and-heir", for example, and thus have an inflated, barrel-like chest as well as an inflated ego, I used a pressure roller and pressure stool to help them stretch their upper torso in order to decompress their inflated, dense-muscle-bound chest. To help clients who have adopted a Seductive Controlling type of Holding Up Defense due to their childhood caretakers exploiting them by seducing them into becoming their caretakers' special "little-hero & surrogate spouse", for example, and thus manage their life from their hyper-active mind while cut off from tapping into their body-wisdom, I have instructed Assist Persons from the therapy group on how to palpate the severe muscle holding at the base of their skull and massage their frozen neck muscles thus releasing the spasms that prevent access to their bodily feelings. I also have them stretch their neck muscles with good effect. (See The Neck Stretch and Fascia Release Protocols below.) For more case examples on how to work energetically with clients who have a Holding Up Defense, see *Innovations in Healing Trauma Vol. I* (Howe, et. al., 2023).

Using Two of My Favorite Energetic Vibration Protocols to Help Clients Release the Muscle and Fascia Holding in Their Body

There are two sets of protocols I use to help clients release the muscle and fascia holding in various parts of their body. One is to use a trampoline and pressure roller/stool to do so, and the second is to put the tense muscles of their body under stress using energetic vibration exercises. The reason why using a trampoline works so well to release muscle tension in the lower body is that clients must stand on a flexible surface that causes considerable stress in their feet, legs, hips and pelvis as these body parts must work much harder in order for clients to maintain their balance. The trampoline also amplifies the lower body movements, especially in the feet and legs, and this amplified stress eventually causes the muscles in clients' legs to vibrate rather strongly. When clients set an intention to move this vibration down into their ankles and feet and up into their pelvis, and even into their torso as well as up into their neck, shoulders, and face, it will help release the muscle and fascia tension and holding in their body. (See below for more on using the trampoline with clients.)

The pressure roller or pressure stool induce vibratory movement in the upper body muscles in a similar way when clients lay back side down on it, so their upper body is suspended in midair, so to speak. This suspending of their upper body creates the stress needed to induce their torso muscles to vibrate which helps to release the tension and holding in them. (See below for more on using the pressure roller/stool with clients.)

Then there are a number of energetic exercises, see below, that can be used by clients to generate a vibration in various parts of their body without resorting to the use of a trampoline and a pressure roller/stool to do so. I also include several Slow Movement Stretching exercises which help clients release the muscle and fascia holding in their body as well. Simply have clients follow the instructions provided.

A Case Presentation: Using Energetic Vibration & Slow Movement Stretching to Help a Client Release Her Muscle Holding

I worked with this client during a weekend empowerment workshop. She was in her early thirties, married with two young daughters, and worked as a computer software programmer. She had been doing trauma healing work for about a year with a body-oriented psychotherapist and had made good progress in restructuring her Holding Out and Holding Back Defenses. However, two parts of her body resisted this energetic restructuring effort, these being her neck and shoulders and her left ankle and leg. She had suffered a concussion in a skiing accident which left her with a stiff neck, tight shoulder girdle, and some pain in both areas as well as with balance problems. Later she lost her balance on a ladder, fell, and broke her ankle and the fibula in her leg which left them stiff with some pain in her ankle and numbness in her lower leg muscles. Her healing intention in the energetic work she did during the empowerment workshop was to regain flexibility in her neck, shoulders, ankle, and leg, get rid of the pain in her neck, shoulders, and ankle, and recover feeling in her lower leg.

After interviewing her during a prior intake session to collect information about her childhood history, it was clear that due to having been reared in a chaotic home in which her alcoholic mother abused her while her absent, workaholic father failed to protect her, she was not able to become energetically well-grounded as a child and this continued into adulthood. This lack of energetic grounding prevented energy from feeding her feet, ankles, and legs and thus made physical healing from the falling injury difficult. In addition, the frequent beatings she suffered as a child from her drunken mother caused her to crunch her shoulders, neck, and head downward thus causing immobility and lack of energy flow in them. This prevented her neck and shoulders from healing fully following her skiing accident and thus they continued to remain stiff and painful.

Her job as a computer programmer added to the stiffness and pain in her neck and shoulders as she sat hunched over the computer for hours each day, nor did it help with her lack of energetic grounding since she did not walk much and was not on her feet for most of every day. She also did no physical exercise, except in sessions with her body-oriented psychotherapist, which contributed to her energetic problems.

Using the Trampoline to Release Muscle Holding in Her Legs

To help her realize her healing intention, I suggested she use a small trampoline to build a good energetic charge in her body, and then develop a vibratory movement and energy streaming in her stiff ankle and numb lower leg. She began by bouncing on the trampoline to deepen her breathing and raise her heart rate thus increasing the energetic charge in her body. Then, she stood on the trampoline with flexed knees, while holding an Assist Person's hands for balance, to develop a vibratory movement in her legs

Chapter 7: Vibration & Slow Movement Stretching Protocols • 165

which served to help energetically ground her. Next, I suggested she stand on the balls and toes of her feet on the trampoline and maintain this position for about 45-60 seconds, then lower herself to rest, and repeat this exercise two more times. Following this, I suggested she stand on her left foot, raise up on the ball and toes of that foot, and maintain that position for 45-60 seconds. This was repeated twice more with a period of rest in between.

To keep her legs in sync, I asked her to repeat the same exercise with her right leg. She had no difficulty doing these energetic ankle and leg exercises and was able to develop a good amount of vibratory movement in them before she tired. She did not report any streaming sensations, but this is not unusual since quite a bit of vibratory work needs to be done to release muscle holding in the legs before streaming occurs. I emphasized she would need to do these trampoline vibration exercises once or twice a day daily if she was to make progress in releasing the muscle holding in her legs and then maintain her gains. She did not have a trampoline at home, so I suggested she use a firm, thick foam sofa cushion instead which works just as well as a trampoline to get a vibration going in tense leg muscles.

Using Slow Motion Exercises to Release Holding in the Fascia of Her Ankle and Leg

Next, I suggested she use slow stretching movements to help release the fascia holding in her ankle and leg. This was done by having her sit in a chair, lift her left foot off the floor and place it inside of a strong resistance loop. (Resistance Loops are long, wide rubber bands of various thicknesses; they are available on Amazon.) One end of the resistance loop was held by an Assist Person while she slowly pushed the ball of her foot forward against the resistance loop, stretching it as far as she could. Then, she repeated the exercise 40-50 more times. This was followed by repeating the exercise in three additional directions with the Assist Person holding the resistance loop—that is, she pushed the ball of her foot against the resistance loop to stretch it toward the outside of her body, then she did the same to stretch the loop toward the inside of her body, and finally she lifted her foot against the loop (as if taking her foot of an automobile gas pedal) toward the front of her body. This exercise was then repeated for her right foot and ankle. Fascia holding often takes weeks of steady, slow movement stretching work to release. I stressed this point with her and suggested that, for homework, she do the slow movement stretching foot and ankle work at least once or twice a day daily.

Using Vibration Exercises to Release the Muscle Holding in Her Neck & Shoulders

Next, I suggested she do vibration exercises to help release the muscle holding in her neck and shoulders. To do this work I asked her to lay on her back on a massage table with the group participants surrounding her. Then I asked her to raise her head high enough to slightly lift her shoulders off the table and maintain that position to develop a vibratory movement in her neck and shoulders. It took time and several rest periods for this to happen. Then she did the same exercise but with her head turned to one side and then the other side. Again, she was able to get a vibratory movement to develop in her neck and shoulders with her head turned to each side.

Following the above vibratory neck and shoulder work, I suggested she do a couple of more energetic vibration exercises. One was to stand, lift her arms and extend them outward while holding a pillow in each hand. This helped develop a vibratory movement in her arms and shoulders. She maintained this position until her arms tired, and then repeated it two more times. Then, laying back side down on a pressure roller, she extended her arms backward while holding the pillows to create a vibratory movement in her neck, arms, and shoulders. She maintained this position until she got tired and repeated it two more times.

Using Slow Movement Stretching Exercises to Help Release the Fascia Holding in Her Neck & Shoulders

Next, I suggested she do slow movement stretching exercises to help release the fascia holding in her neck and shoulders. Sitting in a chair, using a resistance loop with one end placed around the top of her head while an Assist person held the other end of the loop, she slowly moved her head forward against the resistance loop, stretching it as far as she could. Then she repeated the forward head movement 20-30 more times, resting in between repetitions as needed. She repeated this resistance loop exercise by moving her head to one side, then to the other side, and finally backward. Then, she did two more full rounds of the exercise. This head stretching exercise helped release the fascia holding in her neck muscles. Then, she followed up by sitting in a chair and slowly moving her shoulders backwards and forwards 20-30 times to stretch them. This exercise was repeated two more times. When she finished the slow movement stretching work, I sent her home with a suggestion she do these stretching exercises as homework.

To help increase her commitment to doing these energetic vibration and slow movement stretching exercises on a regular basis, since she admittedly had difficulty sticking to a physical exercise routine, I suggested she sign a contract with an Assist Person from the group which stipulated she would do the exercises at least three times per week and check in with her Assist Person by phone once per week to assess her progress. She did so for several weeks and reported making good progress toward reaching her healing intention of releasing the muscle and fascia holding in her neck and shoulders as well as in her ankle and leg. In fact, she later reported the stiffness and pain in her left ankle and leg as well as in her neck and shoulders had largely disappeared.

Following are a number of Vibration & Slow Movement Stretching Protocols with instructions on how to use them.

The Energetic Vibration & Slow Movement Stretching Protocols

The Trampoline Protocol to Release Muscle Holding in the Lower Body

One of the great tools for helping clients work energetically to release muscle tension in their lower body is the small trampoline; it is well worth the investment to get one. However, you can also have clients stand on a 4-inch thick, firm foam pad, (or a firm sofa seat cushion, a firm foam mattress, or a large pillow) as a substitute for the trampoline.

To use this protocol, follow the steps below:

1. Have clients bounce on the trampoline or do vigorous exercise off the trampoline for a minute or so to increase their breathing, heart rate, and blood flow. This helps to develop an energetic charge in their body which they can use to challenge their muscle and fascia holding.

2. Then have clients stand on the trampoline while holding onto an Assist Person's hands or a chair back, or a pole, to help keep their balance. Have them bend their knees until they feel a stretch at their Achilles while keeping their back straight. Then instruct them to rotate their weight very slowly and gently from one

foot to the other, side to side, then back and forth from front to back, and then in a circle one way and then reverse to the other way. Have them do this with rest periods as needed, until their legs begin to vibrate and tire. Then they are to step off the trampoline to rest.

3. When rested, have them step back on the trampoline and repeat the above exercise movements, adding standing on the balls and toes of their feet to the mix; have them maintain standing on the balls and toes of their feet for 20-45 seconds. For the second and third round of standing on the balls and toes of their feet, suggest they do one foot at a time by raising the opposite foot off the trampoline. Whenever they encounter pain, have them stop the exercise, rest, and then resume the exercise as the pain disappears. Also, have them check to see if their pelvic floor is relaxed while doing this exercise. If not, suggest they relax it by pushing outward as if they are having a bowel movement. Tightening of their pelvic floor will inhibit muscle holding release.

The Pressure Roller Protocol to Release Muscle Holding in the Upper Body

The pressure roller helps release muscle tension in clients' back, chest, diaphragm, belly, shoulders, and neck. You can easily make a pressure roller by covering a 12" diameter concrete-form tube that is 16" long with a layer of 1 to 2 inches of foam and then a layer of carpet wrapped around it held in place with glue and plywood caps wedged into the tube at each end.

1. Before using the pressure roller, have clients build a good energetic charge in their body by doing some

vigorous exercise such as hitting a pillow with a tennis racket, for example.

2. Then have clients lay back side down on the roller at shoulder blade level, with their knees bent and feet placed flat on the floor. They can clasp their hands behind their head to give it support.

3. Instruct them to roll back and forth so very slowly and gently that the roller presses into their upper back and shoulders, and then roll downward on their lower back muscles. Have them slowly and gently roll up and down the length of their spine several times.

4. Then, have them roll on the pressure roller until they reach a point with it centered on their lower back, so their head and upper body extend as far in that direction as possible without being too uncomfortable. Have them maintain this suspended position for as long as possible and then roll into a comfortable position on the roller to rest. Using and repeating this suspended position will eventually generate a vibratory movement in their upper body. Whenever they encounter pain, ask them to roll to a less challenging position, rest, and then resume the suspended position after the pain dissolves. When clients tire, have them rest by rolling into a sitting position on the floor and lean back against the roller to rest. Have them repeat this roller exercise at least one or two more times.

5. To increase the stress of this roller exercise, clients can reach their arms backward away from the roller while in the suspended position. Even more stress can be generated by having them hold small dumbbell

weights in each hand as they extend their arms or hold onto the hands of an Assist Person who gently pulls on their arms to stretch them.

The Pressure Stool Protocol to Release Muscle Tension in the Upper Body

The pressure stool is similar to the pressure roller with regard to helping release muscle tension in the upper body but has the advantage of putting even more pressure and increased stress on the targeted tense muscles. The pressure stool I use is homemade from wood and measures 16" x 16" long and wide at the base, 24" tall, and 10" wide and 16" long at the platform top with a small 90-degree lip fastened to the platform edges so a blanket roll can be placed on the platform without slipping off. The blanket roll is made by rolling up a large firm wool blanket and has a circumference of 24" and is 16" long. I use the pressure stool in the same way that I use the pressure roller by having clients lay back down on the blanket roll except they are unable to roll back and forth on it. In order to change the pressure point on clients' bodies, they must reposition themselves on the blanket roll.

The Energetic Vibration Protocols to Release Muscle Tension in the Upper & Lower Body

The following energetic vibration protocols require clients to lay back down on a carpeted floor or workout pad unless otherwise noted in the specific exercise instructions. Clients are to do 10 repetitions of each exercise and then repeat each exercise 3 times. Clients must relax their pelvic floor and breathe deeply while doing these exercises. If clients have difficulty developing a vibration and then streaming movement in a part of their body, they can try tightening and relaxing the body part several times. It may take repeating this tightening and relaxing movement a number of times for a vibratory or streaming movement to develop. Also, clients might need to develop a stronger energetic charge in their body by doing some vigorous energetic exercise. This increased energetic charge can help challenge the holding in the body part's musculature. It is also possible the fascia in that part of the body may be preventing the muscles from releasing. If this is the case, have clients use the slow movement stretching exercises for that part of the body.

The Pelvic Lift Stretching Protocol

Have clients lay back down on the floor, bend their knees, and place their feet flat on the floor about 10" apart. They are to raise their butt off the floor into a stretch and then lower their butt, so it remains above the floor about an inch or so. Have them check to make sure their pelvic floor is relaxed. They are to maintain this position until they tire. The aim is for them to develop a vibratory movement in their legs, pelvis, and lower torso. When clients tire, they are to lower their butt to the floor and rest. Then have them repeat the exercise several times. Also, having them lift their pelvis off the floor into a good stretch several times during the exercise can help them develop a vibration in the legs.

The Open Clam Shell Stretching Protocol

To use this protocol, have clients lay back down on the floor and place their feet flat on the floor to raise their knees. Their feet should be touching each other. Then, they are to lower their knees to the floor to stretch the muscles on the inside of their thighs. Next, they are to slowly bring their knees up until they reach a point about halfway closed which will produce a vibratory movement. They are to maintain this vibratory position until their legs tire at which time they can stop the exercise and rest. Opening and closing the clam shell slowly several times can help get this vibratory movement started. Then have them repeat the exercise several times.

The Closed Clam Shell Vibration Protocol

Clients assume the same position as in the Open Clam Shell above, lower their knees into a stretch, and then bring their knees together on a thick pillow placed between them. They are to squeeze their knees together on the pillow to develop a vibratory movement in their legs and pelvis. They are to maintain this position until their legs tire. After a rest, have them repeat the exercise several times.

The Butt Squeeze Protocol

Clients are to stand and squeeze their butt cheeks together as tightly as possible as well as tighten their pelvic floor. They maintain this squeeze position until a vibratory/streaming movement develops in their pelvis. Squeezing and relaxing their buttocks several times can help get the vibratory movement started. When they tire, they are to relax their buttocks and pelvic floor to rest. Then have them repeat the exercise several times.

The Leg Lift Stretching Protocol

Clients lift one leg off the floor as high as they can to achieve a good stretch. They are to lower the leg, keeping it straight with their knee unbent and the heel slightly off the floor. They are to maintain this raised leg position to develop a vibratory movement in the leg and pelvis. When this leg tires, they are to lower it, rest, and then repeat the leg lift stretch exercise with the other leg. Having them rotate their feet inward and outward will affect different muscles in their legs. Then have them repeat the exercise several times.

The Torso-Pelvic Lift Stretching Protocol

Clients are to lay on their back on the floor, bend their knees and place their feet flat on the floor. They are to lift their torso and pelvis off the floor so only the upper part of their shoulders and their feet touch the floor into a good stretch. They also lift their head off the floor and support it by clasping their hands behind their head. Then they are to lower their pelvis-torso a bit and maintain this position to develop a vibratory movement in their upper and lower body. When they tire, they are to lower their torso-pelvis and head to the floor to rest. Then have them repeat the exercise several times.

The Reverse Belly Bow Lift Stretching Protocol

Clients are to lay belly down on the floor. They are to lift both their head-torso and feet-legs upward into a reverse bow stretch so their weight rests on their belly. They are to maintain this belly bow lift position to develop a vibratory movement in their upper and lower body. Using this position may take some time and repeated effort to get the vibratory movement started. When they tire of this position, they are to lower their full body to the floor and rest. Then have them repeat the exercise several times.

The Standing Bow Protocol

Clients are to stand with their feet placed shoulder width apart. They are to make fists and place them together in the lower mid-section of their back. Then they are to lean back over their fists thus creating a reverse arch with their body that resembles a drawn, curved bow from the side view. They are to maintain this bow for a couple of minutes or more until a vibratory movement develops in their body or they tire of holding the position.

The Head Lift Protocol

Clients are to lay back down on the floor, bend their knees, and place their feet flat on the floor. Then, they are to lift their head, so it is slightly off the floor. They are to maintain this head lift position without supporting their head to develop a vibratory movement in their shoulders and neck. When they tire, they are to lower their head and rest. Having them turn their head to one side and then the other will affect different muscles in their neck and shoulders. Then have them repeat the exercise several times.

The Arm Lift Protocol

Clients are to lay back down on the floor, bend their knees, and place their feet flat on the floor. They are to extend their arms outward and then lift them off the floor slightly while holding 2-pound weights. They are to maintain this arm lift position to develop a vibratory movement in their arms and shoulders. When they tire, they are to lower their arms to the floor and rest. Having them rotate their hands upward or downward will affect different muscles in their arms and shoulders. Then have them repeat the exercise several times. This Arm Lift exercise can be done while standing. Clients are to extend their arms outward from their body, lift pillows or 2-pound weights in each hand, and maintain this position until a vibratory movement develops or their arms tire. They are to rest and then repeat the exercise several times.

The Jaw Drop Protocol

This exercise may be done standing, laying down, or while sitting. Clients are to drop their jaw into a stretch, so their mouth is as wide open as possible. They are to maintain this jaw drop position for as long as possible. Then, they are to relax their jaw while still leaving their mouth open and maintain this jaw position to develop a vibratory movement in their jaw and face. It can be difficult to get a vibration going in the jaw so having clients move their jaw in and out and/or bite down hard on a form hand gripper or folded washcloth can help get the vibratory movement started. When they tire, they are to close their mouth, relax their jaw, and rest. Then have them repeat the exercise several times.

The Jaw Bite Protocol

Clients are to bite down firmly on a foam hand gripper or folded washcloth. They are to maintain this jaw bite to develop a vibratory movement in their jaw and face. Have them stop the bite when their jaw tires. Then have them repeat the exercise several times.

The Slow Movement Stretching Protocols to Release Fascia in Various Body Parts

Slow, gentle, stretching movements of various body parts will begin to release the fascia and muscle holding in these body parts and eventually, with patience, it will release and reform rather than staying stuck. Using a resistance band can help with this fascia release process for several parts of the body such as the neck and ankles, for example. Resistance bands come in various colors with each color providing a different level of resistance. They also come in closed loops such as the Bandismo Resistance Loop Bands which I use or in long length bands and cords which are open at the ends. (Resistance Bands can be purchased on Amazon.) To use the resistance band, bring the ends together to create a loop (if the band is open at the ends) and then place the loop around the body part to be worked with. Follow the instructions for using them with the various protocols below that require them.

The following slow movement stretching exercises are designed to be given to clients as homework and therefore the instructions are written directly to them. First, demonstrate the protocol or protocols given as homework and then simply have clients follow the instructions provided. Make sure they fully stretch into each exercise, and then repeat the exercise many times over the course of weeks and even months to help release the fascia holding.:

The Releasing Fascia in Your Feet & Ankles Protocol

While sitting, place the loop of a medium resistance band around your foot while an Assist Person holds the ends of the band to pull on it in the appropriate direction to create the resistance needed. (If the medium resistance band provides too little or too much resistance, choose the appropriate color to provide the resistance needed.) Next, move your foot very slowly and gently backward pointing your big toe at your head 20 times and hold the backward movement of your foot at least 5 seconds on each repetition. Then reverse direction to push your foot forward, pointing your big toe away from your head 20 times with 5 second holds in between each foot push. Do the same exercise by moving your foot inward and then outward. Now, rotate your foot in a circle 20 times and then reverse the rotation 20 times. If you encounter pain at any time, stop the stretching movement, rest, and then resume the stretching slowly and gently. Repeat this set of exercises one or two more times to help release the fascia holding in your feet and ankles. Also, gradually increase the number of repetitions for each foot exercise from 20 to 50 if possible.

The Releasing Fascia in Your Knees & Hips Protocol

Wrap the loop of a resistance band around your right foot and then lay on your back on the floor. Lift that foot and leg off the floor into a good stretch. Lower your leg and have an Assist Person hold the ends of the resistance band and pull on it to create the resistance needed. Slowly and gently rotate your raised leg in a wide circle 10-20 times, and then reverse the direction of the rotation 10-20 times. Next, lower your leg to the floor to rest, and then, do the same rotation exercise with the raised left leg. If you encounter pain, back off and then resume the stretching movement as the pain disappears. Repeat this exercise 1 to 2 more times to help release the fascia holding in your knees and hips.

The Releasing Fascia in Your Shoulders & Arms Protocol

Sit on a stool or stand on your feet. Using a 2-pound weight in each hand, lift and extend your arms outward from the sides of your body to shoulder level. Then slowly and gently rotate your arms in a wide circle 10-20. Next reverse the direction of the arm rotation 10-20 times. Then, using both arms, slowly and gently move it as if you are doing a freestyle swim stroke 10-20 times. Next, reverse the direction of your arms by doing a backstroke swim movement 10-20. If you encounter pain, back off and resume the movement as the pain disappears. Repeat this exercise 1 to 2 more times to help release the fascia holding in your shoulders and arms.

The Releasing Fascia in Your Neck Protocol

Sit on a stool or stand on your feet. Using a resistance band with the loop around your head while an Assist Person pulls on the ends to create the resistance needed, slowly rotate your head in a wide circle 10-20 times. Then, reverse the rotation of your head 10-20 times. Next, slowly lower your head so your chin touches your chest and then reverse the direction of your head so the back of your head points downward toward your spine. Do this back-and-forth movement of your head 10-20 times. Then do this stretching head movement side to side with your ears pointing downward toward your shoulders on each side-to-side movement. Do this side-to-side head movement 10-20 times, and then repeat it 1-2 more times to help release the fascia holding in your neck.

The Neck Stretching Protocol

Move your chin slowly downward toward your chest as far as possible. Then, reverse and move your head backward toward your spine as far as possible. Do this 10 times. Now move your head slowly, tipping it toward your right ear as far as possible. Then, move your head slowly, tipping it toward your left ear as far as possible. Do this 10 times. Finally, slowly rotate your head to the right, looking over your right shoulder, as far as you can. Then, slowly rotate your head to the left, looking over your left shoulder, as far as you can. Do this ten times. Repeat this neck stretching exercise 1 or 2 more times daily for at least 4 weeks. For maximum results, hold each stretch 3-5 seconds or more.

The Releasing Fascia in Your Back & Chest Protocol

Sit on a stool or stand on your feet. Slowly bring your shoulders forward by rounding your back and hold for 5 seconds. Then reverse your shoulders in the opposite direction by slowly thrusting your elbows backward to crunch your shoulder blades together and hold for 5 seconds. Do this forward and backward stretching movement of your shoulders 20 times. Repeat this exercise 1 to 2 more times to help release the fascia holding in your back and chest.

The Resistance Bands Without an Assist Person

The resistance bands can be used to stretch and release fascia holding in various parts of the body as described below. I prefer to use a 3-foot length of 3/8 inch surgical tubing or the open-ended type of resistance band because these can be threaded around a table leg to use them as described below, for example.

For the neck: fold the resistance band by bringing the ends together and then place the loop end around your head, at forehead level. Hold the ends of the resistance band in one hand and pull on it in the direction for which you want to create resistance and move your head in the opposite direction. For instance, to help release the fascia in the left side of your neck, pull on the ends of the resistance band away from that side while you move your head in the opposite directions to your left. However, pulling the resistance bands to the rear of your head may be too difficult unless you have great flexibility in your shoulder and elbow in which case you will need to find a creative way to do the forward stretch such as fastening the ends of the of the band together and then using a hook screwed into a wall to hold one end of the loop with the other end of the loop placed around your forehead, for example.

For the ankles: place the loop end of the resistance band around a table leg, for example, and then sit in a chair near the table leg and pull on the ends of the band to create tension in it. Place your foot on a short stool near the table leg so you can move it in various directions against the stretched tense band. To help release the fascia holding on the inside of your ankle, place the instep side and ball of your foot against the resistance band and push against it to do 20 to 50 repetitions with a 5 second hold between each repetition. To help release the fascia holding on the outside of your ankle, place that side of your foot against the resistance band to push against it. To help release the fascia holding on the front side of your ankle, place the top side your foot against the resistance band so you can pull against it with that foot while you place the bottom of your other foot against the band a little way further from the table leg to push against it thus creating the resistance needed. To help release the fascia holding in the back side of your ankle, place the loop of the resistance band around the bottom ball of your foot while pulling on the ends and push into the band with that foot.

The Shake-Rattle-And-Roll Trauma Release & Healing Protocol

When your Energetic Therapy progress taps into the frozen core of your trauma, it will begin to thaw and release naturally, if the right conditions are provided, causing you to tremble and shake as it discharges its compressed energy. Allowing and encouraging it to do so will be very healing. (See Peter Levine's *Waking the Tiger* [1997] for more on this.) To use this protocol, follow these steps:

1. Allow yourself to collapse into frozen immobilization as your natural trauma healing process moves you to do so. Take in your Therapist's or Assist Person's encouragement and support while you are in this frozen immobilized state. These are the necessary conditions for your frozen core trauma to begin thawing and discharging its compressed energy.

2. When your frozen trauma begins to thaw, allow yourself to tremble and shake as your body naturally heals itself by discharging its frozen trauma and fear.

3. Allow your body to tremble and shake for as long as is needed. Do not stop or interfere with it by trying to stop or slow it down or speed it up. Let your body release the trauma in its own time and way.

4. Allow your Assist Person to help you sort out and resolve any confusion, guilt, or shame that may arise in your mind during or after this trauma discharge process.

5. When you're trembling and shaking ceases of its own accord, allow your Assist Person to help you reactivate

your fight and flight responses which were shut down by the trauma. To help reactivate your fight response, hit a pillow with a tennis racket or kick a pillow around the room while imagining fighting off the threat of the trauma. This will help mobilize your shut down aggression. To help reactivate your flight response, flee the imagined trauma by running from the room or run in place while imagining you are fleeing from the trauma.

The Classical Stretch Protocols

For another great exercise program using slow movement stretching exercise protocols to release fascia and muscle holding in the body, see Miranda Esmonde-White's Classical Stretch on PBS TV. She also has numerous classical stretch DVDs available for sale on Amazon. She is also author of *Aging Backwards* [2018].

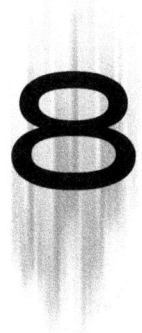

Creating a Spiritual Bridge to Help Clients Heal Trauma

Our body's inner wisdom can occasionally knock on our door summoning us to heal our childhood and adult trauma. All we need to do is listen for the knock and then heed its call to heal. If we choose to ignore our body's call or fail to follow where our inner wisdom directs us, we do so at our own peril. Let me give you an illustration of how this worked in my own life.

My rags to riches and then back to rags story occurred early in my adult life and set the stage for my anger at God and the development of these Spiritual Bridge Protocols to help me, and later, my clients heal our childhood and adult trauma. It is not uncommon for trauma victims like me to be either angry with God, estranged from God or a Higher Power, or completely indifferent to the existence of a Spiritual-Religious Presence. As trauma victims, we have been physically abused, sexually exploited, and/or gravely interfered with during our childhood development and therefore, tend to lack a strong belief in a caring, loving, benevolent God or Higher Power. We did not have loving, benevolent childhood caretakers so why should we believe in such a Spiritual-Religious Presence! This was certainly my case.

From Rags

I started life as a farm boy, the oldest of five children. My parents, when I was born, did not have two nickels to rub together. As a young boy, if I wanted a candy bar or bottle of pop, I had to search the roads for pop and beer bottles, return them for the bottle deposit, and then use that money to buy what I wanted. There was never any extra money for anything, nor a college fund for me, so when I decided to go to college, I had to apply for scholarships, work at odd jobs, and pay my own way, and I just scraped by until I graduated with a BA in Social Science.

To Riches

Following college, I taught English and Social Studies as a high school teacher and used that income to put myself through graduate school, eventually earning a PhD in psychological education and organizational development. This was followed by taking an Assistant Professorship at Temple University teaching psychological education. Within three years, I had co-authored a best-selling psychological education handbook for teachers and started a very lucrative consulting business based on that successful book. I followed up by writing and publishing three additional best-selling books, and the consulting jobs poured in. I was on a roll with more money and recognition than I had ever dreamed of having.

Back To Rags

Within seven years, I lost everything. Temple University cut a deal with the State of Pennsylvania to swap its College of Education, giving it to the Pennsylvania State Colleges, in return for a Law School, so I lost my professorship. My consulting business dried up as Pennsylvania Public Schools embraced the move Back to Basics and away from personalizing students' learning. And my marriage ended in a divorce. Thus, my life was shattered leaving me angry, bitter, and in despair. I returned to live near my parents and began an intensive body-oriented psychotherapy and personal growth program to heal myself. I retrained as a psychotherapist earning a Master's in Social Work degree, while working part time on my parents' family farm, with the goal of starting my own successful energetic trauma healing private psychotherapy practice, which I soon did.

I Am Angry with God

It was during a weekend body-based training for my numerous trauma clients that I heard the leader, whom I had hired to help me run the workshop, speak about how the early Jews believed it was a great sin to be separated from God. He explained they believed that not taking their anger at God, to God caused them to be separated from God. This got my attention! If what he said was true, it made sense to me why I was feeling so alone, separated from others, angry, and in despair. I did not subscribe to the 'being in sin' part, but perhaps I was angry with God for abandoning me. I came to this awareness slowly as I was not raised in the church, and my father had a great deal of skepticism and even dislike of organized religion which he passed on to me. As I came to this awareness, I realized many of my Energetic Therapy clients were also feeling alone and separated from others. I knew they were in despair and their depression was the main reason they were in Energetic Therapy with me. I decided to explore with them the possibility they too were angry with God or feeling cut off from a Higher Power. As I did so, they responded with a lift in their depression. It showed me there really was something to this idea of needing to take one's anger at God, to God. So, I began to speak about this idea to colleagues and at psychological meetings. As a result, a group of local ministers retained me to speak to them on the topic of 'Taking Ones Anger at God, to God'.

While doing this speaking engagement for these religious leaders, I heard about a minister of a local church who had recently lost a four-year-old girl in his congregation. The death of this healthy, beautiful little girl was so unexpected it rocked him as well as his whole congregation. His response, when he delivered the sermon at her funeral, was to take his anger at God, to God, for allowing this little girl to die. The effect of his sermon helped members of his congregation follow his lead and take their anger at God, to God for allowing this little girl to die. In fact, it eventually had a profound healing effect on nearly everyone in his congregation including the parents of the dead four-year-old girl. In addition, many others outside of his church were deeply moved by this story and began to take their anger at God, to God as word of his funeral sermon traveled widely from person to person in the community.

I was deeply moved by this story and knew immediately I had to do something about resolving my own anger by taking my anger at God, to God. So, one afternoon when I was alone, I gathered up some large stones and began hurling them onto the ground and at a tree in the yard to vent my anger at God. I did so for quite some time screaming, "Why God?! Why have you abandoned me?!" and so on, over and over again each time I crashed a stone onto the ground or into the tree. When I finished and lay exhausted on the ground, I began to feel energy move through my body. I felt alive and connected to things around me and to myself. My depression and despair lifted. I was amazed! There definitely was something to this notion of needing to take my anger at God, to God.

Over the next few weeks, as my depression and despair came back, I began to regularly take my anger at God, to God in a similar way. I put a baseball bat and a large piece of thick foam mattress in my car. Then I'd stop on a deserted road, place the thick foam pad on the hood of my car, and beat on it with the baseball bat as I screamed my anger at God. Each time I did so, my depression lifted for a while, and I felt alive and well again for a short time until my depression returned again. So, I kept repeating this exercise each time my depression and despair settled over me. Slowly but surely, I began to climb back out of my dark hole.

Then I had a setback. I missed my children terribly. This was especially true in the mornings and evenings. I had always cooked breakfast for them and eaten it with them when we were living as a family. And, in the evenings, I had often put them to bed, read them bedtime stories, and sang them to sleep as I played my guitar. One morning, about a year after separating from my wife by moving out of our home, I was cooking my breakfast and eating it alone when I burst into tears. I missed my children so much I thought it would tear my heart out. That evening, as I missed reading the bedtime story to them and singing them to sleep, I went into a very deep despair. Without them, life seemed pointless and hopeless.

I was so depressed I could not even find the energy to get angry with God and beat on the foam pad with my baseball bat. I did not know what to do or where to turn to rid myself of my despair and hopelessness. Then, for some reason, which was a mystery to me at that time, I remembered meeting a man outside of my Bioenergetic psychotherapist's office who had impressed me. He was a drug and alcohol addictions counselor who was seeing another Bioenergetic psychotherapist in the same office. After briefly talking with him that day, I remembered having had an intuitive feeling he knew something I needed to learn, but I did not follow up on it. However, it now seemed imperative I talk with him. So, the next morning I phoned to ask if we could meet with him for an hour or so during the coming week.

During my meeting with him, I poured out my story of fear, loss, and despair. When I finished my story, I waited for him to respond. He did, but not in the way I expected or wanted. Very matter of fact he said, "Tonight, when you get back home, I want you to get on your knees and ask God for help."

"That was it!" I screamed inside. I drove an hour to this man's home, spent another hour pouring out my heart-breaking story, paid him a fee for listening to me, and all he had to say was, "I want you to get on your knees and ask God for help!" I could not believe my bad luck. I quickly ended my appointment and left his home very angry. Here I was, deeply in debt with only a little income, finishing up a nasty divorce, saddled with huge child support payments, and my mental and physical health deteriorated. And he had the gall to tell me to get on my knees to ask God for help—a God who certainly had not paid me much attention over the years except recently when my depression lifted from throwing rocks on the ground and beating the hood of by car with a baseball bat as I yelled at God for abandoning me.

My anger got me home that evening at ninety miles per hour. But as I lay down to sleep, the worst feeling of terror, hopelessness, helplessness, and despair I had ever felt descended upon me. I wished I was dead, but I didn't have the courage to end my life.

As I twisted and turned trying to sleep, this man's last words began ringing in my ears, "I want you to get on your knees and ask God for help," I tried in vain to put those words out of my mind. But the more I tried, the more I tossed and turned in my bed, and the more his parting words haunted me. I simply could not sleep nor get those words out of my mind.

On My Knees

"Ok!" I yelled silently in my mind, "You win." I found myself rolling out of bed and dropping to my knees on the floor beside my bed. In a whisper, full of emptiness, loneliness, hopelessness, and despair I said the words, "God, if you exist, please show me the way".

I was instantly hit by a bolt of energy, as if lightning had struck me. I was so startled I wasn't sure what had happened. When I recovered a bit, I whispered the words again, "God, please help me." Another bolt of energy surged through my body. "What is going on?" I asked myself in a surprised and confused state of mind. This made no sense to my rational mind. But I liked the surge of energy I felt in me. I felt alive! And something heavy lifted off me. I did not know what was going on, but I liked it, whatever it was.

I decided to say the words another time. "God, please help me," I repeated. The same bolt of energy was there again. And, I was feeling wonderfully alive, transformed in some unexplained way. After enjoying this feeling for a while, I climbed back into bed and slept soundly for the first night in months.

When I awoke the next morning, I felt everything alive around me and in me. The sunshine radiated in the window as if it was the first sunshine in my life. The sounds of the morning birds were as if I was hearing them for the very first time. I felt wonderful, alive, and at home in my body. I felt connected to everything around me. I was part of it, and it was part of me. I felt miraculously uplifted and transformed.

This uplifted and transformed sense of myself helped me uncover the rouge lie that lay behind my disabling fear, emptiness, loneliness, and despair. In my next Bioenergetic psychotherapy session I realized this rouge lie had to do with my feeling of being an outsider wherever I was—that I had to do life alone. During that break-through therapy session I was flooded with memories which made it clear to me why this was the case.

I Am an Outsider Even with God

In that therapy session, I realized I had always felt like an outsider. I was quite shy as a young boy, and although I did well in school in terms of my studies, I had few close friends and did not engage in sports or after school activities on a regular basis because I had to work on the family farm before and after school, especially during the Spring and Fall months when my father kept me busy after school doing the Spring planting and Fall harvesting.

I remembered as a boy, standing in our front yard looking up at the stars in the night sky and asking God to step in and stop my father from taking his anger and rage out on me for not moving fast enough and working hard enough. I just could not please my father no matter how hard I tried. But God did not step in to stop my father from beating me with his belt when I made what he called "stupid mistakes" or did not do his exact bidding fast enough, so I thought of myself as an outsider even with God. As a young man, I would go to church after seeing a religious movie like *The Ten Commandments*, and then walk out disgusted when the preacher started ranting about needing to repent our sins so we would be saved from going to hell, or when he delivered a sermon about how the more submissive women are to their husbands, the more their husbands would love them, for example. So, I felt an outsider with the church as well.

When I began my personal Bioenergetic psychotherapy, I was divorcing my wife because I felt like an unwanted, not worthwhile, outsider husband with her. I always felt something was wrong with my marriage but did know what it was until my wife left me alone with our young children for two weeks when she went to care for her dying father who lived in a distant city. It was the best two weeks of my life. When my wife left for her trip, our young children clung to her skirts and cried their eyes out which made it very difficult for her to leave them with me. However, soon after she departed, our children resumed their normal activities just as if she had not gone away. The best part for me was they turned to me for what they needed. I loved it as I cared for them and played games, read them books, and told them stories. It was the most wonderful two weeks of my life because for the first time in my life I no longer felt like an unwanted, outsider father. However, that all changed when my wife returned. When she walked back into our house, our children ran to her crying and sobbing their eyes out just as they had done when she left. She gave me a withering look as if to say, 'how could you' and then immediately took over the parenting role with our children that I had fully assumed thus leaving me once again excluded and feeling like the unwanted, outsider father in my own family. It was one of the worst days of my life.

As a result of all this, I started taking my anger to God on a regular basis, and I often got on my knees to ask God to show me the way. I always got an answer, if not right away, then later in a dream or a flash of insight, for example. And, when I got on my knees to ask God for help, I still got a surge of energy moving up and down my spine. It still does this to this day. I have often asked myself why this happened for me. One explanation I have given myself is that perhaps God exists only in my imagination—that I just needed to surrender and not try to do my life alone. Thus, when I take my anger to God and get on my knees to ask for God's help, I surrender and this is what sends energy surging through me, renewing my spirit and body. This may be the correct explanation; however, I prefer to believe there really is a God, a

Higher Power, that responds to me when I take my anger to God and then get on my knees to ask God for help. But then I wonder, is this just my attempt to not feel alone in the world? Perhaps when I take my anger to God and get on my knees to ask for God's help, and I get a message back, I am really only tapping into my own internal wisdom in order to find the answers I need. Perhaps this is the case. All I know is when I take my anger to God and get on my knees to ask God for help, it works for me.

Since taking my anger to God and getting on my knees to ask God for help worked for me, I started sharing my story with clients and suggesting they take their anger to God and get on their knees to ask God for help. And, to my supersize, it seemed to work for many of them as well.

God's Given Forgiveness

Taking my anger at God, to God as well as getting on my knees to ask God to show me the way worked for me, that is for sure. Yet, there was another part of my life where I still felt cut off from God. I had made a lot of mistakes in my life and hurt a number of people along the way, people I loved very much. So, I carried regret and guilt. I could not forgive myself for my trespasses. Nor could I take my regrets and trespasses to God. In fact, it did not occur to me to do so or that such a thing was possible. When I married again, I carried the burden of my 'sins' into our marriage—although I did not call my trespass "sins" or think of them that way. They were simply emotional scars that constantly reminded me I was not worthy because of the pain I had caused others. This constant nagging reminder of feeling less than worthy, and therefore being less than fully lovable, created a level of distance with my new wife whom I married about ten years after my second divorce which had eventually became intolerable just as my first marriage had become, and for the same reason, my second wife put our child first leaving me feeling as the outsider in our family. It was a repeat of my first marriage!

One day I got fed up with feeling unworthy with my current wife. So, I went to her and unburdened myself, telling her all of my 'sins', regrets, and about my inability to get the nagging reminders of them out of my mind. In response, she told me I needed to forgive myself. I agreed with her but replied this would be very difficult for me to do. In fact, I said I did not know how to begin to forgive myself. She replied perhaps I needed to get on my knees and ask God to show me how to forgive myself. "Of course," I thought to myself, "how could I have missed such a simple answer?" So, that night I got on my knees and asked God to give me an answer. The answer I received came to me in a dream that night in which God kept repeating the words, "I forgive myself," and, "I forgive others."

When I awoke from the dream the next morning, I made a list of all my trespasses and ways I had hurt others as well as a list of the ways others had hurt me and trespassed against me. Then, I read the first item on my list of trespasses and ways I had hurt others and repeated the words, "For this I forgive myself," over and over until I began to believe my words. This took many repetitions for me to accept and believe my own words, "For this I forgive myself." Then, during the following months, I worked my way down my list of 'sins', repeating over and over the words, "For this I forgive myself." Next, I began doing the same with my list of the ways others had hurt and trespassed against me. For each name and item on this list, I repeated over and over the words, "For this, I forgive you." This exercise was very helpful in getting rid of the nagging reminders of my sins in my mind. Yet, I still felt something was missing.

When I pondered what was missing, I realized at a very deep level in me I still felt less than worthy and less than fully lovable. So, I got on my knees again to ask God to show me the way to solve this problem. The answer I got the next morning was like a lightning bolt surging through me, much like that lightning bolt which had hit me the first time I got on my knees to ask God to show me the way. The answer was, "God has already forgiven me!" As I let this realization sink into me, I felt a wave of love and peace wash over me like I had never experienced before.

Thus, whenever I begin dwelling on a mistake I have made, or a trespass I have committed, or a hurt I have caused to another person, I say the words, "For this, God has forgiven me." These words immediately bring me peace of mind and move me into a self-loving, self-forgiving state of being. As well, whenever I begin obsessing over another person's mistake, trespass, or injury to me and/or my loved ones, I say the words, "For this, God has forgiven you." These words also immediately bring me peace and move me into a loving, forgiving state of being.

No License to Trespass

Now, you might think since God has already forgiven me for any trespass or hurt I cause others, I might feel I have a license to trespass or hurt others at will. In fact, I find the opposite is true. The peace and loving, forgiving state I am in because of God's Given Forgiveness helps make me less likely to trespass and hurt others.

Using The Spiritual Bridge Protocols with Clients

Following please find four energetic protocols designed to help trauma clients create a spiritual bridge by 1. taking their anger at God, to God, 2. getting on their knees to ask God for help, and 3. accepting God's Given Forgiveness.

A Word About Using the Spiritual Bridge Protocols

In order to overcome feelings of being totally alone in the world, it is important for trauma victims to find a safe place to express their anger at having been abused, abandoned, and betrayed as well as ask for help to heal their trauma. These kinds of safe places are not easy to find. For some, God or a Higher Power is the only safe place available. If clients resonate with the words God or a Higher Power, then use the Spiritual Bridge Protocols presented here as they are written.

However, for others, there simply are no safe places. I resonate with this view also. At times I've had my doubts about the existence of God or a Higher Power, especially when I see so much violence and evil in the world, especially violence to innocent children and helpless people. So, if taking their anger to "God" or a "Higher Power" is a turn off for clients, suggest they try using terms like, "Source, The Universe," or, "The World," instead, or use another less loaded term like, "Nature," for example, which is more acceptable to them. This can have the same effect as using the words God or a Higher Power when taking their anger to Source, The Universe, The World, or Nature, for example, and asking this Power for help. It is the act of surrendering and not trying to go it alone that is important here. At least, that is what was important for me to do. It was the act of surrendering to a Benevolent Force and not trying to go it alone that gave me new energy and lifted me out of despair.

The Spiritual Bridge Protocols

To use The Spiritual Bridge Protocols to help clients heal their trauma, simply have them follow the instructions provided for each protocol.

The Take Your Anger at God, to God Protocol

1. Identify the anger you have with God or a Higher Power (or if you prefer another name such as Source, The Universe, or Nature, for example).

2. Express your anger at God, (or your name for this Power), as you take your anger to God by yelling at God and simultaneously hitting a pillow with a tennis racket, stomping on a large pillow, throwing a temper tantrum while lying on a mattress, or hitting a punching bag with your fists, for example. If you believe God does not exist, yell, "I don't believe you exist God!" while energetically expressing your anger.

3. Keep voicing and energetically expressing your anger at God until you are exhausted. Doing this will help lift your depression.

4. Rest and recover from this exercise and then check-in with yourself, and your Assist Person, or your Therapist, by reflecting on the experience and how you feel in your body as a result of taking your anger at God, to God. Did it help lift your depression and your spirits? If not, repeat the above steps.

The Getting on My Knees to Ask God for Help Protocol

1. Explore, reflect upon, and express your despair regarding your present life situation. You can do this in your mind, by writing down your thoughts and feelings, or sharing your thoughts and feelings with an Assist Person or Therapist.

2. Then, get on your knees and ask God or a Higher Power for help. Use words like, "Please help me God," or, "Show me the way God." Ask for this help by voicing it out loud.

3. Tune into your body and yourself by reflecting and reporting on what is happening internally, emotionally, and physically as a result of asking God for help. Repeating this exercise one or more times may be helpful.

4. Share with your Assist Person or Therapist what is happening inside your body and yourself as a result of being on your knees and asking God for help.

5. Consider making this act of 'Getting on your knees to ask God for Help' a regular practice in your life.

The God Has Forgiven Me Protocol

When you begin to obsess about something you have done to hurt others, or the mistake(s) you have made in your life, or the ways you have trespassed, simply say the words, "For this, God has forgiven me." Repeat these words until they bring you peace as well as move you into a self-loving, self-forgiving state of being. You may wish to substitute the words "Higher Power" or "Universe" or "Source", for example, for the word "God". You can also change the wording to, "God forgives me for this." for instance.

The God Has Forgiven Them Protocol

When you begin to obsess about something another has done to hurt you or your loved ones, or an egregious mistake they have made, or a way they have violated and trespassed on your space, for example, say the words, "For this, God has forgiven you." Repeat these words until they bring you peace as well as move you into a self-loving, self-forgiving state of being. You can also change the wording to, "God forgives you for this," for example.

Learning the Life Lessons that God Gives Us

I have often questioned why God, Source, or my Higher Power allows so much evil and misery to exist in the world. With all the mass shootings, abuse of children and women, oppression of Blacks, Native Americans, and minorities, and the greed that is destroying our climate and planet, it is enough to shake my faith at times. And then, add to this all the suffering I and my loved ones have endured over the years, and it all seems too much. The only way I have been able to handle all this evil and misery is to say to myself each time I am confronted with or reminded of the evil or misery, "God is giving me or us a life lesson to learn," and then set about learning to master it. Sometimes this required me to get involved in political or civil rights activities, for example, and other times it required me to address more personal issues. Without fail, if I did not learn the life lesson that was being put in my face, especially on a personal level, it would keep appearing in my life until I finally did learn the lesson.

The Major Life Lesson Which Kept Reappearing in My Personal Life

For example, one of the major personal life lessons that I was given had to do with all the women whom I instantly fell in love with only to have those love relationships fall apart later. I worked on this life lesson for a long time during my personal psychotherapy. Finally, it came to me that the women to whom I was instantly attracted and fell in love with were clones of my childhood mother. It was my childhood mother's elusive love that I was trying to capture in those problematic love relationships. As I reviewed the character traits of those women, they all had one thing in common with my mother. At some point, each of those women were really not available to me just as my childhood mother had not been available to meet my needs as a child. For instance, my first wife was available to me in the beginning until our first child was born and then she turned all of her attention and affection toward our newborn daughter. This continued with our other two children. Unfortunately, my wife refused to go see a marriage counselor and it became intolerable for me to continue our marriage as it left me out in the cold and the outsider in our family. Unexpectedly, the same almost exact thing happened in my second marriage.

Next, I got involved with a woman from Brazil who loved me like crazy but refused to come live with me in the U.S. because she did not want to be away from her family. Nor would she have me come to live with her in Brazil because she feared that, for a while, I might have to be dependent upon her until I found work as a psychotherapist. Thus, she was only available to me for brief periods when we visited each other in our respective home countries. Eventually this arrangement became unacceptable to me, and I left the relationship.

When I realized that my women were unavailable to me just as my childhood mother had been unavailable to me, it was an 'aha' moment! I had been searching for my childhood mother's love in all those unavailable women. To correct this, I began looking for a different kind of woman and found my current wife as a result. However, when I met her and we began dating, my first thought was that, although she was very attractive and I liked her a lot, she was not the kind of woman with whom I could quickly fall in love with since she was so reserved. Therefore, I almost stopped dating her. Fortunately, I ignored my impulse to drop her and made a conscious decision to keep on dating her. It took some time for her to open herself up to me but when she did, I was blown away. She had overcome so much pain and abuse in her childhood I was amazed at how well she functioned in her adult life. She had an abundance of faith, courage, and grace. Of course, I also learned she had done a good deal of psychotherapy to heal and free herself from her painful, abusive past which I greatly admired. As a result of learning this, I developed a deep respect for her, and this then became the solid basis for really falling in love with her. The best part was she was always available to me, and I was able to make myself available to her. Thus, we have been happily married for over 20 years. Finally, I learned the lesson God had repeatedly put in my face which was to stop looking for my unavailable childhood mother's love in all of those unavailable women and find the love of my life in a woman who was available.

When I do learn the lesson I have been given, then without fail, another life lesson will take its place. I don't know why I am being given these life lessons, but I assume there is a reason for it beyond my own self-improvement. This gives me hope and helps me push on trying to create good in the world. Perhaps the reason I am being given these life lessons may be revealed to me at some later time, such as in an after-life, if there is one. So, I keep on learning the life lessons I am given. And, I keep taking my anger at God, to God for allowing such evil and misery to exist in the world. As well, I keep getting on my knees to ask God to show me the way to learn the life lessons I am given about how to deal with this evil and misery. And, I keep repeating the words, "God has forgiven them for this evil and misery making," and, "God has forgiven me for any part I have played in keeping evil and misery alive in the world."

I use The Learning Life's Lesson Protocol below on a regular basis. Whenever I am facing a difficult time or crisis in my life, or I am perplexed by an evil act or the misery making in the world, I ask myself and my Higher Power, "What is the life lesson I am being given here?" I always get an answer which helps me negotiate the difficult time or crisis and learn a new lesson in my life.

The Learning Life's Lesson Protocol

1. When you are facing a difficult time or crisis in your life, ask yourself the question, "What is the life lesson I am being given here?"

2. Then, get on your knees to ask your Higher Power to help you learn the life lesson you are being given. Or ask loved ones or your Therapist for help in doing so.

3. Use the life lesson you are given to help guide you in navigating the difficult time or crisis you are facing and thus give more hope, purpose, and meaning in your life as well.

Helping Clients Let Go of a Trauma Memorial

When clients create a memorial to their trauma as a way to stay connected to the traumatic loss of a loved one or the loss of their identity such as getting a divorce or becoming a fired employee, the trauma memorial can take various non-physical as well as physical forms. Clients may engage in compulsive rituals, have recurring dreams, or repeat certain behaviors. These are examples of creating a non-physical trauma memorial. Or they may publicly display cherished artifacts of their lost loved one, refuse to remove the belongings of their former loved one's chest of drawers, or keep old boxes of work papers after being fired from their job. These are examples of creating a physical trauma memorial.

The problem is these non-physical and physical trauma memorials can have very negative effects such as interfering with clients' sleep, disturbing their concentration and peace of mind, and preventing them from living in the present moment, for example. To help clients let go of their problematic trauma memorials, I have them use and follow The Releasing Your Trauma Memorial Protocol which is presented below.

The Releasing Your Trauma Memorial Protocol

To use this protocol, if you are a trauma client, follow the steps below. If you are a Therapist, have your client follow these steps:

1. Jump Start a good energy charge in your body by engaging in strong physical activity such as hitting a pillow with a bat or tennis racket.

2. Ground your energy charge by doing energetic grounding such as using the Hair-Pin or Downhill Ski Energetic Grounding Protocols.

3. Identify the nature of your Trauma Memorial—how it operates to negatively affect your life (such as interfering with your sleep, disturbing your concentration and peace of mind, or preventing you from living in the present moment, for example).

4. Imagine your lost loved one or your embodied lost identity standing in front of you.

5. Do one or more of the following. Say "Goodbye" to your Lost Love or Lost Identity, turn your back on your Lost Love or Lost Identity and walk away knowing you will never see your Lost Love or Lost Identity again, and/or bury your Lost Love or Lost Identity by covering it with a sheet, for example. The goal here is to get in touch with and express your grief about losing your loved one or your identity. You can also use the Spontaneous Movement Protocol to find the best way to say goodbye to your lost loved one or identity—that is to say, the best way to get in touch with and express your grief.

6. Ask your Higher Power (God/Source/The Universe) to help you let go of and release your Trauma Memorial. For instance, you might get on your knees and say the

words, "God, show me the way to let go." Or use other words which resonate to ask your Higher Power for help in releasing your Trauma Memorial.

Here is a case example of a client using this protocol to say goodbye to her lost loved one.

Saying Goodbye to Her Granddaughter

She consulted me to treat a sleep disturbance. She complained of having dreams about losing her granddaughter. The nightly dreams left her feeling anxious and depressed. She also talked in her sleep while having these dreams and this disturbed her husband's sleep. She felt very confused because she had actually lost her granddaughter at age twelve, about six years prior to seeing me, due to a nasty divorce in which the mother turned her granddaughter against her as well as against the father who was her son. In her disturbing dreams, she was trying to reach out for her granddaughter who was always disappearing on the periphery of her vision as a kind of shadowy figure. "I feel like I am losing her," she explained, "but that makes no sense to me since I have already lost all contact with my granddaughter for the past six years."

She explained that before her son's divorce, she had been very close to her granddaughter who loved her dearly. "So, when the divorce happened and the mother turned my granddaughter against my son and me, and would not allow her to visit us, I was heartbroken," she said. "I was the loving grandmother to her that I never had. But following the divorce this was no longer possible. I felt completely helpless to do anything about it because the mother hated me for my son's having left her. My son took her to court and won visitation rights so my granddaughter could visit me, but the mother successfully ignored the court order due to the elected judge having had a political conflict of interest in the case, and thus, the court order was never enforced." She finished her story with tears in her eyes. "The worst part of it was I never had the chance to say goodbye to my granddaughter," she lamented.

To begin this client's Energetic Therapy aimed at helping her let go of the trauma memorial she had created in the form of nightly dreams in order to stay connected to her beloved lost granddaughter, I suggested she jump start a strong energy charge in her body by repeatedly hitting a pillow with a tennis racket while yelling the word, "No." This also helped her mobilize her aggression and anger at the mother for turning her granddaughter against her. I then had her follow-up by grounding her energy charge using the Downhill Ski Energetic Grounding Protocol.

While using the Downhill Ski Protocol, she reported not feeling her feet and legs. I noted her weight was mostly back on her heels which raised her toes slightly off the floor. I suggested she shifted her weight onto the balls of her feet which started a small tremor in her legs and thus allowed her to have more feeling in them. When she was better energetically grounded, I suggested she set an intention for what she wanted to have happen in her therapy session. She immediately replied she wanted to stop dreaming about her granddaughter. I then suggested she go to a still point in her body and mind to be followed by letting a spontaneous movement come from her body that would help her realize her intention. Her spontaneous movement was to rapidly blink her eyes.

I pointed out the fluttering movement of her eyes and asked her what her eyes were saying. "I want to see my granddaughter," she replied. I then asked what wanting to see her granddaughter had to do with her nightly dreams. She answered by saying, "My dreams are my only connection to my granddaughter." She followed this statement by reporting she felt sick to her stomach. "I feel like throwing up," she said. I pushed a waste can toward her and encouraged her to throw up if she needed to do so. She grabbed the waste can and began retching into it. She had not eaten anything all day so she only dry heaved several times. When she finished, she set the waste can down and stayed standing in a silent crouched over position.

I observed her shoulders were crunched forward as if she was protecting her chest and heart. As a result, I asked her if she would like some support. She glanced up at me trying to decipher my meaning. "Who would you like to back you up in this painful process?" I asked. She answered by saying, "My husband." I responded by saying since her husband was not available at the moment, I would like to step in to support her in his place. She nodded her agreement, so I asked her if I could place my hand on her back below her shoulder blades near the rear of her heart. She nodded her assent. As I did so, she raised her crunched over body into a taller stance and took a deep breath. My words to her at that point were, "I am so sorry you did not get a chance to say goodbye to your granddaughter." My words brought tears to her eyes. However, she quickly choked back the sobs which were threatening to erupt with her tears.

I followed-up by asking her if she would still like to say goodbye to her granddaughter. "Yes, of course," she replied. With her assent, I suggested she imagine her granddaughter standing in front of her and then say 'goodbye' to her. As she reluctantly did so, a flood of tears and sobs erupted from her body. She also began to tremble and shake as the frozen trauma of losing her granddaughter thawed and discharged itself from deep within her body. In alarm, she looked to me for an explanation for what was happening. I reassured her that her trembling and shaking was her body's natural way of healing the trauma she had experienced when she lost her beloved granddaughter, and she should continue to let it do so. After a while, her trembling and shaking subsided and she relaxed. I then suggested she let another spontaneous movement arise from her body that would move her further along in realizing her intention to stop dreaming about her granddaughter

Her spontaneous movement was to shake her arms as if she was shaking something off from them. Her words that came with this shaking off movement were, "Get off me! Leave me alone!" I suggested she amplify the shaking off movement and her 'leave me alone' words by exaggerating them. This helped get her whole body involved as she forcefully shook her arms, shoulders, head, torso, legs, and feet to get rid of the burden she had been carrying for so long. When she finished shaking her whole body, she reported she felt very alive and free. I suggested she anchor her feeling of aliveness and freedom by doing energetic grounding using the Hair-pin Energetic Grounding Protocol.

Finally, I suggested she ask her Higher Power to help her realize her intention to stop dreaming about her granddaughter. She did this by raising her arms skyward and asking her granddaughter's Better Angel to help her granddaughter get free and be herself. This brought closure to her therapy session. She later reported she no longer had the disturbing dreams about her beloved granddaughter.

10

Using The Toxic Shame Busting Protocol to Help Clients Get Rid of Their Debilitating Toxic Shame

Feeling shame can be a useful thing. It tells people that they have crossed a social barrier and that they need to reconsider their actions. Toxic shame, on the other hand, is a disabling and crippling feeling and thing. It overtakes people with self-attacks which make them feel unworthy, unlovable, and fundamentally bad. As well, it affects people's behavior by making them withdraw and isolate from others, greatly reduces their self-esteem, and leads them to become very depressed, so much so that they may begin to contemplate suicide.

Quite by accident I discovered a method to help clients get rid of their debilitating toxic shame after reading Byron Brown's practical approach to "Liberating Yourself from The Judge Within." In his book, *Soul Without Shame*, (Brown, 1994), he sets forth dozens of techniques to help clients live without toxic shame. His book title promises a soul without shame, but I found this to be a bit of a stretch. In actual practice, the shame reduction exercises that he offers had the effect of attenuating clients' toxic shame but in no way did these practices reduce their toxic shame to zero. However, clients did find his idea of "The Inner Judge," very helpful in conceptualizing how this mechanism works in the mind to keep feeding one's toxic shame. And the specific protocols of, "Dis-identifying With The Inner Judge," and, "Defending Against The Inner Judge," were also very useful in helping clients reduce their toxic shame. Unfortunately, he does not address the idea of getting rid of people's, "Inner Victim." I found that getting rid of my "Inner Victim" mindset was the key to purging my "Inner Judge" and thereby jettisoning my toxic shame for good. Let me share the story of how I did this which then set the stage for creating The Toxic Shame Busting Protocol to help others do the same.

Jettisoning My Toxic Shame Shroud

While co-leading an empowerment workshop, I was rudely yanked back into the shame of my past by an incident with one of my staff members. Upset with my stance on a procedural issue near the end of the workshop, she began dumping out her cold rage on me during a staff meeting designed to clear the air and resolve things between us. It was evident to me, as the cold rage poured forth from her eyes, that the insistence that my staff be present and on time for the daily briefing meetings during the workshop, had re-stimulated negative feelings she apparently still harbored toward her own father for his tyrannical treatment of her as a child.

As she continued to pour out her cold rage on me, which was the same kind of cold rage that my own tyrannical father poured out on me as a boy, I was unable to look in her eyes just as I had been unable to meet my father's eyes as a boy. It felt as if her eyes would pierce mine, so I felt forced to look away. As I did so, I felt myself shrink in size and power as if I was once again ten years old facing my judgmental childhood father. It was a feeling that

I had felt many times while growing up as a boy. It seemed that no matter how hard I tried, I could not measure up to my father's expectations and demands, and consequently, I often faced his wrath for failing to do so.

What surprised me about this clearing incident was how helpless and intensely shameful it made me feel as well as how long my shame and helplessness lasted after the workshop. For several weeks I was not very present or productive. I found myself withdrawing from people and obsessing over what had happened during the clearing with this woman. When I replayed the incident in my mind, it left me feeling deeply ashamed. Yet, on a rational level, I was aware that I had nothing to be ashamed about. Although I had been demanding of the staff, it was clear to me that I had not acted the part of a tyrant with them. It was also clear to me that this woman was projecting her own issues regarding her tyrannical father onto me as the workshop leader and this had re-stimulated my boyhood shame thus preventing me from effectively dealing with this woman in the clearing incident.

What helped deepen the feeling of shame was the way my staff reacted to me following the workshop. I think that most of them were very uncomfortable with the conflict that this woman had with me and my inability to successfully resolve it because I had gotten hooked by her shaming of me during the clearing. I think that they chose to distance themselves from me to deal with their own discomfort. This, of course, helped feed my feeling of shame. In one case, a staff member was quite open about his negative judgment regarding my failure in handling the clearing successfully. He was a younger staff member whom I had been mentoring. He sent me a letter indicating that it was time for me to step aside from leading the Women of Fire & Men Step into the Fire empowerment project and let him take over as the project leader as well as replace me as the male co-leader of the empowerment workshops. The reason he gave for wishing to replace me was because it was quite clear to him that I did not know how to do a successful clearing and blessing of that woman. My failure, he indicated, was unacceptable to him. Although on one level, I knew that a competitive motive lay behind his letter, on another level, his words about my 'not being able to bless the woman' touched a raw nerve and served to feed the feeling of shame. What I should have done with this staff member was point out that his job had been to monitor the clearing process and step in to help if the clearing did not follow the clearing protocol, and this he had failed to do. But I did not take him to task because I was too stuck in the shame to do so.

A Visit to My Therapist

Over the years, prior to that fateful workshop, I had acquired a lot of skill and tools for dealing with shame, especially from Brown's *Soul Without Shame* (1999). I had faced shaming incidents in the past and overcame them, but in this case, none of my skills and tools for handling shame seemed to work. As a result, I decided to consult my former energetic Therapist by scheduling a session with her. During the session, as I explained what had happened to me in the workshop clearing with that woman staff member, I felt totally ashamed and just wanted to evaporate. Fortunately, I was still present enough to say out loud to my Therapist that I just wanted to disappear. She suggested that I use one of my own Energetic Therapy protocols—namely The Spontaneous Movement Protocol—to let a spontaneous movement arise from my body that would help me move forward with healing my toxic shame; the movement was to reach for a bed sheet and ask her to place a sheet over my head to cover me. When she did so, I relaxed my tense body, let down, and breathed more fully. This had a miraculous effect on me. I was able to become much more present and move out of my shame shroud temporarily. It allowed me to discuss my shame much more openly with my Therapist and as a result, I moved a step closer toward shedding the shame shroud which had shut me down for the past couple of months.

However, after leaving my Therapist's office, the feeling of shame returned, and trying as I might to shed it, I was unable to do so on my own. Then several interesting things happened to help me understand the nature of the toxic shame problem that I was facing. Two of them seemed quite trivial at the time but in retrospect, they were the things that helped me solve the puzzle of how to get rid of my "Inner Victim," and its counterpart, my "Inner Judge," thus allowing me to get rid of the toxic shame shroud for good.

The Two Incidents Which Helped Me Solve the Puzzle of How to Get Rid of the Toxic Shame Shroud

First, while serving as a consultant for an empowerment training for high school students and their adult mentors, I introduced myself using a microphone in a small room. As I spoke, I was surprised by the strong sound of my voice coming back to me in this cramped space. My voice sounded full and deep, not at all the way I experienced it when I spoke without a microphone. As I heard my voice in this positive way, the shame shroud lifted momentarily.

Second, the staff member who wrote me the letter about not being able to bless the woman in the clearing incident called to tell me that he had just been certified as a leader in the New Warrior Men's Adventure Training project. His call accidentally got recorded on my answering machine when I picked up the phone after the fourth ring. As I listened to the recording following the call, I was again surprised by my voice which sounded very upbeat. It was not the way I had experienced myself when I spoke to him on the phone. Again, the shame shroud lifted for a moment as I noted the positive quality reflected in my recorded voice.

These two incidents of using a microphone in a small room and hearing my recorded voice, which surprised me by their positive quality, provided me with a clue about why I could not seem to shake off the shame shroud. I say this, because shortly thereafter, during a phone conversation with a colleague about how to help clients get rid of their toxic shame, I argued that perhaps using Brown's strategy of having clients dis-identify with their Inner Judge was not the right answer to the problem. Rather, I argued that an outside positive experience might be needed to help shift clients out of their toxic shame shroud. I used the experience of hearing my own voice reflected to me in a positive way, and the fact that it had momentarily lifted my own shame shroud on two occasions as an example of the kind of outside positive experience that was needed. I continued the argument by explaining that what I felt I needed to shake off the toxic shame shroud permanently was a deeper positive experience of some sort which must come from outside of myself.

Following our conversation, my colleague sent me an e-mail. In it she wrote: "I want to make it quite clear that it was not my intention to minimize the impact or difficulty you had in dealing with your shame. I also want to point out that you are one of the most beautiful beings that I know and that I have enormous love and respect for you. The thoughts that elicit this shame in you are lies, my friend, utter and absolute lies."

She had heard me! Her extolling and validating words to me brought tears to my eyes and with it, I felt the toxic shame shroud lift totally off me! And it did not come back. So, here was outside confirmation from my colleague and good friend, whom I respected and admired, which absolutely refuted my father's judgments of me as failing to measure up to his standards and therefore, being unworthy! And here was confirmation of the intuitive feeling that I had needed an outside positive experience—validation and high praise—to help lift the toxic shame shroud off me, and to be rid of it permanently. What a lesson that was!

The Essence of the Lesson and the Proposed Cure for Toxic Shame

Here is the essence of that lesson as I now see it. Toxic shame, when it is deeply internalized as a sense of worthlessness and taken over and maintained by one's Inner Victim and Inner Judge, can be dispelled by the extolling and validating of one's true essence from an outside respected source. Perhaps this is the only way that toxic shame can be eliminated. Certainly, my own efforts to confront my Inner Judge and change its self-attacks on me as well as get rid of the disabling Inner Victim' voice to remove the toxic shame shroud was feeble indeed. Yes, the sheet that I asked my Therapist to cover me helped bring me briefly out of the debilitating shame and be able to think more clearly about the issue. Yes, hearing my own voice reflected in a positive way also helped lift the shame shroud momentarily. And yes, these were useful tools. But it was only when an outside respected source, the voice of my colleague and friend whom I greatly admired, spoke words extolling and validating me that my Inner Victim identity was sent packing, and therefore, my Inner Judge identity no longer had my Inner Victim to attack in my mind and so also disappeared, that the toxic shame shroud lifted permanently. It also confirmed the suspicion which I had that the first English award that I received as a sophomore in high school as well as later writing awards had lifted my childhood toxic shame shroud enough to allow me to bloom during my junior-senior high school years, succeed in graduating from college, and later, shine in my higher education career.

As I saw it, the key to getting rid of the toxic shame permanently was receiving those validating actions and words from what I saw as external respected sources—that is to say, the action of my high school English teacher giving me a writing award, then interestingly to be followed by winning third place in a fiction writing contest sponsored by the English Department at Michigan State University, and subsequently having several best-selling and award winning psychological education handbooks published, as well as the final extolling words of my colleague and good friend when she sent me her email full of high praise. Those validating and extolling actions and words were enough to counter my childhood view of myself—that is, my Inner Victim identity—as being unworthy with the result that the toxic shame shroud and Inner Judge totally disappeared and have remained so until this day.

Creating The Toxic Shame Busting Protocol

As a result of that final miracle experience of being validated by my respected colleague and friend, I created The Toxic Shame Busting Protocol which features the process of validating and extolling toxic shame-filled clients. (See this protocol below.) I began using it with great success in my trauma healing practice as well as in my Energetic Therapy training seminars, workshops, and speaking engagements which I was increasingly asked to do.

The Toxic Shame Busting Protocol

Part I: Covering the Shame Filled Client

When trauma clients encounter toxic shame that shuts them down during their trauma healing work, suggest that they allow themselves to be covered with a sheet or blanket. If they agree, simply place the sheet or blanket gently over their head so that the top half of their body is completely covered. Then, allow them to experience being under this covering. Often shame filled clients who are covered in this way will visibly let down and relax as well as comment on how good it feels to not be seen, both of which confirm the benefits of the covering. If these clients do not relax or find the covering not to their liking, check in with them to ask about what is going on for them. Then, simply respond to their feedback as appropriate. At some point, the clients who like the covering will want the covering removed and can then proceed forward with their trauma healing work. If they do not ask to have the covering removed, again check in with them to ask how they want to proceed. One possibility is to ask if you can join them under the covering and do the validating and extolling in Part II below. Whatever their response is, take your cue from them. Go to Part II when and if they are ready.

Part II: Validating and Extolling the Shame Filled Client

Using this validating and extolling part of the Toxic Shame Busting Protocol requires that the Therapist, group members, or family members know the client/Focus Person who is to be validated and extolled quite well. If this is not the case, then the Therapist, group members, or family members will need to do a research interview with the client to learn the strengths, abilities, and accomplishments of the client in order for this part to work.

The validating and extolling steps are quite simple. Step 1 is for the client/Focus Person to agree to receive the validating and extolling statements—that is to say, to receive high praise from the Therapist, family members, and/or group members. Step 2 is for the Therapist, family member(s) and/or group members to validate and extol the client—that is to give the client high praise and validation for his/her strengths, talents, abilities, accomplishments, values, and character traits. If this protocol is used in a family or group setting, then all the family or group members are to validate and extol the Focus Person by giving her/him their high praise and validation. Step 3 is for the Therapist to check in with the Focus Person to see if he/she was able to take in the high praise and validation. If the client was unable to take in the extolling and validation, then some therapeutic work must be done with the client to remove the block(s) that prevents him/her from taking it in.

The ground rules for this part of the client validating and extolling exercise are as follows: 1. In a group or family setting, those giving the high praise to the Focus Person are to each take a turn doing so and to not use qualifying words like, "sometimes, mostly, usually," and, "on-the-other-hand," for example. 2. The Focus Person receiving the high praise is not to respond except to take in the validating and extolling words, say thank, and refrain from commenting on the high praise received by diminishing it, downplaying it, and explaining it, for example.

How I Use the Toxic Shame Busting Protocol in My Energetic Therapy Practice

To use The Toxic Shame Busting Protocol in an individual therapy session, I ask the client if I can share some positive words about her/him. Then, I simply validate and extol the client with all the high praise that I can lavish on him/her. To use it in a group setting, I have each client be the Focus Person who then receives the other group members' validating and extolling words.

A Case Example of Using the Toxic Shame Protocol

I want to share a case example of how I use The Toxic Shame Busting Protocol to help clients who suffer the debilitating effects of living with a toxic shame shroud. The client in this case example was an addictions counselor in his early 40's. He was married and had one son of college age. He joined my on-going Energetic Therapy group with a complaint that he often felt overwhelmed by life even though he was happily married and loved his job.

In terms of his childhood history, he reported that when he was a very small boy, his father referred to him as, "That Little Bastard," and accused his mother of being a whore. His father also called him a "mama's boy," and made fun of his interests in drawing, painting, and music. His father was an alcoholic who regularly beat his mother when he returned home late at night from the bar. When the client had tried to stop his father from abusing his mother as a boy, his father slapped him silly, laughed at his attempts to intervene, and called him a "feeble little shit".

As an adolescent, his father was always trying to make a man out of him and would repeatedly challenge him to an arm-wrestling match. When he failed to win the arm-wrestling contest, his father told him to, "get his thumb out of his ass," and dismissed him with a kick to his butt. On his birthdays, his father took a candle from the cake which his mother had baked for him, made him hold it in his fingers, lit it, and laughed as it burned down dripping hot wax on his hand. When he dropped the burning hot candle, his father called him a sissy and then used his belt to thrash him.

When he graduated from high school at age 18, his father told him that it was time for him to join the family construction business, but he refused. His father then kicked him out of the house and forbade him to ever show his face at home again. Fortunately, he was able to obtain a full ride scholarship to the State University and studied to become a high school music teacher. Upon graduation he secured a high school teaching position as a music teacher in a nearby school district and married a female math teacher whom he met at the high school.

When their son was born, his wife devoted all her time and attention to their son, and he soon found himself as an outsider in his own home. His regret was that he became very jealous of his son and one day, when his son refused to clean his room, he used a plastic bat to beat his son's butt. He said that it was the only time he was violent with his son and was very ashamed of his unforgivable, angry behavior. He and his wife soon divorced, and it was not long after this that he found and married a woman with a better fit since she was an art teacher at a nearby school and he dabbled in painting. Thus, they had more in common.

His son developed an alcohol problem as a teenager and was treated at a local addiction and rehabilitation center. During this period, the client became very involved in his son's alcohol rehab work. As a result, he later decided to change his career by going back to school to become a social worker and then secure a position as an addiction counselor at the same rehabilitation center where his son had gotten sober.

When he consulted me, he reported that he had always felt like an outsider in the world and recently had lived in a constant state of feeling depressed and overwhelmed with life despite having a meaningful career as well as a happier marriage and family life. I suggested that he join my ongoing Energetic Therapy group to help him overcome his feeling of being an outsider and a loner in life. The members of this group made him feel very welcome which helped him make steady progress in dealing with his depression and feelings of being overwhelmed by life. At a turning point in his therapy, he admitted that he felt very unworthy and sometimes contemplated ending his life because he was often ashamed of not being able to measure up to the high standards of behavior which he imposed on himself. To help him deal with his feelings of shame and unworthiness, I suggested that he use The Toxic Shame Busting Protocol. I explained that this was a tool which I used to help people overcome their feelings of not being worthy and failing to measure up in life. He agreed to give it a try.

To use this powerful protocol with him, I first asked group members to do Energetic Grounding using the Downhill Ski Protocol. Then, with the client serving as the Focus Person, I asked each group member to take a turn validating and extolling him by giving him high praise about his positive qualities, behavior, actions, and character traits which they had witnessed. He was instructed to respond only by saying thank you and not to diminish, downplay, or explain away the group members' validating statements in any way. For examples of the validation and high praise statements that were given to him, see the Box entitled "Validation Highlights" on the next pages.

My Client's Toxic Shame Busting Outcome

When I suggested that my client use the Toxic Shame Busting Protocol exercise, it was my sense that he immediately put on a stoic face and continued his stoic behavior during the validation exercise. I surmised that he did this so that he would not be emotionally touched by the high praise that he received. When the validation exercise was finished, I asked him if he was able to take in the high praise that group members gave him. In response, he instinctively tensed his body, withdrew eye contact, and lowered his head. My sense was that he had again gone into shame. I responded by telling him that I wanted the group members to cover him with a sheet unless he protested. He did not, so they put the sheet over him. At that point he broke into sobs. Several of the group members simply crawled under the sheet with him to give him comfort. They stayed that way for a long period of time. When his emotions settled, he admitted that the high praise he received was difficult for him to hear and take in, not because he

Validation Highlights

1. **Validation Around Courting His Second Wife:**

    Background Information: After meeting his future second wife, my client courted her by asking several of his musical friends to put on an evening performance of her favorite violin-piano concerto and invited her to attend it with him. He picked her up in an old 1956 Cadillac limo that a friend owned, and this friend drove them to performance as their chauffeur. She reported to everyone that it was the highlight of their courtship.

    Example Validation Statements: The group members gave him high praise for his creativity and inventiveness in courting his future wife. They also gave him high marks for his loving, emotional spontaneity, and connection to his love to be, as well as being really tuned into her.

2. **Validation About His Personal Growth Work**

    Background Information: In a men's adventure weekend retreat, part of his center work was to climb a 15-foot-tall ladder to the top and, in spite of his fear of heights, fall backward off the ladder into the linked arms of the men below who caught him. His courage in doing this feat became legendary.

    Example Validation Statements: His group members gave him high praise for his courage to let himself fall off the tall ladder and for his ability to trust and put himself in the hands of the men who cradled him after his fall off the ladder. He also received high praise for overcoming his extreme fear of heights and surrender to the ordeal.

3. **Validation About Forming a Rock Band**

    Background Information: Soon after he was married to his second wife, he formed a rock band in which he played lead guitar and sang as the featured vocalist. The rock band played at local venues and developed a large and loyal following.

    Example Validation Statements: He received high praise from group members for following his musical passion and throwing caution to the wind by starting a rock band at such an advanced, but 'young in attitude' age.

4. **Validation Around His Passion for Painting**

    Background Information: He pursued his painting hobby and was invited to display his paintings at a prestigious art gallery in a nearby city. This resulted in the sale of several of his paintings and earned him the reputation of being 'an up-and-coming artist to keep an eye on'.

    Example Validation Statements: He received high praise for following his passion for painting even though he had no formal artistic training as well as for being willing to take the risk of showing his work in public.

5. **Validation About His Volunteer Fireman Work**

    Background Information: He served as a volunteer fireman in the small town in which he resided and was considered a beloved member of that small fire department.

Example Validation Statements: He received high praise for his volunteer effort and his ability to connect with the other volunteers, most of whom were skilled laborers rather than being college educated and professionally trained as he was.

6. **Validation Regarding His Support for His Son's Addiction Recovery**

    Background Information: When his son entered an addictions recovery program, he stepped up to support his son's recovery effort and stood by him in the difficult days that lay ahead.

    Example Validation Statements: He received high praise for his empathy and compassion as well as his perseverance in supporting his son during such a trying time and challenge.

7. **Validation for His Empathy**

    Background Information: He bought his young son from his second marriage a pet rabbit which was kept in a small, sheltered cage that he built outside to house the pet. During an unexpected cold snap, the pet rabbit, which was affectionately named Peter, froze to death. Following a funeral ceremony for the pet rabbit, he helped his son write letters to Peter Rabbit telling him how much they missed him, which his son then mailed to Peter Rabbit, Heaven, USA.

    Example Validation Statements: He received high praise for his empathetic response to his young son's grief in losing a 'loved member' of the family and his creative response in helping his son heal from the trauma of his pet's death.

8. **Validation for His Contributions to Others**

    Background Information: He had spent over two decades as a music teacher and addiction counselor.

    Example Validation Statements: The group members gave him high praise for his commitment to helping his music students and addiction patients achieve their goals and live better lives. He also received high marks for his empathetic understanding of his charges and willingness to always go the extra mile to care for them.

9. **Validation for His Energetic Therapy Work**

    Background Information: He was in Energetic Group Therapy for more than a year.

    Example Validation Statements: The group members gave him high praise for all the trauma healing work he had done and especially for volunteering to do the Toxic Shame Busting Protocol exercise and said that it demonstrated his strong desire to continually better himself. They also said that he inspired them to do their own healing work.

did not want to hear it, but because it tapped into a deep personal longing for acceptance, recognition, and validation, none of which he received from his childhood father.

Thus, the high praise that was lavishly heaped on my client was something that he longed to receive but was also very painful for him to hear. He also added that the cover over him felt safe because his childhood father could not see what a sissy he was for crying. This elicited a pained expression from his group members, and they rushed to give him high praise and validation for being able to express his deep sadness and that he was no less of a man for doing so. In fact, they added that he was more of a man. It was then that he removed the sheet covering and emerged to bask in his group members' love, admiration, and cheers.

During the reflective processing that followed, the client said that the whole validation experience had a profound effect of lifting him out from under his toxic shame shroud for the first time in his life, and for this he was very grateful to everyone.

Knowing that my client had avoided any time in therapy dealing with his mother's role in his childhood trauma, I invited him to do a session with my female colleague, who is also a co-author of this article. By employing Rogerian active listening to gain his trust and repeatedly using, over time the validation strategy described above to extoll his revelations, she was able to help him successfully face and heal the toxic shame trauma that he suffered as a young boy when his father sexually abused him while his mother turned a blind eye.

Other Methods of Helping Clients Lift Their Toxic Shame Shrouds

There are some other methods for helping toxic shame victims get out from under their shame shrouds, at least on a temporary basis. My experience is that clients are often not ready to embrace the Toxic Shame Busting Protocol with its validating and extolling process. For one thing, receiving validation and high praise from others can bring up buried and painful feelings that may be overwhelming even for seasoned trauma therapy clients. For another, there can be a prohibition on the part of many clients about receiving high praise as reflected in such parental statements like, "Don't get too full of yourself." When this kind of resistance is encountered, there are some alternative methods of helping clients alleviate and deal with their toxic shame. In the box below, I cite a few resources that contain ideas and methods that I have used successfully with toxic shame filled clients who were reluctant to engage in the validating and extolling process prior to using The Toxic Shame Busting Protocol.

Additional Resources for Healing Toxic Shame

Byron Brown, in his handbook *Soul Without Shame*, describes a number of practical strategies for dealing with the workings of the mind which cause people to go into shame and to unwittingly perpetuate it in their lives. (Brown, 1999.)

Bernard Golden in his April 22, 2017, Psychology Today article, *Overcoming the Paralysis of Toxic Shame*, identifies a number of key strategies for getting rid of toxic shame.

Michael Lewis has written a very informative and helpful book on dealing with toxic shame entitled, *Shame: The Exposed Self* (1995), New York: Simon & Schuster.

More on Innovations in Healing Trauma & Client-directed Energetic Therapy

Including:

1. Using the Bilateral Tapping Protocol to Heal Trauma: A Case Example

2. Using the Energetic Peer Co-counseling Therapy to Help Trauma Clients Heal: A Case Example

3. Using the Trauma Sleep Disturbance Remedy Protocol to Help Clients Fall Asleep AT Night

4. Energetic Therapy for Survivors of Childhood and Adult Trauma on Zoom

5. Training for Therapists, Assist Persons, And Clients on Using Energetic Trauma Healing Therapy on Zoom

6. 6. Tips and Cautions for Therapists on Helping Clients Restructure Their Energetic Holding Defenses

7. A Recommended Energetic Therapy Progression Sequence

8. Our Energetic Therapy Outcome Results

Using The Bi-lateral Tapping Protocol to Heal Trauma: A Case Example

This client used The Bi-lateral Tapping Protocol to help work through his internal resistance which was keeping him from moving forward with his trauma healing work.

Client's Background History

At the time of this intervention, this client was in his mid-50s, divorced, with no children, and working as a manager of a large vehicle repair company. He entered Energetic Therapy with me about a year prior to this case example. He had made good progress in healing his childhood trauma caused by his demanding father, a Calvinistic protestant minister, who expected him to perform above and beyond with heroic effort.

Client's Therapy Session

I began his therapy session by asking him what he wanted to have happen in the session. His response was he was feeling overwhelmed in his life. "I feel swarmed by pressures that feel too great to handle," he said.

"What are these pressures?" I asked.

"I don't know," he said. "It is not work, or the church. Nor is it my family life. I just don't know what it is."

"So, is it some kind of internal pressure you are putting on yourself?" I asked.

"I guess so since I cannot think of any outside pressures that are causing me to feel overwhelmed." he replied. "But I don't know what the internal pressure is. So, I feel stuck."

To help him get unstuck, I suggested he stand or sit and use bi-lateral tapping of his body to access hidden thoughts, feelings and memories which might be keeping him mired down. I further instructed him to alternately slow tapping of one side and then the other side of his body in a repeated sequential fashion and let any thoughts, feelings, emotions, memories, and/or spontaneous movements arise from his body and mind as they would. In addition, he was to speak his thoughts, feelings, and memories aloud, note his spontaneous movements, and follow them wherever they led.

While standing, he chose to tap the top of his right leg with his right hand followed by tapping the top of his left leg with his left hand. He repeated the taps at a little less than one second intervals. As he did so, he began shifting his weight from one foot to the other. "My right side feels weaker than my left side as I shift my weight back and forth," he observed."

"Yes, I see your right ankle is pronated inward," I responded. I then suggested he use The Spontaneous Movement Protocol to go to a still place in his body and mind, and then let a spontaneous movement arise from his body that helps him strengthen his weak right ankle. He immediately rocked his ankles outward to stand on the edges of his feet.

"Wow, that feels a lot stronger," he said.

He then continued tapping his legs. "The word that comes to mind is obligation," he said. "I always felt a huge obligation being placed on me as a boy by my childhood father. 'Do this and then do that to better the world and to be great—win the Nobel Prize,' were his words over and over again while I was growing up."

"So, you felt obligated to do 'this and that' at his bidding in order to better the world and be great," I repeated back to him.

"Yes, that is it!" he exclaimed. "My father was greatly energized by his overwhelming obligation to help others and make the world a safer, better place. It was his ministerial crusade. But that did not energize me! I felt burdened by it all."

"What energized you as a boy?" I asked.

"I got energized by learning new things, and by creating a fantasy world in which I was the hero such as writing fictional stories and theatrical plays where I was the central heroic character." As he said those words, his whole demeanor changed from looking burdened and defeated to looking alive, animated, and fully present in his body.

I then suggested he continue tapping to get out from under his burden and stuck place. As he started tapping again, a big smile lit up his face. "Yes, I need to take time to learn new things and be creative. I need to start writing fictional stories again, "he said. "I don't have to feel obligated to make the world a better place or feel pressured to do great things. Nor am I obligated to become a great person by winning the Nobel Prize. Those were Dad's personal obligations and pressures which he then put on me. They were not my obligations and responsibilities!"

With this statement, he continued tapping his legs. Then, he suddenly stopped as if surprised by something. "But why do I feel so guilty and ashamed?" he asked. "I realize my father sold me a big lie as a boy! Yet, I still feel I should have measured up to his expectations. That is nuts!" He shook his shoulders as if trying to remove the frozen burden of his boyhood guilt and shame. "It is all too confusing and crazy."

In the next session, he worked on thawing out his frozen guilt and shame core which had resulted from the trauma shock of his boyhood father's threat to his existence. First, I suggested he stand on a small trampoline to ground using The Downhill Ski Energetic Grounding Protocol. Then I suggested he stand on the floor and try to activate his body's innate, natural healing process by inducing a trembling, shaking muscle response to begin thawing out his frozen core. To help him do this, I ask him first to recall a time when his boyhood father did something so traumatizing to him that it scared him to death. Then I instructed him to picture the event in his mind while bi-laterally tapping his legs and concurrently to simulate a trembling, shaking fright response in his body. As he did so, the simulated trembling and shaking turned to real, spontaneous trembling and shaking. I encouraged him to let his body tremble and shake until it subsided of its own accord.

"Wow, that was intense," he said, looking at me with questioning eyes. I explained his spontaneous trembling and shaking was his body's way of healing the trauma shock that he had experienced at the hands of his demanding, overpowering, boyhood father. I asked him how he felt following the experience. He reported he was less dissociated and more present in his body.

He continued, during the next several Energetic Therapy sessions, to move his trauma healing therapy forward by using The Bi-lateral Tapping Protocol, The Spontaneous Movement Protocol and The Trembling-Shaking Protocol (which can be found under the name of what I fondly call, The Shake-Rattle-And-Roll Protocol) to work through and resolve the burden of his boyhood guilt and shame which had enveloped him like a giant, frozen shame shroud.

Reflecting On His Therapy Session

Clearly his use of the Bi-lateral Tapping Protocol (see below) helped my client face his traumatic boyhood, which was characterized by having to deal with his demanding, overpowering father who expected him to perform at heroic levels and look at it in a new light. It was as if the bi-lateral tapping allowed him to finally see the lie his childhood father had sold him—that he was obligated to follow in his father's footsteps to help make the world a better place and to do great things like winning the Nobel Prize. It helped him thaw out his frozen core of guilt and shame which had burdened him for failing to measure up to his father's overwhelming expectations as a boy. Furthermore, it helped him access his own inner wisdom to find what energized him thus allowing him to begin moving out from under the burdened, stuck place in his life. It helped him move forward with his Energetic Therapy and trauma healing, to resolve the shame shroud which had continued to envelop and dog him as an adult.

The Bi-lateral Tapping Protocol

Instructions: To use The Bi-lateral Tapping Protocol with your client, follow these steps:

1. Have your client tap one side of his/her body and then tap the other side in a slow repeated sequential fashion as if mimicking the swinging pendulum of a clock as it swings back and forth from one side of the clock to the other side. Have your client choose the area of the body on which to tap such as the sides of the temple, the sides of the chest, the sides of the hips, or the tops of the legs, for example. This tapping can be done standing or seated.

2. As your client taps her/his body, suggest that he/she give voice to any thoughts, feelings, emotions, memories, and/or spontaneous movement that emerge or arise from her/his body-mind. Your client can use these elicited thoughts, feelings, emotions, memories, and spontaneous movements to help move his/her trauma healing therapy forward.

3. If a spontaneous movement arises from your client's body, have her/him note the spontaneous movement. This movement can be a large movement like shifting his/her weight from one foot to the other or closing her/his hand to make a fist, for example, or a small or tiny movement

such as lifting an eyebrow or dropping the corner of his/her mouth, for example. Then instruct her/him to voice any thoughts, feelings, or memories connected to the movement. Also, you can suggest your client amplify or study the movement by exaggerating it, forcefully repeating it, or repeat it while watching herself/himself do so in a mirror, for example. Another spontaneous movement might arise following your client's initial spontaneous movement. If this happens, have your client voice any thoughts, feelings, and memories connected to the movement as well as to any further movements, and so on.

Notes: This client suffered from having adopted an Energetic Holding Out Defense which he used to help protect himself by dissociating from his body and living in a fantasy world of his own creation as a boy. His mother was not available to him as a child as she was dying from cancer nor was his father available as he was continually on 'ministerial crusades'. The exception was to place unreasonable demands and expectations on him which he could not hope to achieve. The main energetic trauma healing work centered around helping him become energetically well-grounded and thaw out his frozen core which had developed from the childhood shock of having his very existence threatened by his unavailable parents.

Using Energetic Peer Co-Counseling to Help Clients Affordably Heal Their Trauma

In this section I will introduce the Energetic Peer Co-counseling Protocol which is designed to help clients engage in longer term trauma healing Energetic Therapy more affordably by doing Energetic Co-counseling rather than engaging in individual and/or group Energetic Therapy which can become expensive over the longer term. Of course, if clients who can afford to do both individual/group Energetic Therapy and Energetic Peer Co-counseling and/or their health insurance will pay for both may do so. My colleagues and I have offered this option to our clients and found those who can take advantage of doing both types of Energetic Therapy move their trauma healing forward at a very rapid and intense pace.

First, provide clients who are going to engage in doing Energetic Peer Co-counseling with some training in how to use the co-counseling protocol. We conduct workshops, or what we call Fire Circle Co-counseling Training, which our clients as well as new participants can engage to learn how to use the Energetic Peer Co-counseling to move their trauma healing forward. Then, have your clients use the Energetic Peer Co-counseling Protocol (presented below) to do their Energetic Therapy.

The Energetic Peer Co-Counseling Protocol

This protocol is used by trauma clients in a peer setting under the guidance of a Coach/Therapist. It can be used in either a Zoom type meeting or in an in-person meeting. To use the Energetic Co-counseling Protocol, follow these steps:

Step 1: Have the clients form peer co-counseling trios.

Step 2: Have the co-counseling trio members decide who will be the Focus Person who will do his/her Energetic Therapy work, which trio member will be the Assist Person who will help the Focus Person work, and which trio member will be the Monitor and Safety Person who will help keep the Energetic Therapy work on track and safe.

Step 3: Have the trio members Jump Start an energy charge in their bodies by engaging in some vigorous physical exercise such as doing jumping jacks. Then have them follow this by doing Energetic Grounding such as using the Hair-pin Energetic Grounding Protocol.

Step 4: Instruct the Focus Person to begin their Energetic Therapy work by stating a healing intention for their work.

Step 5: Suggest the Focus Person use the Spontaneous Movement Protocol to direct their Energetic Therapy work to realize their stated healing intention and move their trauma healing work forward with the help of their Assist Person and Monitor and Safety Person.

Step 6: During the Focus Person's Energetic Therapy work, as the Coach/Therapist, suggest the use of various Energetic Therapy Protocols (presented in this handbook) as needed to help them work through any internal resistance encountered and move their therapy work forward.

Step 7: When the Focus Person finishes their Energetic Therapy work, or their allotted time is up, have the Focus Person energetically ground themselves by using one of the Energetic Grounding Protocols (also found in this handbook).

Step 8: Repeat the above steps with new trio members taking a turn at being the Focus Person, Assist Person, and Monitor and Safety Person.

Step 9: When each trio member has taken a turn at being the Focus Person, Assist Person, and Monitor and Safety Person, end the session by having everyone do Energetic Grounding.

For more information on using the Energetic Co-counseling Protocol, see the chapter on using this protocol in *Innovations in Healing Trauma, Vol. I* (2023).

A Case Example

Here is a case example of my client who used the Energetic Peer Co-counseling Protocol to move his trauma healing forward. He was 40 years old, married, and worked as a product development manager in a large tech company.

To jump start a good energy charge in their bodies, the trio members kicked a large, heavy pillow back and forth between each other. Then they followed the kicking by doing Energetic Grounding using the Downhill Ski Energetic Grounding Protocol.

When it was my client's turn to be the Focus Person, he Ground he stated his healing intention was to take better care of his health.

Here is the way the remainder of his co-counseling session went.

"Over the Christmas holidays I let go of taking care of myself," he said. "I stopped running and working out each day as I had done before Christmas. I ate poorly, consuming a lot of sweets and carbohydrates as well as drinking a considerable amount of alcohol. Thus, I put on a lot of weight in a short amount of time. I also began to feel depressed and fall asleep during the day while having difficulty sleeping at night. On a mental level, my Inner Judge began attacking me in my mind for being such a slacker and yelled at me to just suck it up and get back in shape." He stopped talking at that point and hung his head in despair.

His Assist Person intervened, asking. "Then what happened?"

Still looking down at the floor, he answered. "I resented being pushed around by my Inner Judge's words to get back in line, and did just the opposite," he replied. "So, I ate more, drank more, and slept more. Now I feel awful and stuck!"

His Assist Person, who was female, suggested he use the Spontaneous Movement Protocol to help himself get unstuck. He reluctantly did so. His spontaneous movement was to make his hands into fists.

"What do you want to do with your fists?" his Assist Person asked.

"I want to punch my Inner Judge in the face," he said.

"I want you to Imagine looking at your Inner Judge's face," she said. "Who do you see?"

He paused for a moment and then answered, "I see the face of my father. My father was always telling me to 'suck it up and get with the program' when he thought I was not behaving the way he wanted me to behave. It was very demeaning, and I felt totally dis-empowered."

"So, what do you want now?" she asked.

He faced her and answered, "I want my power back!"

His Assist Person turned to the trio Coach who was very experienced in using the Energetic Peer Co-counseling Protocol. The Coach suggested they use the Tug of War Protocol to help him regain his power. To accomplish this, the Assist Person handed him a towel with which to use like a rope in doing the tug of war.

At that point, the Monitor and Safety Person, who was also female, intervened to ensure the Tug of War Protocol was done in a safe manner by placing chairs behind each of them in case they accidentally let go of the towel. Thus, they would fall back into the chairs rather than crashing to the floor and hurting themselves. She also instructed them to keep their body weight balanced over their well-spaced legs rather than let their tail ends hang backward without leg support underneath them.

When all was in place to ensure safety, the tug of war proceeded with the Focus Person trying to take the towel away from the Assist Person while yelling, "Give me back my Power! It is mine! I am taking it back!" and so on. The tug of war ended when he took the towel away from his Assist Person.

After they had rested, the Assist Person asked him, "How was that?"

"It felt good," he answered, standing erect with his shoulders uplifted, a grin on his face. and a gleam in his eyes.

The Coach intervened at that point to suggest the Assist Person ask the Focus Person what blessing or validation words he would have wanted to hear from his childhood father after taking back his power. He responded, saying, "I would have wanted my father to have said, 'I admire your strength, persistence, resilience, and power. I know you will solve the issue you are facing. You always have and you will do so again. You have great stuff inside you. You have great courage and fortitude."

Then his Assist Person repeated back his blessing words he would have loved to have heard from his father. As she did so, tears began to stream from his eyes. When she finished repeating the blessing words he would have wanted to hear, he was sobbing. She and the Monitor and Safety Person moved to embrace him while he cried. When his crying subsided and they ceased embracing, they ended the session by doing energetic grounding.

My client reported, following his Energetic Peer Co-counseling Session, he had returned to his prior to Christmas routine of taking care of himself and his health.

Using The Trauma Sleep Disturbance Remedy Protocol to Help Clients Fall Asleep At Night

Trauma clients often complain of not being able to fall asleep at night and waking up from a nightmare dream and not being able to fall back asleep. This protocol can help them remedy such a sleep disturbance. Here is a case example of a client who used The Sleep Disturbance Remedy Protocol to get a better night's rest whenever she encountered such sleep disturbances.

I Am So Tired: A Case Example

While doing Energetic Therapy work, my client ceased all movement, closed her eyes, and was mute for several moments. When I asked her what was going on, she let out an exhausted sigh and whispered, "I am so bone tired." She paused for another few moments, and then said," I am not sleeping at night. I can't fall asleep for hours and then when I finally do sleep, I wake up from a nightmare and can't fall back asleep for hours." I asked her how long this had been going on. She answered, "For my whole life, it seems to me."

I followed up by suggesting the client use The Trauma Sleep Disturbance Remedy Protocol in order to help her get some better rest at night. To practice using the protocol, I asked the client to lay backside down on a mat with her knees in a raised position and her feet placed flat on the floor spaced about twelve inches apart. Then, I asked her to raise her pelvis off the floor into an arched stretch and then lower her butt, so it was about an inch above the floor. Next, I asked her to relax her pelvic floor by pushing outward as if having a bowel movement and to maintain this position until she was tired of doing it. I also suggest she imagine a babbling brook running beneath her bridged body which fed her energy and spirit. As she did so, she developed a vibratory movement in her lower body and reported a pleasurable streaming in her pelvic musculature as she maintained the position.

After a time, she lowered her butt to the floor and rested. When she was rested, I suggested she do the exercise two more times, resting in between each round.

When the client finished doing the third round, I asked her how she felt. "I feel really relaxed and rested," she said with a big smile on her face. I then suggested whenever she had difficulty sleeping at night, she use The Trauma Sleep Disturbance Remedy Protocol while lying in bed to help her fall asleep, or to fall back asleep whenever she awoke during the night.

In a later therapy session, I asked the client, who I noticed was looking much more alive and present, how she was sleeping at night. She replied that, thanks to using The Trauma Sleep Disturbance Remedy Protocol, she was finally getting a good night's rest almost every night.

The Trauma Sleep Disturbance Remedy Protocol

If you are a client, follow the steps below. If you are a Therapist, in order to teach and have your clients practice using this protocol in your office, give them these instructions:

1. Lay back side down on a mat with your knees in a raised position and your feet placed flat on the floor spaced about twelve inches apart.

2. Raise your pelvis up off the floor with your back in an arched stretch and then lower your butt so it is about an inch above the floor.

3. Relax your pelvic floor by pushing outward as if having a bowel movement and maintain this position until you're tired of doing so.

4. Imagine a babbling brook running beneath your bridged body which is feeding your energy and spirit.

5. Let a vibratory movement develop in your lower body which will eventually cause a pleasurable streaming in your pelvic musculature as you use and maintain the position. Let this pleasurable streaming move down into your legs and feet and up into your torso/upper body as it will.

6. When you tire of maintaining the position, lower your butt and back to the floor and rest.

7. When you are rested, repeat the above steps at least two more times, resting in between each round.

8. Use this raised bridge protocol whenever you have difficulty falling asleep, or when you awake during the night and have trouble falling back asleep. The best part is you can use this protocol while lying in bed to help you fall asleep. Thus, there is also no need to get out of bed to use this protocol or do Energetic Grounding when you awake during the night and want some help falling back asleep.

Zoom Energetic Therapy for Survivors of Childhood and Adult Trauma

The Center for Innovations in Healing Trauma has developed a Zoom Energetic Therapy Program for survivors of childhood and adult trauma who want the help of an energetic Therapist trained in the Innovations in Healing Trauma Approach presented in this handbook. For more information on this training visit the Innovations in Healing Trauma website at www.innovationsinhealingtrauma.com.

Zoom Training for Therapists, Assist Persons, And Clients on Using Energetic Therapy To Move Trauma Healing Forward

The Center for Innovations in Healing Trauma has developed a Zoom training for Therapists, Assist Persons and clients who want to get Energetic Therapy Training in the Innovations in Healing Trauma approach presented in this handbook. For more information on this training visit the Innovations in Healing Trauma website at www.innovationsinhealingtrauma.com.

Tips & Cautions for Helping Clients Restructure Their Energetic Holding Defenses

The following Tips and Cautions for helping clients restructure their Energetic Holding Defenses, presented below, come from more than two decades of doing Energetic Trauma Healing Therapy with clients.

General Tips & Cautions

Their Energetic Holding Defenses

1. When clients set a healing intention and then use the Spontaneous Movement Protocol to self-direct their Energetic Therapy, if you as the Therapist, Assist Person, or client miss the initial spontaneous movement that arises from the client's body, simply follow the next spontaneous movement wherever it leads. The client's body will keep yielding spontaneous movements which if followed wherever they lead will move the client toward realizing her/his healing intention(s).

2. Introducing clients to the Restructuring of the Energetic Holding Defenses Protocol too early in their trauma healing therapy can shift them into intellectualizing about

their healing process as they dwell on trying to identity their specific holding defense(s) rather than letting their therapy unfold organically in its own way and time and move them to do the energetic restructuring of their holding defense(s) as their inner body wisdom dictates.

3. Clients may need to be reminded they are not their holding defense(s) but rather, persons who adopted the holding defense(s) as children to stop the pain of their childhood trauma and prevent it from happening again in the future.

4. Clients need to work with a strong energetic charge in their body otherwise their trauma healing progress may stall or slow to a crawl. Having them do intense energetic exercise like bouncing on a trampoline, hitting a pillow with a tennis racket, or running in place, for example, will build a strong energetic charge in their body as their breathing deepens and blood pumps through their body.

5. Clients and Therapists need to do energetic grounding at the beginning of a therapy session, during the therapy session such as before engaging in an energetic activity, at the end of an energetic activity, for example, and at the end of the therapy session so they do not leave in an ungrounded state which might cause them to be distracted and have an accident or get lost while traveling home.

Tips & Cautions for Working with Clients with a Holding Back Defense

1. Therapists' understanding of the basis for the Holding Back Defense is vital to the successful restructuring of this defense. Johnson [1994], discussing this issue regarding the Willful Determined sub-type, writes, "Getting the

story straight about the history that motivates this extreme need for control and proper functioning in all realms can yield the kind of sympathetic understanding for the self that these individuals require." (p. 67).

2. It is important to keep clients with a Holding Back Defense in the present "here and now" moment in the restructuring process and to encourage greater attention, exploration, and expression of feelings rather than thoughts.

3. The realness of the Therapist in the therapeutic restructuring process with these clients is very important to its success.

4. Clients with a Holding Back Defense need to access their spontaneous feelings, thoughts, movements, and behaviors regarding the expression of their sexuality and animal nature which were stifled, cut off, and banned by their caretakers. They must come to see and accept these feelings, thoughts, movements, and behaviors as normal, healthy, and good.

5. One of the most serious mistakes Therapists make with these clients is to collude with them by treating them in a distant, non-feeling, intellectually oriented mode of therapy. Therapists who have a Holding Back Defense can be prone to make this mistake. In addition, these clients do not respond well to cognitive and behavior therapy which may prove to be counterproductive because it does not help them access their real feelings and emotions.

6. Vital to the success of the restructuring of the Holding Back Defense is the energetic body work. For example, a pressure roller/stool is used to release the holding in the muscles of the back, chest, diaphragm, and pelvis. Biting

on a hand gripper or folded washcloth helps to release the holding in the jaw and neck muscles. Taking a towel away from an Assist Person while yelling, "I want your love," for example, is effective at mobilizing clients' aggression. Rapid kicking on a thick pillow while lying back down on the floor releases the holding in the pelvis. Having clients reach out to an Assist Person's face with their hands while saying, "I love you," helps open their heart.

7. Clients with a Holding Back Defense often complain of back pain. The long muscles of their back tend to be extremely rigid as they stand ramrod straight with their shoulders pulled back. This puts severe stress on their back muscles thus producing the back pain. Releasing the muscle holding in their back will help get rid of this back pain, however, helping them create a strong body foundation will also release their back pain. Therefore, I suggest they do a body foundation basic workout on a regular basis. This basic workout is found in *Foundation: Redefining Your Core, Conquer Back Pain, and Move with Confidence* by Eric Goodman & Peter Park (2011). I also suffered back pain until I began using these five core exercises in the *Foundation Basic Workout* three times per week. Now, I am back pain free as are the clients who do this *Foundation Basic Workout* regularly.

Tips & Cautions for Working with Clients with a Holding In Defense

1. Therapists working to help these clients restructure their Holding In Defense lifestyle of self-defeating behavior, pessimism, distrust, and depression can be defeated by being invested in successfully therapy outcomes with them. Rather, Therapists must be detached from the

therapy outcomes and make it clear to these clients they are responsible for the success and failure outcomes in their therapy.

2. These clients are very difficult to work with. If they make progress, it will be a slow, halting, grinding process. As a result, Therapists may get frustrated and fed up with these clients who work tirelessly to defeat the therapy. This can cause Therapists to have feelings of incompetence, pessimism, anger, and hopelessness as these clients try to defeat the Therapist just as they were defeated in childhood by their caretakers. Thus, infinite patience and tolerance is required on the part of Therapists during the long, hard trauma healing process.

3. Vital to a successful outcome of the therapy with these clients is the energetic body work that must be done to release the muscular holding and tension in their expressive organs—face, arms, hands, pelvis, legs and feet. Doing this will allow them to discharge the enormous, compressed energy in their torso and express the anger and rage at having suffered such intolerable intrusion and over control abuse from their childhood caretakers. For example, having them twist a towel while imagining they are wringing the neck of their abusive caretaker, while yelling, "No", or taking a towel away from an Assist Person who resists giving it up while yelling, "I want it!" will help release the holding in their hands, wrists, and shoulders. Having them drink a glass of water on an empty stomach and then use the tail end of a toothbrush to gag themselves to throw up the water helps release the holding in their throat, jaw, tongue, and mouth muscles. Having them bite on a towel held in their mouth while an Assist Person tries to pull it free will help release the

holding in their jaw and throat. Having them stomp on a pillow and kick it around the room will help release the holding in their feet, legs, and pelvis. Squeezing foam hand grippers will help release holding in their hands and wrists. Hitting a pillow with their fists while yelling, "No, I won't!" helps to release holding in their hands and shoulders and will mobilize their aggression. Having them throw a temper tantrum on a thick foam body-length pad helps to mobilize their aggression and release their bottled-up anger and rage.

Tips & Cautions for Working with Clients with a Holding Up Defense

1. Clients with a Holding Up Defense have a deep narcissistic wound and therefore exhibit all the character traits narcissists are famous for displaying. The most important thing Therapists can do to help them heal the traumatic loss of their real self in favor of adopting a false self is to really listen to them in an empathetic and compassionate way, so they feel genuinely understood. In this regard, Johnson [1994] writes, "It is very therapeutic for the narcissistic client simply to show vulnerability and confess his grandiosity in a setting where he can be emphatically understood." Further he writes, "A narcissistic individual will often express surprise that another person is genuinely interested and caring, and after that surprise, will begin to experience the extraordinary longing that she has always had for such concern." In my experience, Johnson could not be more right on.

2. Another very important task Therapists need to attend to with these clients is to help them grieve their childhood trauma injury as well as the loss of their true self.

3. Therapists should not immediately confront these clients with a narcissistic diagnosis or work quickly to deflate their grandiose self-image and inflated vision of themselves. Doing so is likely to generate a great deal of anxiety in them and may prematurely end the therapy as they head for the hills. I also suggest that body-centered Therapists using the energetic trauma healing approach presented in this handbook, not use the Start-up Protocol and the self-diagnosis Energetic Holding Defenses checklist with these clients until considerable energetic trauma healing work has been completed and a strong bond of trust has been developed with the Therapist.

4. Clients with a Holding Up Defense develop energetic blocks in the body to restrain or make unconscious impulses and behaviors that were deemed unacceptable by their childhood caretakers and stop feeling the pain of their caretaker exploitation and abuse that was inflicted on them very early. Both the Power-controlling and Seductive-controlling sub-types have a pelvis that is tightly constricted and rigidly held with the pelvic floor exhibiting severe muscle contractions preventing awareness and release of their sexual charge which is weak in the former sub-type and much stronger in the latter sub-type. For example, having them do rapid kicking with the legs and feet on a thick pillow while laying back down on the floor helps release the holding in the pelvis. Having them repeatedly tighten and relax the muscles of the pelvic floor helps release this holding. There is often a constriction at the waist that also reduces awareness of their sexual impulse as well as blocks awareness of their lack of energetic grounding. In addition, there is often a constriction of the muscles around the diaphragm which

inhibits full respiration as well as awareness of bodily feelings. These areas of holding can be addressed by having them lay over a pressure roller/stool to soften and release this holding. This will also help deflate the puffed-up chest of the Power-controlling sub-type. The lack of energetic grounding needs to be addressed by having them do grounding exercises such as standing on a small trampoline to get a vibration moving in their legs and feet which strengthens them, or doing the Wall-sit Protocol, for example, which will have a similar result. There is often tightness in their fear-raised shoulders which can be released with the use of the pressure roller/stool. There is usually tightness in the muscles of the neck, and always severe contractions in the muscles at the base of the skull. Both areas of holding prevent the flow of feelings from the body to the head and brain. This blocks awareness of the emotional and physical pain they suffer from having had to give up their real self in favor of a false self. Vibratory and slow movement stretching can also help release this holding.

However, the release of the severe holding at the base of the skull may require a skilled massage or cranial-sacral Therapist to address it in a gradual manner. Immediate unskillful release can cause these clients to go into a rage as they get in touch with how their childhood caretakers exploited them. Finally, there is often an eye block, along with the ocular block at the base of the skull, which prevents them from seeing the truth of their painful childhood situation as well as keeps them from seeing others as real human beings instead of human objects. This eye block can be worked with by having them follow a finger which is moved slowly back and forth and up and down just in front of their eyes. This can generate strong feelings of fear and terror, especially as the finger begins to move out of sight range.

5. These clients tend to become indignant or angry with Therapists who do not make themselves immediately available at a moment's notice, or do not give them extra time for the therapy session, or charges them extra for running overtime in a session. Or they may become jealous and openly resentful of Therapists for seeing other patients. Thus, it is important to set firm boundaries and limitations with them, so they do not continue to see themselves as special and entitled.

6. These clients are very likely to show up in Therapists offices exhibiting multiple Energetic Holding Defenses in addition to their Holding Up Defense. They are especially likely to show a Holding Out Defense, and a Holding On Defense. This is because they were reared by narcissistic caretakers who are notorious for being poor parents at all ages and stages of their children's development. Therapists simply must address and restructure the energetic holding defense that presents itself at any given time. Therapists must, however, be aware they are in for a long haul if these clients make the choice to stay in therapy to resolve and restructure all their several Energetic Holding Defenses.

7. Clients with a Holding Up Defense can present themselves as very high functioning as they try to be the best and most perfect at all they do, including being the perfect client. However, this high state of energetic charge in their upper body and head tends to keep them in a continually revved up condition which can eventually lead to burnout, collapse, and illness. Helping them learn

to play, relax, let down, and achieve balance in their life is very important for their physical and mental health.

Tips & Cautions for Working with Clients with a Clinging Holding On Defense

1. These clients tend to be very needy and thus cling to the Therapist. Therapists can easily get irritated and fed up with such clinging and sucking behavior which then can cause these clients to become even more clinging or cause them to terminate therapy early.

2. Therapists who are themselves needy may promise more than they can deliver to these clients which will eventually defeat the therapy as these clients become disappointed once again thus repeating their childhood trauma of disappointment.

3. These clients have underdeveloped, undercharged musculature which must be developed using energetic exercises such as bouncing on a small trampoline while holding their breath which develops their respiration, and then standing on it with flexed knees to create a vibration in the muscles of the lower body which will, over time, build up these muscles and strengthen them. This will also greatly increase their energetic grounding which is sorely lacking. Using a pressure roller/stool to create vibration in the upper body will have the same effect upon these undercharged and underdeveloped muscles, building them up and strengthening them.

Tips & Cautions for Working with Clients with a Joined-at-the-Hip Holding On Defense

1. The main aim of Energetic Therapy with these clients is to resurrect and develop their true, real self. The

energetic work must lessen their sense of obligation and accommodation to others, increase their capacity for self-expression, alleviate their fears of hurting others by being separate and different from them, and increase their ability to find pleasure in their lives, give them a solid understanding of their childhood history and the arrested development their childhood caretakers caused them by their symbiotic holding on to them which prevented them from separating and individuating, and help them answer the question, "Who am I?" with regard to their likes and dislikes, preferences, aptitudes, abilities, ambitions, values, and beliefs.

2. These clients develop energetic blocks in their body to keep their real self from emerging, prevent self-expression, accommodate others at their own expense, and stop feeling the pain and trauma caused by their childhood caretakers who thwarted and delayed their natural separation and individuation process by prolonging their dependency and symbiotic attachment. These clients lack energetic grounding and have underdeveloped and undercharged lower bodies with weak legs and feet that prevent them from really standing on their own two feet. Having them do an energetic grounding exercise such as standing on a small trampoline to induce vibration and streaming in their lower body, especially in their legs, will help strengthen, charge, and develop these muscles. They will have muscle tension, contractions, and constrictions in their pelvis, around their waist and diaphragm as well as in their chest. Having them use the pressure roller/stool to release this holding will improve their sexual feeling and functioning and allow them to experience a fuller and deeper respiration thus creating more energy

and feeling in their body. They will have muscle holding in the parts of their body that prevent self-expression and natural aggression to reach out for what they want. Having them to hit a pillow with a tennis racket while yelling, "No, I won't give up myself for you!" or, taking a towel away from an Assist Person while yelling, "I want my real self back!" or, twisting a towel as if to wring their childhood caretakers' neck while yelling, "How dare you steal who I am just to accommodate you!" or, kicking a pillow around the room while yelling, "No, I won't take care of you at my expense!", for example, will help to release the holding in these parts of their body, mobilize their aggression, and discharge their held in anger and hostility. They have severe holding in their neck and at the base of their skull to prevent their bodily pain and the awareness of their abusive situation from reaching their head and brain. Having them do neck stretching and vibratory release exercises to discharge the holding there as well at the base of their skull will allow them to realize and feel the damage that has been done to them and grieve the loss of their real self. They have holding in their shoulders, arms and hands which block their impulse to reach out for what they want. Having them do vibratory strengthening and stretching exercises to release this holding will allow them to reach out for real relationships, interests, activities, and experiences that can be truly satisfying and fulfilling for them.

3. Using the Spontaneous Movement Protocol with these clients is very important. It helps them spontaneously express their real feelings and emotions. It also helps them identify their real self preferences, likes and dislikes, interests, values, and beliefs. These clients are

not known for being spontaneous, so it helps them in this area as well.

Tips & Cautions for Working with Clients with a Holding Out Defense

1. With clients who have a Holding Out Defense, Therapists working to release the frozen, blocked energy at the base of the skull, around the diaphragm, and in the pelvic joints, must do so slowly and carefully to prevent the compressed energy in these areas from flooding and overwhelming their defenses and exploding into retaliatory rage. For example, my Bioenergetic trainer reported that his Therapist tried to release the holding at the base of his skull by giving it a karate chop which immediately sent him into rage and later turned his brown and gray head hair completely white.

2. Therapists who conduct therapy with these clients in an impersonal, totally rational, and behavioral or mechanical way without feeling, empathy, and compassion will collude with them and deepen their pain of having been reared by impersonal, mechanical caretakers.

3. Therapy which is too affectively oriented can re-traumatize these clients and cause a deepening of their dissociative defense.

4. Therapists who become impatient with these clients due to their slow, halting therapeutic progress will stall the therapy and run the risk of ending it prematurely.

5. "As it is above, so it is below" is a truism in Energetic Therapy. This applies to these clients who lack mental and emotional grounding in reality—the above—as they necessarily lack energetic grounding in their lower body—

the below. Thus, Therapists must practice due diligence to help them become energetically well-grounded in order to stop them from dissociating and thus live in reality. This is a long haul; energetic grounding exercise must be repeated over and over again before it will become well established in these clients.

6. Therapists must provide these clients with a corrective emotional experience in therapy by being attuned, emphatic, and compassionate while being careful not to push them into more closeness, intimacy, and self-understanding than they can safely handle.

An Energetic Therapy Progression Sequence to Help Clients Heal Their Trauma

We have found the following progression of steps below very beneficial in helping clients heal their childhood and adult trauma:

Step 1: The Energetic Therapy starts with the Therapist interviewing and listening to clients' personal histories about what brings them into trauma healing therapy at that point in time. This includes noting clients' complaints and problems which they are having in their life by using empathetic and reflective listening as well as words like, "Tell me more," and, "Can you give me an example of how this problem affects you?" for example. The Therapist also asks questions about clients' current and past physical and emotional health, childhood history including caretakers' interference in their natural developmental stages as well as physical and sexual abuse, current family situation, work and financial situation, relationship issues, spiritual/religious orientation, present limitations, losses, fears, and joys, as appropriate, for example. At the same time, the Therapist observes the client's body and its muscular holding, posture, the angles of head and limbs, skin color and tone, eye clarity, grace of movement, body symmetry including disparity between the size of the upper and lower body, the level of energetic charge, and the flow of energy in the body, for example.

Step 2: The Therapist introduces clients to The Client-Is-In-Charge Protocol by having them review, discuss, amend, and sign The Client-Is-In-Charge-Agreement. Although the client-is-in-charge Energetic Therapy is client-centered and client self-directed, the Therapist is very active in clients' Energetic Therapy providing them with suggested protocols to use and guiding them as they move along in their trauma healing process. Most clients come into Energetic Therapy with little knowledge and skill in how to heal their childhood trauma so in the beginning the Therapist needs to actively teach them how to self-direct their Energetic Therapy using the Spontaneous Movement Protocol. Client self-directed Energetic Therapy is the opposite of using the current medical model of psychotherapy with its reliance on the Therapist diagnosing clients' problems and prescribing treatment interventions. Rather, client self-directed Energetic Therapy proceeds by having clients use the Spontaneous Movement Protocol process to self-direct their therapy which is introduced to clients at the appropriate time in step 3.

Step 3: The Therapist introduces clients to the Spontaneous Movement Protocol. This is the main tool clients use to direct their own trauma healing therapy. It is designed to help them set a healing intention for each Energetic Therapy session, uncover their hidden childhood trauma, and move their trauma healing forward. Movement is connected to every part of the human brain, so when clients let a spontaneous movement arise from their body after setting a healing intention, their movements naturally tap into childhood memories, feelings, emotions, thoughts, and behaviors that produce quick and satisfying results and progress with very little internal resistance in the beginning of their therapy.

Step 4. The Therapist introduces energetic grounding. Energetic Therapists have a saying, "You can only go as deep as you are grounded." There is a good deal of truth in this. Clients need to have a solid foundation from which to overcome the pain and trauma their childhood caretakers caused them by interfering with their natural stages of child development. There is another saying about traumatized and abused children which is, "Childhood caretakers cut their children's legs out from under them." This is true too. The energetic muscle holding in the body that this interference caused them as children prevents energy from feeding their lower body—that is, the muscular contractions and tensions, especially in their chest, diaphragm, waist, pelvis, legs, and feet to stop them from feeling the pain of this trauma thus keeping energetic vibration and streaming from strengthening their legs and feet in order to provide them with the solid foundation they need to face their childhood trauma, overcome it, and heal it. There are numerous energetic grounding protocols that Therapists can teach clients to help them do this. (See the chapter on using the Energetic Grounding Protocols.)

Step 5: The Therapist introduces the Restructuring of the Energetic Holding Defenses. Using the Spontaneous Movement Protocol to self-direct their Energetic Therapy will only take clients so far in healing their trauma. At some point, as clients near the core of their trauma pain, their unconscious and conscious fears will kick in to stall them in their therapy progress. This is because their defense against their childhood trauma and pain is literally structured into the musculature of their body as an energetic holding defense(s). This childhood energetic body holding, at the stage of development around which the caretaker(s) interference occurred, triggers an emotional brain alarm signaling danger of resurfacing the childhood pain of being rejected, over controlled, exploited, neglected, or annihilated depending upon the age and stage of the caretaker(s) interference. These Energetic Holding Defenses must be restructured so the muscular holding can be modified in such a way clients can live their life in a healthy way, free from the effects of the emotional and physical trauma they suffered. The Therapist can teach clients how to self-diagnose their limiting energetic holding defense(s) using the Start-up Protocol and then help them do the energetic restructuring of their holding musculature that is needed to be free from it.

Our Innovations in Healing Outcome Survey Results

The former clients who responded to the outcome survey included twenty-three women and fourteen men. They ranged in age from their mid-20s to their mid-70s with the bulk of clients being in the age range of between 35 to 55. The length of their Energetic Therapy ranged from 2 years to 8-plus years.

Here is a summary of the survey respondents' responses to the agree-disagree statements that were posted. Respondents were asked to respond to each statement by selecting only one of five strongly agree to strongly disagree ratings to indicate how their Energetic Therapy affected them with regard to that statement; 1=SD represented their strong disagreement, 2=D represented their disagreement, 3=D/A represented a response somewhere between disagreement and agreement, 4=D represented disagreement, and 5=SA represented their strong agreement. The top row for each statement rating is the number of individuals who selected the rating, and the bottom row is the corresponding percentage.

Statement:	SD	D	D/A	A	SA
It increased my personal sense of well-being.	0 0%	0 0%	0 0%	5 13.5%	32 86.5%
It increased my sense of well-being for my family and close relationships.	0 0%	0 0%	2 5.4%	11 29.7%	24 64.9%
It increased my sense of work/school satisfaction/ performance.	0 0%	0 0%	8 21.6%	13 35.1%	16 43.2%
It increased my sense of well-being and satisfaction for my friendship connections.	0 0%	1 2.7%	3 8.1%	9 24.3%	24 64.9%
It increased my physical well-being.	0 0%	0 0%	2 5.4%	9 24.3%	26 70.3%
It helped me forgive others & myself.	0 0%	1 2.7%	1 2.7%	11 29.7%	24 64.9%
It increased my awareness and acceptance of my body.	0 0%	1 2.7%	0 0%	4 10.8%	32 86.5%
It worked the best for me compared to other therapy approaches.	0 0%	0 0%	4 10.8%	5 13.5%	28 75.7%
It enhanced my other therapy work.	0 0%	0 0%	4 10.8%	3 8.1%	33 81.1%
It increased my overall satisfaction with my life.	0 0%	0 0%	0 0%	4 10.8%	33 89.2%

REFERENCES

Brown, B. (1999). Soul Without Shame: A Guide to Liberating Yourself from the Judge Within. Boston: Shambhala Publications.

Cherry, K. (2020). Child Development Theories and Examples. <verywellmind.com/child-development-theories>

Danial, C. (2016). Bioenergy Healing: Simple Techniques for Reducing Pain and Restoring Health Through Energetic Healing. New York: Helios Press.

de Shazer, S. (1994). Essential, Non-Essential: Vive La Difference. In J. K. Zeig (Ed.), Ericksonian Methods: The essence of the Story. New York: Brunner-Mazel.

Dreikurs, R., & Soltz, V., (1991). Children: The Challenge, New York: Plume Books.

Duncan, B., Miller, S., & Sparks, J., (2004). The Heroic Client: A Revolutionary Way to Improve Effectiveness Through Client-Directed, Outcome-Informed Therapy. San Francisco: Jossey-Bass.

Emmons, R. (2007). Thanks!: How the New Science of Gratitude Can Make You Happier. New York: Houghton Mifflin.

Emmons, R., & McCullough, M.E. (2003). Counting Blessings Versus Burdens: An Experimental Investigation of Gratitude and Subjective Well-Being in Daily Life. Journal of Personality & Social Psychology, 84, 377-389.

Erickson, M. H., (1980). The Use of Symptoms as an Integral Part of Hypnotherapy. In E. Rossi (Ed.), The collected papers of Milton H. Erickson on hypnosis (Vol. 4). New York: Irvington.

Esmonde-White, M. (2008-2022). Classical Stretch: The PBS TV series on video tapes. Produced by The Esmonde Technique, www.essentrics.com.

Esmonde-White, M. (2014). Aging Backwards: Reverse the Aging Process and Look 10 Year Younger in 30 Minutes a Day. New York: Harper Wave.

Firestone, R. F., & Catlett, J. (1999). Fear of Intimacy. Washington DC: American Psychological Association.

Frued, S. & Brill, A. A. (2012). The Basic Writings of Sigmund Freud. New York: Modern Library.

Gerber, R. (1988). Vibrational Medicine: New Choices for Healing Ourselves. Santa Fe: Bear & Company.

Goodman, E. & Park, P., (2011). Foundation: Redefining Your Core, Conquer Back Pain, and Move with Confidence. New York: Rodale.

Golden, B. (2017). Overcoming the Paralysis of Toxic Shame, Psychology Today, April 22.

Goleman, D. (1994). Emotional Intelligence: Why It Can Matter More Than IQ. New York: Bantam Dell.

Gordon, J. S. (2019). The Transformation: Discovering Wholeness and Healing After Trauma. New York: HarperOne.

Hendrix, H. (1988). Getting the Love You Want: A Guide For Couples. New York: Henry Holt.

Hoffmann, L. (1904). Later Magic. New York: Dutton & Co.

Howard, P. J. (2000). The Owner's Manual for the Brain: Everyday Applications from Mind-Brain Research. Atlanta: The Bard Press.

Howe, L.W. (2011). Grab the Tiger by the Tail: The Revolutionary Spontaneous Energetic and Trauma Healing Process. Leslie, MI: EWH Press.

Howe, L.W. (2011). The Companion Guide to Grab the Tiger by

The Tail. East Lansing, MI; Self-published.

Howe, L.W. (2021). Innovations in Healing Trauma. Lyons, MI, Self-published.

Howe, L.W. (1977). Taking Charge of Your Life. Niles, IL: Argus Communications.

Howe, L.W., et. al. (2023). Innovations in Healing Trauma Vol. I, Lyons, MI: IHT Press.

Howe, L.W. & Howe, M.W. (1980). Personalizing Education: Values Clarification & Beyond. New York: Hart Publishing.

Howe, L.W. & Solomon, B. (1979) How to Raise Children in a TV World. New York: Hart Publishing.

Hubble, M., Duncan, B., & Miller, S., (1999). Directing Attention to What Works. In M. Hubble, B. Duncan, & S. Miller (Eds.), The Heart and Soul of Change: What Works in Therapy. Washington, DC: American Psychological Association.

Jackins, Harvey. (1970). Fundamentals of Co-Counseling Manual, Revised edition. Seattle, Washington: Rational Island Publishers.

Johnson, S.M. (1985). Characterological Transformation: The Hard Work Miracle. New York: W.W. Norton & Co.

Johnson, S.M. (1994). Character Styles. New York: W.W. Norton & Co.

Jung, C. (2021). Psychology of the Unconscious. Digireads.com.

Keleman, S. (1975). The Human Ground: Sexuality, Self and Survival. Berkeley, CA: Center Press.

Kurtz, R. (1990). Body-Centered Psychotherapy: The Hakomi Method. Mendocino, CA: LifeRhythm.

Kurtz, R., & Prestera, H., (1984). The Body Reveals: How to Read Your Own Body. New York: Harper Collins.

Lamia, M.C., (2011). The Downside of Success: Guilt or Shame? <psychologytoday.com>

Lehrer, J., (2009). How We Decide. New York: Houghton Mifflin Harcourt.

Leitch, M.L. (2007). Somatic Experiencing Treatment with Tsunami Survivors in Thailand. The Foundation for Human Enrichment.

Leitch, M.L., et. al. (2009). Somatic Experiencing Treatment with Social Service Workers Following Hurricanes Katrina and Ritam. The Foundation for Human Enrichment.

Levine, P. A., with Frederick, A., (1997). Waking the Tiger: Healing Trauma. Berkeley: North Atlantic Books.

Lewis, M. (1995), Shame: The Exposed Self. New York: Simon & Schuster.

Lewis, R. (1998). The Trauma of Cephalic Shock. In Bioenergetic Analysis (Vol.9, No. 1). New York: The International Institute for Bioenergetic Analysis.

Lowen, A., (1975). Bioenergetics. New York: Penguin Books.

Lowen, A., (2004). Honoring the Body. Alachua, Florida: Bioenergetics Press.

Lowen, A., (1958). The Language of the Body. New York: Macmillan Publishing Company.

Lowen, A., & Lowen, L. (1977). The Vibrant Way to Health: A Manual of Bioenergetic Exercises. New York: The International Institute for Bioenergetic Analysis.

Luna, A. (2019), What is Toxic Shame? <lonewolf.com>.

McIlroy, A. (2011). Researchers Looking at How the Brain Mutes the Inner Critic to Allow Ideas to Flourish. Saturday's Globe and Mail, January 28, 2011.

Melrose, R., (2009). Not ADHD, Not Bipolar, Not Learning Disabilities – Trauma. Ezine Articles, January 9, 2009.

Modell, A. (1965). On Having the Right to Life: An Aspect of the Superego's Development. International Journal of Psychoanalysis, 46, 323-331.

Modell, A. (1971). The Origin of Certain Forms of Pre-Oedipal Grief and Implications for a Psychoanalytic Theory of Affect. International Journal of Psychoanalysis, 52, 337-346.

Myss, C. (2002). Sacred Contracts: Awakening Your Divine Potential. New York: Three River Press.

Nigg, J. T. (2006). What Causes ADHD: Understanding What Goes Wrong and Why. New York: Guilford Press.

Parker, C., et. al. (2008). Somatic Therapy Treatment Effects with Tsunami Survivors. The Foundation for Human Enrichment.

Nigg, J. T. (2017). Getting Ahead of ADHD: What Next Generation Science Says About Treatments That Work—And How You Can Make Them Work for Your Child. New York: Guilford Press.

Nigg, J. T., (2006) What Causes ADHD: Understanding What Goes Wrong and Why. New York: Guilford Press.

Pelzer, D. (1995). A Child Called It: One Child's Courage to Survive. Deerfield Beach, FL: Health Communications, Inc.

Pierrakos, J. C. (1990). Core energetics: Developing the Capacity to Love and Heal. Mendocino, CA: LifeRhythm.

Prior, E. (2017). Toxic Shame: How to Survive and Heal. (professionalcounseling.com), July 14.

Ramachandran, V. S. (2011). The Tell-Tale Brain: A Neuroscientist's Quest for What Makes Us Human. New York: Norton & Company.

Randolph, J. (2020). The Brain Health Book: Using the Power of Neuroscience to Improve Your Life. New York: Norton & Company.

Ratey, J. J. (2001). A User's Guide to the Brain: Perception, Attention, And the Four Theaters of the Brain. New York: Pantheon Books.

Ravilochan, T. (2021). Could the Blackfoot Wisdom That Inspired Maslow Guide Us Now? Apr. 4, <gatherfor.medium.com>.

Reich, W. (1961). Character Analysis. New York: Farrar, Straus, & Giroux. (First English edition published in 1945. Originally self-published in German in 1933.)

Sack, D. (2015). 5 Ways to Silence Shame, Psychology Today, January 13.

Schafer, C. E., & Geronimo, T.F. (2000). Ages and stages: A Parent Guide to Normal Childhood Development. New York: John Wiley & Sons.

Seung, S. (2012). Connectome: How the Brain's Wiring Makes Us Who We Are. New York: Houghton Mifflin Harcourt.

Simon, S.B., Howe, L.W. & Kirschenbaum, H. (1972). Values Clarification: A Handbook of Practical Strategies for Teachers and Students. New York: Hart Publishing.

Stone, H., & Stone, S., (1993). Embracing Your Inner Critic: Turning Self-Criticism into a Creative Asset. New York: Harper Collins.

Tallman, K., & Bohart, A. (1999). The Client as a Common Factor: Clients as Self-Healers. In M. Hubble, B. Duncan, & Miller, S., (Eds.), (1999). The Heart and Soul of Change: What Works in Therapy. Washington, DC: American Psychological Association.

Thera, N. (1973). The Heart of Buddhist Meditation. York Beach, Maine: Samuel Weiser.

Wampold, B. E. (2001). The Great Psychotherapy Debate: Models, Methods, And Findings. Hillsdale, NJ: Erlbaum.

Zeig, J. K. (1980). A Teaching Seminar with Milton H. Erickson. New York: Brunner-Mazel.

About the Authors

Leland W. Howe, Ph.D.

Leland W. Howe, PhD, is Director of The Center for Innovations in Healing Trauma and has a private psychotherapy practice doing Energetic Trauma Healing Therapy in Lyons, Michigan. He is author & co-author of numerous professional books and articles including the ground-breaking *Grab the Tiger by the Tail* as well as the best-selling *Values Clarification Handbook* which sold nearly one million copies and was the winner of the Pi Lambda Theta Outstanding Book of the Year Award. He has served as a consultant and speaker to over 125 universities, public & private schools, government agencies, and health organizations in the U.S., Brazil, and Europe on a wide range of psychological, health, and educational topics. He was a Professor of Education at Temple University doing research in psychological education, Director of the Temple University Doctoral Program in Humanistic Education, and winner of the Temple University Lindback Distinguished Teaching Award. He also has an MSW and is trained in Family Systems Therapy.

Rev. Karen Arndorfer, MA

Rev. Karen L. Arndorfer, MA, has worked for over 30 years in the delivery and management of health and wellness services in her jobs in hospital settings, outpatient substance abuse programs and in her "Transformation Pathways" private counseling practice. Karen has a Master's in counseling psychology, is ordained as a trans-denominational minister, and has received training in Esoteric Healing, Psychodrama, Neurolinguistic Programming, Bioenergetic Analysis, and Toltec Energy Work to name a few. She has led personal and corporate workshops on body-centered approaches to change and grow. Karen assisted Leland Howe in the development of Innovations in Healing Trauma (IHT) approach to Energetic Trauma Healing Therapy. She worked with Leland as an individual and group counseling co-facilitator and as a co-trainer in the IHT workshops and training programs.

Terrie MacNicol, CET

Terrie MacNicol has been on a spiritual journey of self-healing and personal transformation for over 27 years. She spent years utilizing traditional therapy plus energy healing and body awareness techniques to work through the effects of significant past trauma. After being introduced to Innovations in Healing Trauma, she recognized its profound impact on her healing journey. Having worked with Leland as an individual and as a co-trainer in the IHT workshops, and as a long-standing member of a leadership circle, she has received practical training in this revolutionary approach to dealing with past trauma. She was also on the team that developed and conducted the first workshop on Spontaneous Energetic Healing. She has received a certification in Energetic Therapy along with training in Esoteric Healing, Reiki and other healing modalities. As an entrepreneur, Terrie has owned and operated several businesses along with EWH Press, which published Dr. Howe's first book *Grab the Tiger by the Tail: The Revolutionary Spontaneous Energetic and Trauma Healing Process*.

For More Information

Scan the above code with a mobile phone camera to go directly to the website, www.InnovationsInHealingTrauma.com, where you will find additional information on:

Energetic Therapy & Training Options

Energetic Peer Co-counseling as well as Trauma Healing & Training in Innovations In Healing Trauma.

Volume I

Innovations in Healing Trauma: Client Directed Energetic Protocols to Move Trauma Recovery Forward with Speed & Efficiency

Handouts

A Client Handout: Using the Start-up Protocol to Help You Self-diagnose Your Energetic Holding Defense(s)

www.ingramcontent.com/pod-product-compliance
Lightning Source LLC
Chambersburg PA
CBHW070637160426
43194CB00009B/1478